FINANCING HIGHER EDUCATION IN TRIPURA

About the Authors

Sanjoy Das: M.Com, Ph.D., did his master's Degree in Commerce from Tripura University in 1990. He obtained Ph.D degree from Assam University, Silchar, Assam in 2017. He is serving as full time faculty in general degree colleges under Government of Tripura since 1996. At present he is Associate Professor, Department of Commerce, Ramthakur College, Agartala. He has authored a good number of research papers and articles in reputed national and international journals. He has participated in many national and international conference / seminar/ workshops.

Kiran Sankar Chakraborty: M. Com. Ph.D, LL.B, is Regional Director, Indira Gandhi National Open University, Regional Centre, Agartala. He has also served as Regional Director, IGNOU, Kolkata Regional Centre. Prior to joining IGNOU in 2002 he has served in different Government Degree Colleges of Tripura for more than 16 years as full time faculty. He has 33 years of teaching and academic experiences. He is also visiting Faculty in the Department of Management, Tripura University. He was associated in many minor and major research projects as Investigator. He has supervised a good number of Ph. D and M.Phil Scholars. He has authored and edited 15 books, and more than 45 research papers & articles in reputed journals of India and abroad. His major contributions include: Anatomy of Overtrading (2003), Entrepreneurship and Small Business Development (ed. 2006), Human Development : Experiences of North East India (jointly ed. 2006), Empowerment and Status of Women in Tripura (ed. 2008), Rural Market and Agricultural Marketing (2009), Food Security and Sustainable Agriculture (Jointly ed. 2009), Reflections on Economy and Society of Tripura (Jointly Authored 2010), Sustainable Food Security (Jointly ed. 2010), Agricultural Development in Tripura (Jointly Authored 2014) and Social Science Research on Tripura(2016). He can be reached by ksc_agartala@rediffrnail.com

Prof. Nikhil Bhusan Dey: M. Com. Ph.D, LL.B, F.I.C.A is Emeritus Professor and Former Dean Mahatma Gandhi School of Economics and Commerce and School of Management Studies, Assam University Silchar. He is also the Former Head Department of Commerce, Assam University Silchar and has 42 years of Teaching experience at the under Graduate and Post Graduate level. He has supervised 25 Ph.D Scholars and 7 M. Phil Scholar successfully. He has acted as UGC Visiting Fellow in Department of Commerce in Mizoram University and Department of Management in Calcutta University. He also acted as Guest Faculty in Assam Royal Global University, Guwahati. Prof. Dey has authored numerous articles and research papers published in national and international journals. He has also presented research papers in many national and international seminars/conferences in India and Abroad. Professor Dey has authored two books and has to his credit two edited books. His current area of research interests are Business Ethics, Corporate Social Responsibility, Corporate Governance and Entrepreneurship.

FINANCING HIGHER EDUCATION IN TRIPURA

Sanjoy Das
Kiran Sankar Chakraborty
Nikhil Bhusan Dey

AKANSHA PUBLISHING HOUSE
NEW DELHI • GUWAHATI • VISAKHAPATNAM

AKANSHA PUBLISHING HOUSE
4649-B/21, Ansari Road
Daryaganj, New Delhi - 110 002
Phones: 011-23263193, 9811582779, 0943116718
Fax: 011-23263193
Email: ektabooks@yahoo.com

Financing Higher Education in Tripura

Edition 2019

ISBN 978-81-8370-493-9

PRINTED IN INDIA
Published by M.P. Misra for Akansha Publishing House, New Delhi.

Contents

PREFACE

Educational attainment in any system demands considerable financial resources. Financing higher education is the most important, yet complex function involving policy making, planning and prudent financial management. If there are deficiencies in the mechanism of financing, the system of higher education, the educational development would be seriously impaired. It is in this context that examination of the entire gamut of financing education, particularly the higher education, becomes an integral part of the overall development strategy. Moreover, finance without its proper management cannot alone ensure the success of higher education. The crux of the above problems basically relates to the management of finance in higher education.

Higher education in Tripura, unlike other major states of India, is largely subsidized as most of the establishments of higher studies are run by the State Government. The colleges in Tripura are mainly financed by the State Government and a very little portion is financed from the fees collected from students and from UGC by the way of different schemes and programmes. The finance is the main issue for most of the colleges. The issues like growth and expansion, sources and applications of funds, cost and expenditure per student, etc. are the other dimensions which have not yet examined in the context of higher education of Tripura. Analysis of these issues backed by adequate data may act as parameters not only to evaluate the financial health of higher education, but also for future decision making in regard to policy formulation.

In this background the book is planned and designed. The book throws some important insight into the problems of financing higher education on one hand and suggested few measures to tackle the problems.

We acknowledge our gratitude to Dr. Raveesh Krishankurty, Assistant Professor, IBS, Hyderabad, Sanjib Banik, Assistant professor, DDM College, Khowai, Debojit Chakraborty, Associate Professor, R.T College, Agartala, Dr. Bhusan Chandra Das, Associate Professor, M.B.B.College, Agartala for their constant support. We would also like to express our sincere gratitude towards Dr. Dipannita Chakraborty, Principal, BBM College, Agartala, Tripura who has magnanimously help us in preparing the book.

Sanjoy Das
Kiran Sankar Chakraborty
Nikhil Bhusan Dey

List of Tables

List of Figures

Abbreviations

AAGR	:	Annual Average Growth Rate
AGR	:	Annual Growth Rate
AJBM	:	Asian Journal of Business Management
BBMC	:	Bir Bikram Memorial College
CABE	:	Central Advisory Board of Education
CAG	:	Controller and Auditor General
CAGR	:	Compounded Annual Growth Rate
CEDA	:	Committee for Economic Development of Australia.
CESIS	:	Centre of Excellence for Science and Innovation Studies
CSES	:	Centre for Socio Economic & Environment Studies
CSHE	:	Centre for Studies in Higher Education
CTR	:	Cash Transfer Report
DDMC	:	Dhasarath Deb Memorial College
EABER	:	East Asian Bureau of Economic Research.
EURYDICE (EACEA)	:	Education, Audiovisual & culture Executive Agency
FICCI	:	Federation of India Chambers of Commerce and Industry

GDC	:	General Degree College
GDC Amarpur	:	General Degree College, Amarpur
GDC Dharmanagar	:	General Degree College, Dharmanagar
GDC Kamalpur	:	General Degree College, Kamalpur
GDC Khumlung	:	General Degree College,Khumlung
GDP	:	Gross Domestic Product
GER	:	Gross Enrolment Ratio
GNP	:	Gross National Product
GSDP	:	Gross State Domestic Product
HEI	:	Higher Education Institution
ICAI	:	Institute of Chartered Accountants of India
ICRA	:	Investment Information and Credit Rating Agency
ICRIER	:	Indian council for research on International Economic Relation
ICVC	:	Iswar Chandra Vidyasagar College
IDRC		:International Development Research Centre
IIEP	:	International Institute for Educational Planning
IJIFR	:	International Journal of Informatic and Futuristic Research
IJIRD	:	International Journal of Informatics Research and Development
IRJFE	:	International Research Journal of Finance and Economics
JSDA	:	Journal of Sustainable Development of Africa
KNM	:	Kabi Nazrul Mahavidyalay
MBBC	:	Maharaja Bir Bikram College

MHRD	:	Ministry of Human Resource Development
MMDC	:	Michel Madhusudhan Datta College
NCAER	:	National Council of Applied Research
NIAS	:	National Institute of Advanced Studies
NIEPA	:	National Institute of Educational Planning & Administration
NSM	:	Netaji Subhas Mahavidyalay
NUEPA	:	National University of Educational Planning & Administration
OECD	:	Organization for Economic Co-operation and Development
RECOUP	:	Research Consortium on Educational Outcomes & poverty
RKM	:	Ramkrishna Mahavidyalay
RTC	:	Ram Thakur College
UGC	:	University Grants Commission
UNESCO	:	United Nations Educational, Scientific and Cultural Organization
UNICEF	:	United Nations Educational, Scientific and Cultural Organization
WC	:	Womens College

CHAPTER 1

Introduction

Background of the Study

Education is a major factor in self-realization and the economic growth of a nation. It is the most crucial input for socioeconomic development. It has the responsibility of transforming human beings into human resource. Development of human resource is the main function of education and the higher education plays an important role in this process. Education provides the link with the past, thus lending necessary continuity and dynamic stability to the development process. Further, it trains the men-power to meet the emerging skill needs. Industrial capacity, financial capital, technology and information can no longer be the driving force of an economy by keeping human resources aside. It is the human capital-human intelligence, talent and creativity and knowledge – that are assuming the pre-eminent places. This underlines the importance of higher education both in developed and less developed countries.

Educational attainment in any system demands considerable financial resources. The success of education in providing quality education with its relevance is dependent upon availability of resources for undertaking new educational programme as well as for maintaining and up keeping the existing infrastructure facilities. If there are deficiencies in the mechanism of financing the system of higher education, the educational development would be seriously impaired. It is in this context that, examination of the entire gamut of financing education, particularly the higher education, becomes an integral part of the overall development strategy. Moreover, finance without its proper management cannot alone ensure the success of higher education. Hence our concern for raising issues in financing higher education with a view to develop proper perspectives on resource allocation and its efficient management.

The Central and State Governments in India have emerged as the main agencies for financing the public system of higher education. The University Grants Commission (UGC) is a statutory organization, which promotes university and college education with financial help under various schemes and programmes. Financial aid for higher education is given to universities and colleges. The UGC gives developmental funds to all types of universities and colleges under plan and non-plan grants. Besides, the UGC has also been providing financial help for the development of higher education under such schemes as vocational education, professional development of university and college teachers, research projects, travel grants, and special grants for women and disadvantaged groups. Apart from UGC, a few other organizations also provide funds to higher education establishments on an occasional basis from time to time.

Financing higher education is one of the most important, yet complex functions involving policy making, planning and prudent financial management. The development of higher education is largely based on the economic conditions of the guardians of the students and government's policy and planning.

The State Government has a role in shaping the economic growth of the State. It depends on the efficiency of the government, economic and environmental conditions and physical or natural ups and downs the State faces. The economy of the State, based on these factors, affects its educational development. The higher education system in any State of our country makes a significant claim on the State's resources.

A document, 'Challenge of Education', brought out by the Ministry of Education, Government of India, in August, 1985, Kaur (2003)[1], highlighted the funding problems for the development of education, It is reported in the document that the budgetary allocation for Plan expenditure for education have gone up substantially over the years, these have not kept pace with the growth in enrollments or rise in prices. As a result, the total expenditure per student per year, by the Centre and the States has declined in real terms. A substantial portion of the expenditure is spent on salaries and wages of academic and non academic staffs.

The expenditure on higher education, including technical and professional education has increased many folds since independence. Consequently, higher education has expanded under different heads such as degrees and diplomas. The data on the pattern of financing education has revealed that the Central and State Government's contribution to financing higher education has been continuously increasing. Thus the strategy for financing higher education needs diversified of sources of finance. Against this background the present study on the financing of higher education in Tripura is proposed and planned.

After Independence there have been marked increases in the number of establishments of higher education in Tripura. At present in the domain of higher education of Tripura, there are three universities, twenty four general degree colleges and twenty one professional and technical degree colleges. Out of these, three establishments, namely ICFAI University and Bhawan's College of Science and Technology and Holy cross college are in private management.

Statement of the Problem

Despite the increase in number of establishments of higher studies in Tripura, their performance is not always up to expectation. Truly speaking shortage of funds and unsustainable increase in enrollment for higher studies make it imperative for most of the institutions to insure the quality of their programmes. Optimum utilization of existing resources is thus need of the hour in a backward state like Tripura where Government to provide education for all.

Higher education in Tripura, unlike other major states of India, is largely subsidized as most of the establishments of higher studies are run by the State Government. As a result the fact is that the colleges in Tripura are mainly financed by the State Government and a very little portion is financed from the fees collected from students and from UGC by the way of different schemes and programmes. The preliminary survey of data of general degree colleges reveals that a substantial portion of the expenses of college education in Tripura is made on salary and wages head. A very little amount is available to upkeep the system. Moreover there is hardly money available for development expenditure. The colleges are facing severe financial crunch due to shortage of funds. The Colleges have not made any attempt to explore an alternative device to finance higher education in Tripura.

The issues like growth and expansion, sources and applications of funds, recurring expenditure per student, capital expenditure per student, etc. have not yet examined in the context of higher education of Tripura. These data may act as parameters not only to evaluate the financial health of higher education, but also for future decision making in regard to policy formulation.

So far as the cost of higher education is concerned, it is known fact that the institutional cost per student for higher education is huge in comparison to primary and secondary education and this cost is rising rapidly. At the same time wastages by the way of dropout, repeaters, uneven deployment of educational facilities etc. cannot be ruled out completely. But we can minimize the wastage, if any, by corrective measures for which economic data regarding higher education are essential.

The implication of the problem and necessity of generating data must be understood properly and dealt seriously by all concerned. Maintenance of proper accounting for financial activities is another dimension of this issue. Proper maintenance of books of accounts can only ensure better MIS which is very much lacking in general degree colleges of Tripura.

In the above situation, a detailed study about the financial aspects of higher education in Tripura, needless to say, is urgently warranted. The crux of the above problems basically relates to the management of finance in higher education.

It seems that the entire gamut of financing in higher education of Tripura is moving towards a aimless direction unless and until the affairs is thoroughly checked and reviewed based on in depth research on this issue. Before doing so review of literature may throw light upon this issue and help to find out the research gap.

Review of Literature

Review of related literature is one of the most important steps in any type of educational research work. Its importance has been established by different researchers on the basis of their fundamental and original work. Review of related literature provides a sound theoretical framework of research and provides the knowledge of the previous research on the problem. It also provides insight into the various method and procedures being used for the objective of research. Financing of education are associated with several theoretical aspects of economics and educational policy of the country. So far as economics of education are concerned lot of studies are found in the literature. Review of Literature as per objectives of the study is prepared into the following three categories. These include growth and expansion, financial aspects, cost and accounting of higher education.

Literatures on Growth and Expansion

A good number of studies relating to growth and expansion of Higher Education with special reference to India have been undertaken by researchers.

Salmi[2] (1997) mentioned that higher education has experienced radical transformation since independence and attempted to look at the current higher education crisis in developing countries and analyzed in the context of higher education reform. It focuses discrepancies between objectives and achievements and attempt to highlight the importance of risk analysis in strategic planning for higher education development.

Tilak[3] (2003) opined that higher education systems, in many developing countries are characterized with a continuing crisis, with overcrowding, inadequate staffing, deteriorating standards and quality, poor physical facilities, insufficient equipment and declining public budgets. This paper reviews some of these widely held presumptions, the relationship between higher education and development, including human development and reports significant effects of higher education on development and public policies, including select policies on financing higher education and privatisation, it underlines the need for increased public financing and warns against excessive reliance on cost recovery measures and privatisation of higher education.

Agarwal[4] (2006) highlighted that higher education in India suffers from several systemic deficiencies such as the unwieldy affiliating system, inflexible academic structure, and uneven capacity across various subjects, eroding the autonomy of academic institutions, and the low level of public funding. This paper also highlighted problems of higher education, growth pattern and focuses on the growth dimension of higher education in India.

Kaul[5] (2006) reviews the prevailing policy environment to evaluate its efficacy in ensuring that India is successfully able to address these challenges in the education sector and also suggested demand based policy.

Thorat[6] (2006) in Nehru Memorial Lecture reflects on the progress of higher education in the country and discusses the emerging needs of higher education and ponder over the possible directions for further advancement of higher education in the country. He mentioned that there is an urgent need to improve the physical and academic infrastructure of these institutions.

Rena[7] (2007) analyzed the sources of finance, the strategies and challenges for higher educational development in the country. The paper provides some implications for the policy purpose to develop higher education so as to curb the use of expatriate manpower in different sectors of the economy.

Mishra & Sharma[8] (2008) critically analyzed the growth of higher education sector in India and identifies the major concerns. It also evaluates the preparedness of the country for the opening up its border for foreign institutions.

NUEPA[9] (2009) highlighted the demand for higher education in India is increasing with the strong growth prospects of the economy and mentioned various ambitious schemes for expansion.

Sinha & Chakraborty[10] (2010) an attempt has been made by that how the concept of TQM can be extended to the institution of higher education for improving quality and suggested to improve financial inputs for improving quality of higher education.

Joshi[11] (2012) opined that there is a serious mismatch between demand and supply in the higher education sector and proposed different reform measure to revamp this sector.

Singh[12] (2012) assesses the growth and development of higher education in the north east region and examine the issues relates to it and also mentioned that GER in this region increased during the 11th plan period and suggested that the central and state government need to improve the infrastructure and attract the talented faculty so that there is a visible improvement in the quality of higher education.

Sreeramamurty & Appalanaidu[13] (2012) examine the inclusive growth in Higher Education in India during the post independence period. He suggested that in order to increase the access to higher education there is a need for sustained efforts both by the government and private agencies to increase Gross Enrolment Ratio among the disadvantaged groups and the government should provide additional facilities to the marginalized sections of the society. Efforts are also needed to bridge the gap between the rural and urban areas in terms of growth in higher education.

Tilak[14] (2012) viewed higher education has suffered in the last couple of decades, including in the areas of policy making and planning. As the above studies have confirmed, a distinctive plan and related policies have always been followed in the Indian educational sector. In terms of quantity of institutions one can observe a steady growth in the sector. But the quality aspect along with the existence of need based infrastructure has Finance –sources, expenditure pattern & alternative sources.

Anand[15] (2013) mentioned that higher education in India has made a significant contribution to economic development, social progress and political democracy. Since independence, there has been a continuous growth of higher education in India, but not comparable to other advanced countries because of regional, social and gender imbalances with respect to access to higher education. She also suggested that a strong need to increase the public spending on higher education.

Joshi & Kinjal[16] (2013) mentioned that the higher education system in India is complex. Quality and efficiency policy responses and their endeavors have been insufficient accompanied by poor regulations and its subsequent implementation. They review the access to higher education and study the financing of higher education in India.

Mondal & Mete[17] (2013) higher education sector is very important for the growth and development of human resource which can take responsibility for social economic development of the country.

Selvam[18] (2013) mentioned that four factors which have an economic impact. Economic development through innovation starts with research and new knowledge which strengthen the ability of enterprise to take advantage of new products, services and processes. Higher education institutions are taking a leading role in economic development efforts. This trend likely to strengthen as the nation moves into era of an innovation economy.

Gupta & Demele[19] (2013) Higher education determines not only the economic condition of a country, but also it's intellectual and social conscience and shows the present and future path of development of the country.

Das,Chakraborty & Dey[20] (2014) highlighted that different aspects of the colleges in Tripura need to be incorporated into policy decision regarding educational inequality. Process and outcomes need to be linked to access to higher educational system. There is an urgent need to synthesize all sorts of disparities to minimise the gap. The establishment of academic institution should be based on sound policy in this regard not political considerations. This perspective would have to account for the relative status in each aspect of the educational system as well as for variation across time and place. In particular, the inequality issue in higher education is a fundamental question for future research.

Literatures on Financing Higher Education

Financing higher education is one of the most important; yet complex function involving policy making, planning and administration. Financing of education are associated with several theoretical aspects of economics and educational policy of the country.

Azad[21] (1976) has examined the issues in the financing of higher education in India. Some of the major findings of the study may be stated as follows;

- The growth rate of expenditure on higher education was 11.9% as against in case of the educational sector as a whole and it was 3.3% of the national income of India during 1947-69.
- There were interstate disparities in outlays on higher education and it had progressively declined over the period.
- As a proposition to the total expenditure, the recurring expenditure of universities and colleges was high. Thus, there was a low level of capital formation in Indian universities.
- The financial resources allocated for the development of undergraduate education at the college level was inadequate. The study has also made a case of rationalizing the grant in aid code meant for higher education.

Psacharopoulous[22] (1986) by reviewing the financial pattern held that in most developing countries, the direct costs of education are financed largely by the taxpayers' money rather than the individual student. It was further held that the tuition fees are substantially higher in certain cases.

Ansari[23] (1988) analyzed the financial health of Indian Universities and estimated the expenditure ratio, per student cost, etc. He also analyzed that the system of higher education cannot be improved unless financial inputs are increased in direct proportion to their requirements which could be worked out on the basis of scientific norms. The author also suggested a mechanism of resource allocation for higher education in India.

Muzammil[24] (1990) showed different sources of financial support for higher education in Uttar Pradesh and the relative role of private and public finance in higher education in Uttar Pradesh. He also analyzes the compound growth rate of the state domestic product, state budget expenditure, total expenditure and higher education expenditure to find out the relative rate of growth in the four variables.

Sulochana[25] (1991) in her study 'Financing of Higher Education in Andhra Pradesh' Showed the plan and non plan expenditure of government of India as well as Andhra Pradesh during the period 1981-82 to 1985-86 and also showed growth of colleges in Andhra Pradesh for the same period. In her work, she also showed low per capita non plan expenditure on university and other higher education in Andhra Pradesh.

Varghese & Tilak[26] (1991) highlighted that optimum utilisation of the existing resources and mobilisation of additional resources become very important for the financing of education in the coming years. The study has attempted to analyse the alternate financing mechanisms is an integral part of the multilevel planning framework and needs to be developed.

Punnyya Committee[27] (1993) observed that 70-75 % expenditure of total allocated fund spend on salaries of teaching and non teaching staff. The committee examined present policy, pattern of providing development and maintenance grants, pattern of allocation of grants between teaching, research and non teaching function, review the existing schemes and also examined patterns of utilization of grants. The committee recommended that UGC may find an appropriate incentive for generating additional resources in universities.

Haggade[28] (1998) in 'Finance and cost of Higher Education in India' analyzed in detail trends, pattern, sources and methods of financing higher education on one hand and the quantitative expansion and expanding higher education in India since independence. He also studied the resource allocation and the pattern of expenditure on education in Karnataka state during 1981-90. It also measured the institutional cost of higher education and studied the management as well organizational problem of higher education in the state of Karnataka. The study, based on primary and secondary data and it is empirical or data based study on higher education of the state Karnataka.

Chatterjee[29] (1999) made a critical analysis of the scenario with special emphasis on financial constraints in higher education done. It revealed from the discussion that the growth rate of higher education expenditure on plan and non plan is declining from year to year.

Majumdar Committee[30] (1999) opined that enhancing the share of investment to 6 per cent of the GNP would be sufficient to provide adequate resources at all levels of the education Cheung Tripathi(2000), mentioned in the article 'Self financing Courses in Universities and Colleges' that financial dependence on central government/state government must be reduced to a minimum level and suggested to start job oriented self financing courses in the universities and colleges so that enable their wards to find a suitable job.

Rani[31] (2002) discussed about that Policy of the Government of India now encourages augmentation of resources for covering a larger portion of the cost of higher education. Public support for higher education remains essential to ensure a balanced achievement of educational and social missions, apart from surviving in the knowledge-based society and also mentioned that funding sources must be diversified.

Bray[32] (2002) focuses on education policy, management, administration, quality, and equity and access and suggested to improve on the quality of education. The work is concerned not only with government financing of education, but also with various forms of private, household, and community financing. Comments are made on distance education, especially at the tertiary level.

Cheung[33] (2003) examines the funding mechanisms adopted by different countries. Funding sources, paths and allocation methods identified and discussed. He also identifies the reasons why governments and higher education institutes keep searching for funding alternatives. Several points have been observed: (1) student enrollment is a common essential element, (2) public authorities have a strong influence on higher education by controlling intake quotas and fund allocations; (3) block grants is commonly used but they only provide the flexibility of internal allocation of funds; and (4) stability and education quality seem to be the fundamental goals of most funding methods.

Kaur[34] (2003) explained about educational attainment in any system demands considerable financial resources. He has analyzed the government expenditure on higher education during the +pre-Independence as well as post-Independence period (1781-2003) in India.

Nair & Kumar[35] (2004) discussed about the development of higher education in India and addresses possible means of financing. The article further says that the financing of Higher Education in the country by the State, is a drain on its exchequer and that more methods have to be found out to move the financial obligations outside the State funds. They suggested that it may become possible to develop several models, which may be accepted by the financial agencies, for funding higher education in India.

Sharma[36] (2004) critically analyses the pattern of funding higher education during the post independence period and discusses the pros and cons of the various alternatives available to augment additional resources for higher education. He also mentioned financial problems in higher education in various respects and suggested strategy for solving financial crisis in higher education. He traces upon the budgeting technique for higher education sector.

Tilak[37] (2004) reviews some of the well-known arguments in favour of, and counters against public subsidies and also reviews the recent trends in public expenditures on education in India. Some of the important issues about the size of the subsidy, targeting versus universalism, and methods of cost recovery are also briefly discussed. It has been shown that the level of subsidies in education in India is not particularly high, nor is the rate of cost recovery, particularly low, in comparison with other developed and developing countries. It has also been found that some of the specific subsidies in education are fairly progressively distributed.

CABE Report[38] (2005) argued that the governments -union and the states- must make a firm commitment to sustain funding of higher education institutions in such a way that basic teaching, research and extension activities are not affected in terms of their quality and quantum due to paucity of financial resources. The state funding for higher education out of tax and non-tax revenues should be the only sustainable way of financing higher and technical education in India.

Chakrabarti & Jogleker[39] (2006) examines patterns and changes in the allocation of government funds for education, particularly higher education, over a span of two decades, before and after the introduction of the new economic policies. It is evident that even after controlling for the economic reform process, privatization exerts a negative significant impact on expenditure on higher education.

Sanyal & Martin[40] (2006) established the reciprocal relationship between the financing of higher education and its mission at system and institutional levels and also touches upon the evolution of the steering mechanism of higher education because of the changes in financing pattern. They showed that how the better allocation of funds, improved management of cash reserves, production, financial indicators, better utilization of resources, evaluation and auditing, and protection from fraud could provide additional funds for higher education.

CEDA[41] (2007) attempt to evaluate the finance higher education evolving financing structure, expenditure pattern, resource mobilization, alternative sources of finance and policy of financing higher education. It entails an in depth analysis of the financing of higher education in the country. In the higher education sector in Nepal financial facilities is limited due to rapid increase of enrollment in higher education sector and also mentioned that the unit cost of higher education is generally high. The study has also shown that both public and private financing is required. The volume of private financing for higher education should be increased with respect to the increasing level of education.

Tulip[42] (2007) discussed about substantial financial barriers to higher education despite large government expenditures aimed at promoting access. Policy makers have proposed addressing these barriers by increasing student grants. In contrast, international best practice seems to be converging on student loans with repayments that vary according to income.

Chakraborty[43] (2007) attempted to provide a brief overview of the educational system in India that the government plays a dominant role not only in providing funds for education, but also in the administration and control of these institutions and also attempted to identify various institutions of repute in India that can be excellent candidates for further consideration.

Srivastava[44] (2008) focuses some issues relating to the financing of higher education in India with special reference to general education.

Chattopadhya[45] (2007) mentioned that the government was the main source of finance for higher education. The other sources of finance have not been tapped. To bring our system to world standards there is a need to identify the additional sources of finance for higher education. This may be in the form of upward revision of fee structure or deregulation of fee structure, education loans, human capital contracts, income contingent loans, graduate tax, education vouchers, self –financing market determined courses as has been suggested.

Prakash[46] (2007) provides expression that the Indian higher education system is presently facing several challenges and gives an overview of trends in the expansion of higher education and examines variations in participation across states, gender and social groups. He also discussed the trends in the financing of higher education and the required resources to meet the target of allocating 6 per cent of the GDP to education.

Woodhall[47] (2007) explains that a major challenge faced by governments everywhere is the reform of finance of higher education (HE) in response to pressures of rising private demand for higher education and heavily constrained public budgets. This paper examines the influence of economic thinking in the last 20 years on debate and policy on HE finance in selected OECD countries (including Australia, Sweden, the U.K. and

U.S.), transition economies (Hungary) and developing countries (Ethiopia and South Africa).

Ahmad[48] (2008) made an assessment of the funds provided by the UGC to universities and colleges in India for maintaining and for further development of higher education during the 10th plan. He clearly mentioned that funds provided for education, especially to universities and colleges by the government through the UGC are not sufficient. He suggested that the UGC need to make necessary efforts to get more funds from the government during the 11th plan and provide the same to universities and colleges to enhance the standard of higher education at all levels.

Azad[49] (2008) attempts to bring into the impact of privatization and mercentization of higher education with particular reference to access, efficiency and equity in the system. The study examines among others, the nature and extent of involvement of the private sector, particularly in the industrial and commercial houses in establishing funding and managing of institutions of higher education. He also analyses the pattern of financing of universities of different types in India.

Bhushan[50] (2008) made an attempt to estimate the investment and expenditure gap and suggested financial gaps need to be managed through a proper strategy. He also explains equity and quality gaps defined in terms of difference between the expected outcome and actual achievement on equity and quality parameters.

De & Endow[51] (2008) analysed major trends in public financing of education in India, including expenditures by the central government, state governments, other local bodies and the NGO sector. The paper examines the level and composition of public expenditure on education and the mechanisms of resource sharing, allocation and utilization, in aggregate as well as separately for the centre and the states. They also analyzed the expenditure trends in seven states to explore the possible impact of expenditure on education outcomes.

OECD[52] (2009) in Higher Education to 2030, Vol-2, explores significant trends in higher education provision, financing and governance, including a specific focus on the future role of market forces, mobility, and quality assurance in higher education. It also focused the themes of higher education provision, financing and governance that have a crucial impact on the capacity of countries, institutions and individuals in the context of globalization.

Patari[53] (2009) observed that increased expenditure on higher education is justifiable as long as the benefits are more than expenditure. He also suggested that government should encourage the institutes of higher education to develop their own initiative and creative method of financing taking into account the condition of the institute and locality.

Suklabaidya[54] (2009) highlighted that higher educational institutions located in semi urban and rural area in Assam are facing tremendous constraints and limitations in terms of finance, infrastructures and information technology.

Tiwari[55] (2009) observed that the higher education system needs organized financing for its proper operation and serious review of all crucial concepts pertaining to the funding of higher education.

Banerjee[56] (2011) mentioned that funding coming from three levels: federal, state, and local. Education in India falls under the control of both the Union Government and the states, with some responsibilities lying with the Union and the states having autonomy for others.

Lbara[57] (2011) examines the present system of funding higher education in Nigeria and draws from the international scene to explore the appropriate route to the challenge of diversifying the funding of higher education to incorporate a more significant role for private funding and also presented mechanism to tune up the income streams of higher education system in Nigeria.

Das[58] (2012) attempt to analyze the present pattern of funding higher education in post-graduate courses of a government-sponsored college, and to discuss the desirability and feasibility of funding the same. In the state of West Bengal, find a huge number of government-sponsored colleges who are getting salary of the permanent teachers and non- teaching staffs as the only financial support from the government. He mentioned that lot of fund is required for maintaining the academic and infrastructural facilities.

Goswami[59] (2011) mentioned that In China, government spends more than 1.5 per cent of its GDP on higher education while India spends less than 0.5 per cent.

Rayal & Kamble[60] (2012) explains the present situation of Higher Education system in India. They mentioned that the system has faced many challenges like inadequacy finances, shortage of faculty and poor infrastructure, lack of Researchers etc. They recommended providing at least 1.5% of the total GDP for the Higher Education in the XIIth plan period.

Das, Chakraborty and Dey[61] (2014) made an effort to analyse the growth and development, policy and plan perspectives of the Governments towards higher education in North East India. An attempt has also been made to discuss the trends of financing in higher education in North East India. They also mentioned that there has been a significant development in the educational scenario of the North Eastern states of India. But few states of this region do not maintain the increasing parity. They also suggested that system of financing higher education in the north eastern states need diversification.

Das, Chakraborty and Dey[62](2015) identified that management of finance becomes necessary when funds allotted are not properly expended or remains unutilized. This call for serious introspection as misutilization or unutilization of funds is against the objectives of fund allocation itself. In their study, they found that around 3 percent of funds remain either unspent or unutilized and suggested that this area needs to be looked into so that a proper utilization of fund takes place.

A look into the above studies is sufficient to conclude that financing pattern in the sector is based on some pre-fixed criteria. In spite of that there may be observed different criteria, like fiscal responsibility in the public expenditure pattern in the educational sector. However the contribution of the private sector in the sector is yet to be analyzed in an effective manner so that a clear picture about the financial sources, utilization pattern and their application may emerge out of such exercise remained an area to be worked upon.

Literatures on Cost of Higher Education

A number of literatures are available related to the level of educational costs in other counties. It highlights the issues related to the various concepts and measurements of educational costs and its estimation.

Kamath[63] (1969) has analyzed the trends and issues in recurring institutional expenditures on higher education with special reference to Poona University. In his study revealed that the institutional recurring costs in case of science courses have been higher than the arts and commerce courses and the recurring institutional costs of technical education like medicine and engineering at undergraduate level was four to five times higher than the undergraduate level general education.

Dey[64] (1969) discussed how to arrive at a correct cost of education. He also mentioned that an amount of depreciation at certain percentage according to the life expectancy of each asset should be included in the revenue account.

Dutt[65] (1969) measures the source of financing of 28 colleges of Haryana which includes four state colleges and 24 private colleges categorized under three headings as the state colleges, private women's colleges and other private colleges. The various sources of financing of higher education were found to be: (i) fee income; (ii) government grants (State, UGC, and local bodies); (iii) other sources (fines, sale of prospectus, etc.); and (iv) funds given by the governing bodies. In all colleges, sources of income were very much different. In the state colleges, the main contributor was the state government, the private women's colleges depend mainly upon state grants-in-aids, and other private colleges depends upon the fees and funds and the UGC grants, if any. After the government grants, among the private sources, the major contributor was fees and funds paid by the students.

Hallak[66] (1969) deals mainly with concepts of cost. In this connection certain distinctions are drawn, especially between money cost and opportunity cost. He also tried to clarify the basic ideas underlying the methods of costing, analysis and the projection techniques used by the costing expert, responsible for estimating expenditure and sources of finance. Again he mentioned that deals with costing as an instrument of economic analysis and outlines the answers to various questions, such as how to assess the total cost of education and discusses methods of establishing total costs and unit costs.

Kulkarni[67] (1969) mentioned that salary and wages of teaching and non teaching staffs are the main items of college expenditure. He also mentioned that unlike the total cost per student, the teacher cost per student has increased year after year.

Pandit[68] (1969) aims to estimate the unit cost of education and locate factors which cause variation in the unit cost of education for different level. He also studies about unit cost in relation to the internal and external efficiency.

Rao[69] (1969) in his paper Educational Cost: Concept and Issues attention is mainly focused on the analysis of the concept of the cost of educations in particular higher education in different aspect. He also discussed the operational significance of these aspects in the context of an underdeveloped economy.

Tilak[70] (1985) has given a detailed account of the variables to be included in the estimation of unit cost of education. He has touched on various aspects such as Resources for Education in India, Educational Finance and Cost Recovery Approaches and also inquired into whether pre-primary education in India is free as it is often claimed.

Paul & Richard[71] (1986) provide information relevant to assessing operational efficiency, planning an investment strategy, evaluating comparative performance, or justifying funding requests and prices charged for services. They also give an idea about cost that could expand the horizon for institutional researchers and point to alternative directions in which they might take their analyses and interpretations of cost. They also highlighted the framework of cost analysis, types of cost, common calculations of cost, and cost measurement.

Mulimani[72] (1990) mentioned that almost all universities are struggling to find funds as the state funding is shrinking to alarmingly low levels because financial stringency and increasing cost of quality higher education. He also suggested various measures to overcome the crisis of higher education.

Bellew & Stefano[73] (1991) investigate the costs and effectiveness of higher education in Pakistan, identify factors that influence those costs and effectiveness, and estimate levels of study subsidies. They find that most colleges and universities are underfunded.

They also mentioned that the higher education sector in Pakistan is underfunded. Existing resources are inefficiently used. Faculty and facilities are less than optimally utilized in many universities. Financing and governance practices contribute to the low resource base and to the inefficient and ineffective use of resources. Cost recovery in colleges and universities are low. Although there is considerable potential to raise student fees, institutions depend heavily on Government funding. The government neither has standards against which to evaluate the productivity of its investment nor does it inspect institutions' budgets, needs, and resource flows. This is an exploratory analysis.

Jenny[74] (1996) mentioned about the cost accounting applications and techniques to institutions of higher education, focusing mainly on the different methods of allocating costs. Its main focus is on accounting costs from the institution's perspective and on the many different ways costs can be allocated to cost centers. Each allocation method tends to produce its distinct cost outcome. He also provided readers with a series of road maps for selected costing applications.

Subbiah[75] (1999) analyzed the central Government expenditure as compared with its total expenditure (Plan and non plan). He also explained the growth rate of expenditure refers to increase in expenditure compared with the expenditure of the previous years. In his study, he mentioned that there is no statistically significant difference in the growth rate of central government expenditure on education and its total expenditure during the period of study. The studies conducted during 1990s generally relating to funding and mobilization of additional resources for the higher education system.

Singh[76] (2003) discusses the theoretical background of the unit cost of education like institutional cost, opportunity cost and private cost and gives the calculations of various costs under study in the tabular form. Comparison of recurring costs per student and the average teaching costs for social sciences, sciences and professional courses is projected. The study finds the courses developed and taught through distance education more cost-effective than those taught at conventional universities.

Vanlalchhawna[77] (2006) examines the growth of public expenditure on higher education, sources of educational finances, unit institutional costs as well as private costs. He highlighted that educational cost analysis provides a powerful tool in the hands of decision-makers to evaluate the efficiency of education institutions in terms of resource allocation and productivity. It is an analytical study and used stratified random sampling.

Johnson[78] (2009) highlighted that with or without a detailed expenditure analysis, the question of degree costs is reasonable and should be taken seriously and can be answered, though the answer will vary depending on the policy motivation and context for the question. The direct and indirect cost of providing instruction for the average bachelor's degree at a public college or university is between $25,000 and $40,000, from a mix of public subsidies and student tuition.

As cost and productivity issues continue to rise on the public agenda-both nationally with the reauthorization of the Higher Education Act and at the state level-policymakers should be sensitive to the challenges inherent in analyzing the costs of an enterprise as complex as American higher education while academics must recognize the legitimacy of their desire to do so.

Patari[79] (2009) observed that increased expenditure on higher education is justifiable as long as the benefits are more than expenditure. He also suggested that government should encourage the institutes of higher education to develop their own initiative and creative method of financing taking into account the condition of the institute and locality.

Kalia[80] (2010) an attempt has been made to highlight the practical problems faced in measuring the costs of professional higher education in the state. She also mentioned that the institutions / governments should bear 75-80 percent of the recurring cost. It is an analytical study and used stratified random sampling.

Obester, Sally & Widener[81] (2011) highlighted that institutions of Higher Education are required to comply with four cost accounting standards (CAS 501,502,505, and 506) and complete a disclosure statement. The study outlines the changes in cost accounting procedure and provides comments gathered a survey of 70 universities with regards to the changes. They also mentioned that the process has been costly in terms of both time and cash expenditure.

Pattern of costing in higher education has been analysed for various institutions and organizations spread over India. A conceivable idea about the cost of education, unit cost, institutional cost and other may be sufficient to let one work upon them on other fields. Since no such study has been undertaken in Tripura the examination of costing pattern in the education sector of the state may provide new insight in this area.

Literatures on Accounting System of Higher Education

Literature reviews relating to the accounting system of higher education are discussed below.

Schaik[82] (2004) mentioned that use of accrual accounting compared with traditional cash accounting seems more desirable, since in accrual accounting, expenditures are compared with the performance objectives not with budgets that have already been agreed.

Thomas[83] (2007) states that accrual accounting possesses advantages for the public sector such as: better facilitation of planning and management of financial resources, performance evaluation, presenting financial position and its evaluation, and also, assessment of financial flexibility and providing required conditions for implementation of operational budgeting.

ICAI[84] (2012) stated that the financial statements of different educational institutions are not uniform or comparable. This has given rise to confusion and misunderstanding among the users of financial information provided by educational institutions. It may be emphasized that wherever the educational institution is incorporated under section 25 of the Companies Act, 1956 they are already required to prepare the financial statements as per Schedule VI to the Companies Act and accounting standards are already applicable to them. In the educational sector, a uniform accounting system has been recommended and it may provide an opportunity for making comparative studies a viable option.

Mahanta[85] (2013) in the sixth chapter of his thesis, accounting process and audit procedure of Gauhati University has been examined. Basic conceptual analysis of accounting like basis of accounting, financial control, compliance with the accounting standards for educational institution, applicability of accounting standard to educational institutions are also carried out. Besides, accounting in higher educational institutions, preparation of annual statements of accounts, audit practice in Gauhati University has also been dealt with.

Gandhi[86] (2015) critically evaluates the role and development of higher education vis-à-vis the role and responsibility, obligations of the Central and State Governments, higher educational institutions, etc. He also highlights the current status of and gaps in practices of higher educational institutions in financial management and disclosure of accounting information to their stakeholders. He argues that the utilization of finance & funds must be strictly in accordance with the set terms and conditions, rules and regulations, and hence, the accounting standards must be widely accepted in practice in which the statutory obligation should be increased and ensured in consultations with the professional and regulatory bodies.

Barman[87] (2012) emphasis on accounting and reporting under the accounting standards of higher educational institute is symptom of innovation in fund and financial management and also as the response to professionalism in higher education institute. Maintaining of uniformity of account and disclosure would indicate more transparency of fund allocation and utilization.

Higher educational institutions need to follow so many standards and guidelines of national policies, policy of UNESCO, UNGC, UNAI principles or so and so.

Wagh[88] (2014) made an attemtp to throw light upon the prevailing accounting practices in the conventional colleges in Mumbai city districts. He also mentioned that some colleges follow Cash Basis of Accounting System whereas a few follow Accrual Basis of Accounting. Even some colleges follow the hybrid or mixed system of accounting for maintaining their accounts. It was found in his study that there are 86.67% of Mumbai City District colleges follow cash basis accounting system and 06.66% follow accrual basis of accounting system whereas 06.67% of the follow hybrid (combination of both bases of accounting) basis of accounting system. Thus it was concluded that majority of colleges prefer cash basis accounting system.

Research Gap

The foregoing review of available literature reveals that the studies on the financial management of higher education institutions are limited, especially in the context of the backward region. The studies on the financial management of government colleges are also found limited. In most of studies, it is also evident that even with regard to the estimation of recurring expenditure major attention was paid to salary (teaching and non-teaching) component. The sources of financing and how it was utilized in case of higher education institutions are not analyzed adequately. The literature on accounting and auditing aspects of higher education in general and government degree colleges in particular are very limited and not properly focused.

The present study makes an attempt to understand the issues associated with financial aspects of government general degree colleges of Tripura. In regards to the state of Tripura, a lot of advanced and comprehensive studies have been undertaken by different researchers and institutions regarding the socioeconomic problems of the state. Unfortunately, unlike the other problems, the financial aspects of higher education have not been able to draw the attention of researchers to any noticeable extent. The survey of the existing literature on different relevant aspects associated with higher education of the state indicates that at present there are a few research articles available. No single intensive and comprehensive study on the above mentioned issues are found. Therefore, a comprehensive study incorporating the issues associated with the financing of higher education is the need of the hour.

Significance of the Study

In specific terms, the present study is significant, in view of the fact that no such study has ever been attempted so far, with reference to higher education of Tripura. More importantly, Tripura is a state where considerable expansion in higher education has taken place in recent years. Despite financial constraints, the State Government is also doing a lot of the expansion of higher education.

Therefore, issues like the expenditure per student for higher studies, graduating cost per student, etc. are to be estimated and be understood by the society in general and the policy makers in particular. On the other hand the issues like an unsustainable increase in enrollment, huge cost involved, subsidization, quality of education pursued by the colleges are also interrelated with the issue of financing in higher education.

In order to formulate sustainable policy frameworks, there is a need for getting relevant data as also studies on the issues associated with higher education finance. The study throws some important insight into the problems of financing higher education on one hand and suggested few measures to tackle the problems. The study may also help to guide the higher education of Tripura for the policy decision. Therefore, a comprehensive study incorporating the issues associated with the financing of higher education is the need of the hour.

Objectives of the Study

Universities, Colleges and other institutions of higher learning are the establishments of higher education. But the general degree colleges constitute its main segment in Tripura. The main objective of the present study is to examine the financial health of higher education in Tripura comprising of general degree colleges and to diagnose the diseases, if any. To achieve this objective, the following component objectives are to be pursued:

1. To analyze the growth and expansion of higher education in Tripura.
2. To examine the sources of finances and expenditure pattern of general degree colleges in Tripura.
3. To analyse the institutional cost, unit cost and expenditure of collegiate education.
4. To examine the accounting system practiced in general degree colleges in Tripura.

Research Queries

The necessity and quantum of public subsidies in education, specially higher education have assumed significance in the context of the new economic climate in India. The market oriented approach aiming at the lessening of the government intervention and shifting emphasis from long- term goal of social justice for short- term goal of financial prudence is adversely affected government allocation to education at all levels. Full cost pricing on education, encouragement of private organizations, emphasizing vocational and technical education instead of general education, searching alternative sources of funds, donation for infrastructure, is the gradual policy shifts in higher education of India.

It perhaps requires no mention that government general degree colleges are the main segment of higher education in Tripura in terms of number of establishments, number of students enrolled and state government's expenditure on higher education.

In this changing scenario of higher education, government general degree colleges of Tripura, is facing several constraints in managing the affairs of the colleges. Financial constraints are the main problem. Most of the government general degree colleges are passing through financial crises, which are becoming more acute day by day.

In this background, the following relevant research questions in connection with present study are identified. i) Is there any disparity or imbalance in the growth and expansion of higher education in Tripura? ii) What are the sources and applications of funds in Government General Degree Colleges in Tripura? iii) What are the components of institutional costs / unit costs in Government General Degree Colleges in Tripura? iv) Is the accounting system in Government General Degree Colleges are adequate and proper as per sound financial accounting system?

Methodology

Based on the survey of literature and the information collected from the Department of Higher Education, Government of Tripura, an analytical method of enquiry has been adopted for the study backed by appropriate statistical techniques wherever needed.

Data Sources

The study is based on both primary and secondary data. For secondary data a number of relevant text and reference books, State Government publications, including the publications of Department of Higher Education, notifications, reports, publications of MHRD (Govt. of India), publications of University Grants Commission (UGC) and other published and unpublished documents relating to the study have been consulted. Educational surveys, research journals, working papers, status reports, etc have also been consulted. The study is also relied upon the data contained in various issues of 'Statistical Abstract' (A Govt. of Tripura publication), and 'Economic Review' (A Govt. of Tripura publication). We have also used the information collected from the office of Controller and Auditor General (Govt. of India), Agartala, Directorate of Audit, Government of Tripura, Department of Finance, Government of Tripura, Department of Planning, Government of Tripura and Department of Higher Education, Government of Tripura.

Basic statistics of government general degree colleges collected from the respective colleges through well-structured proforma, comprising of four parts namely academic, staff, financial and accounting. After obtaining the required information through structured proforma duly signed by the Principal of the respective colleges, the data have been analysed carefully.

Clarifications on any information provided by the colleges, if required, are obtained through discussion with the Officials of the respective colleges. To a great extent data so collected are verified with the information available with the office of the Directorate of Higher Education and Directorate of Statistics, Government of Tripura. Registration and Evaluation related information are also checked and verified with Tripura University as affiliating university.

To understand the issues dealt in the present study the perception of the Principals / Principals in charge, Drawing and Disbursing Officers and Academics associated with financial related activities of the sample colleges were also taken. A set questionnaire was designed to gather response. The responses are analysed in the context of higher education of Tripura. Furthermore the discussion was held with all respondent Principals and DDOs, besides other respondents, if found necessary.

Population and Samples

At present there are 24 general degree colleges in the State of which 22 colleges are exclusively run by the state government under the Department of Higher Education. The two general degree colleges, namely Bhavan's College of Science and Technology and Holy Cross College are run by private management. 15 general degree colleges out of 22 government colleges have been considered for the study purpose as the remaining 7 government general degree colleges were established only after the period of present study. Therefore 15 general degree colleges are the population for the study. The population will adequately represent the higher education of Tripura not only in terms of number of establishments or the financial outlays but in term of enrolment in higher education also.

Tools and Techniques

The data is being expressed in the form of ratios, percentage and then tabulated followed by analysis. Data are suitably represented by using graph, chart and diagrams. To understand the perception of respondents weighted index calculated on the basis of 5 points likert scale and Pearson correlation has been calculated.

To understand the responses of the respondents regarding the factors responsible in providing quality education, factor analysis has been carried out using SPSS 17 software for extracting the factors. To avoid the cross loading among the factors of the variables Eigen Value criteria (greater than one) and Varimax Rotation criteria has been used. Before conducting the factor analysis the reliability of the questionnaire has also been checked.

Period of Study

The study analyses the available data on higher education of Tripura from 1950-51 to 2010-11 pertaining to explain growth and expansion. However, for the purpose of estimating cost of higher education, institutional cost, sources of income and expenditure pattern of the colleges, the study has taken five years from 2007-08 to 2011-12. The government degree colleges, the population in the study, get UGC assistances on the basis of the plan period. The 11th plan period duration is 2007-2012. Therefore, these years are taken into consideration while selecting the period of study pertaining to cost estimation and analyzing finance data. Furthermore, the 3 years general degree courses with every year final examination system under Tripura University was introduced in the year 2004 in colleges of Tripura instead of two year general degree courses. To maintain the uniformity among the years under study, the study has chosen the said reference period of five years from 2007-08 to 2011-12.

Organization of the Study

The discourse is divided into six chapters, including the introduction and conclusion.

Chapter 1 Introduction

Chapter 2 Growth and Expansion of Higher Education

Chapter 3 Sources of Finances and Expenditure Pattern

Chapter 4 Cost of Higher Education

Chapter 5 Accounting System of Government General Degree Colleges

Chapter 6 Summary of Findings, Suggestions and Conclusion

Limitations of the Study

It perhaps requires no mention that the study chalked out in a nutshell. Therefore the relevant concerned issues as per objectives of the study are only dealt in the discourse. 7(seven) government general degree colleges are kept out of the scope of the study as these are established only after the study period.

Due to the limited scope of the study certain areas may be left out in the course of discussion. Moreover, it is an uphill task to get proper response from the sample colleges and other respondents. This is mainly because of non availability of data and the indifferent attitude of the respondents. The data collected by means of discussion and questionnaires are bound to have some errors, such as personal bias of the respondents, etc.

However, attempts have been made to overcome the limitations by visiting the sample colleges personally and interacting with the respondents. Care also is taken to the extent possible to elicit correct information by means of cross checking.

REFERENCES

1. Kaur, K. (2003). *Higher Education in India (1781-2003).* New Delhi: University Grants Commission. P-79.
2. Salmi, J. (1991). *The Higher Education Crisis in Developing Countries (Phree* Paper Series, Document No. Phree/91/37 (10601). The World Bank.Pp-1-19.

3. Tilak J.B.G. (2003). Higher Education and Development in Asia. *Journal of Educational Planning and Administration Volume XVII No. 2.* Pp-151-73.

4. Agarwal, P. (2006). *Higher Education in India- the Need for change* (Working Paper No. 180). New Delhi: Indian Council for Research on International Economic Relations (ICRIER). Pp-1-179.

5. Kaul, S. (2006). *Higher Education in India: Seizing and opportunity* (Working Paper No-179). New Delhi: Indian Council for Research on International Economic Relations (ICRIER). Pp-3-25.

6. Thorat,S. (2006). *Higher Education in India Emerging Issues Related to Access, Inclusiveness and Quality*. Nehru Memorial Lecture, University of Mumbai.Pp.1-27.

7. Rena, R. (2007). *Financing education and Development in Eritrea– some Implication. Manpower Journal, Vol. 43, No. 1.* New Delhi.Pp-73-97.

8. Mishra, J. K., Abidi, N. & Sharma, R. (2008). *Indian Higher Education: Global Challenges and Local Issues* (JBS Working Paper Series, W.P. No. JIITU/JBS/2008/01).Pp-1-14

9. NUEPA. (2009). Facing Global and Local Challenges Country Report: India. In Sub-*regional Conference for South, South West and Central Asia on Higher Education*.Feb.25-26, Vigyan Bhawan, New Delhi.

10. Sinha, A & Chakraborty, K.S. (2010). Management of Higher Education Institutions in Tripura. In *Reflection on Economy & Society*. Akansha Publishing House, New Delhi.Pp-104-112.

11. Joshi, S. (2012). *Sustainable Development of the Higher Education Sector in India for Catalyzing Services-Driven Growth* (Working Paper No. 2012/01). Maastricht School of Management.Pp-2-20.

12. Singh, K.P. (2012). Taking Stock of Higher Education in the North-East. *Economic and Political Weekly, Vol-XLVII-No-38*.Pp-24-27.

13. Sreeramamurty, K., Sailaja, K. & Appalanaidu, D. (2012). Inclusive Growth and Higher Education In India. *International Journal of Multidisciplinary Educational Research, Volume 1, Issue* 2.Pp-21-29.

14. Tilak, J.B.G. (2012). Higher Education Policy in India in Transition, *Economic & Political Weekly, Vol XlVII No- 13*,Pp 36-40.

15. Anand, S. (2013). Access to Higher Education in India: Cross State Analysis. *University News, Vol-51(31),* Pp-18-22.

16. Joshi, K.M & Kinjal, V. A. (2013). Indian Higher Education: Some Reflections. *Intelektinė Ekonomika, Intellectual Economic. Vol. 7, No. 1(15).* Pp-42-53.

17. Mondal, A. & Mete, J. (2013). Higher Education and Quality Research in India: An Overview. *University News, 51(19)*.Pp-3-10.

18. Selvam,P.S.K. (2013). Higher Education and entrepreneurship in India, *University news*, 50(44) Oct.- Nov. Pp 11-15.

19. Gupta, k & Demele,M.(2013). Contemporary challenges in Higher education. *University News, Vol-51, No-32,* Aug.Pp-11-18.

20. Das,S..,Chakraborty,K.S. & Dey, N.B.(2014). Opportunity of Higher Education in Tripura: A Study With Reference to Disparities among General Degree Colleges. *International Journal of Informative & Fututistic Research, Vol-II,* September-2014. Pp-57-65.

21. Azad, J.L. (1976). Financing Institutions of Higher Education in India: The Need for a Realistic Fee Policy. *Higher Education, 5 (1976).*Pp- 1-7.

22. Psacharopoulos, G. & others. (1986).*Financing Education in Developing Countries: An exploration of policy option.* The World Bank, Washington, DC 20433.Pp-1-41.

23. Ansari, M.M. (1988). Financial Health of Universities: A Diagnostic Study. *Journal of Higher Education, Vol- 14*, UGC, New Delhi. Pp-84-86.

24. Muzammil, Md. (1990). Financing of Higher Education in Uttar Pradesh. *University News,* Dec.24.Pp-5-10.

25. Sulochana,M. (1991). Financing of Higher Education in Andra Pradesh. *University News,* April.Pp-4-12.

26. Varghese, N.V &Tilak, J.B.G. (1991).The Financing of Education in India (XIIIP Research Report No -92). *International Institute for Educational Planning* (UNESCO), Paris. Retrieved from unesdoc. unesco.org /images /0009/ 000902/090282eo.pdf on 15.02.2013. Pp-1-64.

27. Punnayya Committee. (1993). *UGC Funding of Institutions of Higher Education*. University Grant Commission, New Delhi.Pp-1-128.

28. Heggade, O.D. (1998). Finances *and cost of Higher Education in India.* New Delhi: Mohit publication.Pp-34-79.

29. Chatterjee.T.K. (1999). Crisis in Higher Education Nature and sources. *University News*, 37(4), Jan.25, Pp 6-8

30. Majumdar Committee. (1999). *Report of the Committee on National Common Minimum Programme's Commitment.* Ministry of Human Resource Development, Government of India.

31. Rani, P.Geeta. (2002). *Financing Higher education In India in the post reform period: Focus on Access and equity* (Occasional Paper -31).NIEPA, New Delhi.Pp.1-49.

32. Bray, M. (2002). The Costs and Financing of Education: Trends and Policy Implications. *Education in Developing Asia, Volume 3,* ADB Publication.

33. Cheung, B. (2003). *Higher Education Financing Policy: Mechanisms and Effects.* Retrieved from www.usca.edu / essays/ vol-5 2003/ cheung. pdf. Dated on 27.09.2014.

34. Op.cit. Kaur, K. (2003).

35. Nair, P & Kumar, D. (2004).*The Financing of Higher Education –A Broader View.* Hyderabad: The ICFAI University Press.PP-21-34.

36. Sharma, N. K. (2004). Importance of Higher Education in Trade, Commerce and Industry. *University News,* May 28-June 03, 45(22).

37. Tilak J.B.G. (2004). Public Subsidies in Education in India. *Economic and Political Weekly.* Jan.24.Pp-343-359.

38. Central Advisory Board of Education Committee. (2005). *Report on Financing of Higher and Technical Education.* National Institute of Educational Planning and Administration (NIEPA), New Delhi.Pp-1-52.

39. Chakrabarti, A. & Jogleker, R. (2006). Determinants of Expenditure on Education: An Empirical Analysis Using State Level Data. *Economic and Political Weekly, VolXLI,* April 15.Pp-1465-1472.

40. Sanyal, B.C. & Martin, M. (2006). Financing Higher Education: International Perspectives. *Higher Education in the World.*Pp-3-17.

41. CEDA. (Tribhuvan University) (2007). Financing the Higher Education in Nepal. *Report submitted to South Asia Network of Economic Research Institutes (SANEI),* Islamabad.Pp-1-153.

42. Tulip, P. (2007). *Financing Higher Education in the United States* (Working Paper-44). ECO/WKP (2007)44, OECD.Pp-5-34.

43. Chakrabarti, A.(2007). Higher Education and Research in India: an Overview. *Sitra Reports 74.* Pp-5-11.

44. Srivastava, R. (2008). Financing Higher education in India –Estimate for 15 % Enrolment under 11th Plan, in '*Higher Education in India Issues Related to Expansion, Inclusiveness, Quality and Finance.* UGC Report. Pp-277-93.

45. Chattopadhyay,S. (2007). Exploring Alternative Sources of Financing Higher Education. *Economic and Political Weekly,* October 20.Pp-4251-4259.

46. Prakash, V. (2007). Trends in Growth and Financing of Higher Education in India. *Economic and Political Weekly. Vol - XLII No. 31,* August 04.Pp-3249-3258.

47. Woodhall, M. (2007). *Funding Higher Education: The Contribution of Economic Thinking to Debate and Policy Development.* World Bank. Retrieved from http://www.socscistatistics.com/tests/pearson/Default2.aspx accessed on 27.03.2012. Pp-10-27

48. Ahmad, S. (2008). Funding to Universities and colleges by the UGC during the 10th plan. *University News, 46(09)*. Pp-9-12.

49. Azad, J. L. (2008). *Financing and Management of Higher Education in India: The Role of Private Sector*. New Delhi: Gyan Publishing House. Pp-29-73.

50. Bhushan, S. (2008). Financial Requirement in Higher Education during XI Plan Period. In *Higher Education In India Issues Related to Expansion, Inclusiveness, Quality and Finance.* UGC Report.Pp-215-276.

51. De, A., & Endow, T. (2008). *Public Expenditure on Education in India: Recent Trends and Outcomes* (Working Paper No-18). Research Consortium on Educational Outcomes and Poverty. Pp-5-6.

52. OECD. (2009). *Higher Education to 2030* (Working Paper No-584). Retrieved from http://www.oecd.org/edu/ceri/44101074.pdf accessed on 27.03.2012.

53. Patari, K. (2009). Financing of Higher Education in Orissa. *University News. 47(13)*.Pp-16-20.

54. Suklabaidya, S. (2009). Quality Assurance in higher Education in Rural Areas in Assam' in NathHemanta Kr. (Ed) *Higher Education in the North East a Perspective*. Guwahati: Purbachal Prakash.Pp-86-95.

55. Tiwari, R.K. (2009). *Financing Higher Education in India*. New Delhi: Neeraj Publishing House.

56. Banerjee, S. (2011). Quality Higher Education, its Status, Problems & Remedial Policy. *International Referred Reseach Journal, VOL-II* Issue 19.Pp-164-65.

57. Lbara, E.C. (2011). Funding Higher Education in a Dwindling Fiscal resource allocation: The Nigerian Perspective. *Journal of sustainable development in Africa. Volume 13, No.3*.Pp-1-9.

58. Das, S.K. (2012). Self-Financing Scheme in Post-Graduate Course of Government-Sponsored College: A case study. *International Journal of Multidisciplinary Management Studies, Vol.2 Issue 1*, January 2012. Pp-94-102.

59. Goswami,D. (2010). *Higher Education in India-Growth Expansion and Issue.* Guwahati: DVS Publishers.Pp-1-150.

60. Rayal, S.K. & Kamble, P.S. (2012). Quality Gaps in Higher Education System in India. *Golden Research thoughts, Vol - I , ISSUE-VIII.* ISSN NO : 2231-5063

61. Das,S.,Chakraborty,K.S. & Dey, N.B.(2014). Development of Higher Education in North East India: An Analytical Study. *International Journal of Informative & Fututistic Research,Vol-I*, August -2014. Pp-86-95.

62. Das,S.,Chakraborty, K.S. & Dey, N.B.(2014). Financing Higher Education: With Special Reference to Government General Degree Colleges of Tripura. *International Journal of Innovative Research & Development, Vol-4,* Sptember-2015. Pp-52-59.

63. Kamat, A.R. (1969). *Efficiency of Education.* In Pandit, H.N. (ed.), *Measurement of Cost, Productivity and Efficiency of Education.* National Council for Educational Research and Training (NCERT), New Delhi. Pp-123-30.

64. Day, B. (1969). On Costing of Education. In Pandit, H.N. (ed.), *Measurement of Cost, Productivity and Efficiency of Education.* National Council for Educational Research and Training (NCERT), Madras. Pp-14-26.

65. Datt, R. (1969). Unit cost of Education- A case study of Haryana College. In H. N. Pandit (ed), *Measurement of Cost Productivity and Efficiency of Education.* NCERT, Madras.Pp-92-113.

66. Hallack, J. (1969). *The Analysis of Educational Cost and Expenditure,* IIEP, UNESCO, Paris.Pp-13-65.

67. Kulkarni, G.B. (1969). Unit Cost of Education in Commerce College of Bombay 1962-63 to 1966-67. In Pandit, H. N. (ed) *Measurement of Cost Productivity and Efficiency of Education,* NCERT, Madras.Pp-114-22.

68. Pandit. H.N. (1969). A Study in Unit Cost at the school stage in India: A Design of the Research Project. In *Measurement of Cost Productivity and Efficiency of Education.* NCERT, New Delhi.Pp-3-13.

69. Rao, H. V. (1969). Educational Cost: Concepts and Issues. In H. N. Pandit (ed) *Measurement of Cost Productivity and Efficiency of Education,* NCERT, Madras.Pp-57-74.

70. Tilak, J.B.G. (1985). *Analysis of Cost of Education in India* (Occasional Paper 10). National Institute of Education, Planning and Administration (NIEPA), New Delhi.Pp-1-67.

71. Paul B. & Richard A. H. (1986). Concepts of Cost and Cost Analysis for Higher Education. *The Association for Institutional Research,* Number-23. Pp-1-9.

72. Mulimani,V.H. (2010). Higher Education in India at Cross Road. *University News 48(09).*Pp-1-8.

73. Bellew, R. & Destefano, J . (1991). *Costs and Finance of Higher Education in Pakistan.* Pakistan: Population and Human Resource Department.

74. Jenny, H. H. (1996). *Cost Accounting in Higher Education. Simplified Macro- and Micro-Costing Techniques.* National Association of College and University Business Officers. Washington, D.C. Pp-1-180.

75. Subbiah, A. (1999). Central Governments Expenditure on Education—A Comparative Analysis with its Total Expenditure. *University News 37(47).*Pp-1-9.

76. Singh, J. (2003). Unit Recurring Cost for Regular and Correspondence Course in Punjabi University. *Journal of Distance Education.*Pp-144-151.

77. Vanlalchhawna. (2006). *Higher Education in North-East India -Unit Cost Analysis,* New Delhi: Mittal Publication.

78. Johnson, N. (2009).*What does a college degree cost? Comparing approaches to measuring "cost per degree".* Washington, DC: Delta Cost Project. Pp-5-24.

79. Parati, K. (2009). Financing of Higher Education in Orissa. *University News,* 47(13), March 30-April 05. Pp 16-20.

80. Kalia, S. (2010). *Cost of Higher Education and Financing Practices among Students in Punjab: A Study of Professional Education.* Unpublished Doctoral Thesis, Punjab Technical University. Retrieved from http://shodhganga.inflibnet.ac.in/bitstream/10603/2094/7/07_absract.pdf accessed on 5.5.2012 CH-5

81. Obester, B. W., Sally, K. & William, M.G. (2011). Cost accounting Standards In Higher Education: Impact of Required Changes. *Journal of Applied Business Research, Vol-17,* No-3.Pp-79-86.

82. Schaik, F. V. (2004). *Mastering the Transformation: New Public Management, Accrual Accounting and Budgeting.* Retrieved from www.deloitte.com, 13, July, 2010.

83. Thomas, H. B. (2007). Does Full Accrual Accounting Enhance Accountability?. *The Innovation Journal: The Public Sector Innovation Journal,* Vol. 12 (3), pp. 9-14.

84. ICAI. (2012). *Report on Implementation of Accounting Standards in Educational Institutions of Department of Higher Education.* MHRD, Government of India.

85. Mahanta, D. K. (2013). *Financial Management of Higher Education -A Study on Gauhati University* (doctoral thesis), Gauhati University. Retrieved from http://shodhganga.inflibnet.ac.in/ dated on 15.08.2015

86. Gandhi, M.M. (2015). Financial management of Higher Educational Institutions. *The Business and management Review, Vol-5,* No-4.

86. Barman, A. (2012). *One Response to Educational institutions to follow ICAI accounting norms. Retrieved Dec. 15.2014,* from www.educationinsight/..../educational-institutions-to-follow-icai-accou.

87. Wagh, A. (2014). Accounting System in Higher Education: A Study of Colleges in Mumbai City District. *Sai Om Journal of Commerce & Management A Peer Reviewed International Journal.* Volume 1, Issue 12.Pp-15- 21.

CHAPTER 2

Growth and Expansion

Introduction

The system of higher education in India has seen an impressive growth sinceindependence. The number of universities has increased from30 in 1950-51 to 564 in 2010-11.The number of colleges has increased from 695 in 1950-51 to 33,023 in2010-11. The totalenrolment increased from 397,000 in 1950-51 to 1, 69,75,000 in 2010-11(UGC, 2012)[1]. The colleges that are affiliated to 131 universities constitute the bulk of the highereducation system in India, which contribute around 89 per cent of the total enrolment.In chapter-II an attempt has been made to analyse the growth and expansion of higher education system, policy and plan perspectives of higher education in Tripura during the period 1950-51 to 2010-11.

India had a good network of universities dealing with higher education during the ancient and medieval period.In ancient times, Indian universities like Taxila, Nalanda, and Vikramsila were renowned seats of higher learning; attracting students from far and near. After these periods the first three universities were set up in the presidency towns of Bombay, Calcutta, and Madras in 1857. It took another 30 years to set up the fourth university at Allahabad in 1887 and yet another 29 years to establish the fifth and sixth universities at Mysore and Banaras in 1916. These universities were established on the pattern of the University of London, and thus, they were basically affiliating, examining and regulating bodies. The existing colleges engaged in teaching and learning were affiliated to these universities. For several decades, only the colleges continued to offer the degree courses. It took a long time before post-graduate teaching and research departments began to be established at the university level around 1920. For over nearly 2000 years the higher education in India developed without royal patronage and financing since imparting higher education was not governed by direct monetary returns to the suppliers and also it was not capital intensive as it is during the modern period. The monasteries and madrasas have played a very important role in higher education during ancient and medieval period. The British imperial rulers were interested in developing the indigenous educated manpower to strengthen its administrative and defense sectors.

Between 1857-1947 several royal families and / or provincial governments in princely states made efforts to set up universities and their constituent colleges. During this period Indian universities had functioned mostly as 'teaching centers' with little concern and facilities for research. Therefore the university education system was in its infancy and highly city centered indicating its imperialist orientation and it was totally funded by British government and princely states(Heggade, 1998)[2].

At present, India possesses a highly developed higher education system which offersfacility of education and training in almost all aspects of human's creative and intellectual endeavors such as arts and humanities, natural, mathematical and social sciences, engineering; medicine, dentistry, agriculture, education, law, commerce and management, music and performing arts, national and foreign languages, culture, communications etc. Today in terms of enrolment, India is the third largest higher education system in the world after China and the USA (Joshi, 2012)[3].

Institutions-Students-Teachers Triangle is Equilateral which signifies that each angle is of the same value and none can be more important component of the higher education than other. The important parameters are student enrolment and teaching faculty in the context of growth of higher education (Komow, Khanna and Sharma, 2012)[4]. Besides growth and expansion an analysis has been made how the concept of TQM can be extended to the institution of higher education for improving quality and suggested to improve financial inputs for improving quality of higher education (Sinha & Chakraborty, 2010)[5].

Since independence, the number of colleges and universities has registered a significant rise. The status on higher education of India reveals that the growth of higher educational institution as well as enrolment isfound to be explosive during the post liberalization period and witnessed a rapid growth in terms of institutions during the post liberalization period compared to the pre- liberalization period.Turning to Tripura it is found that growth and expansion of higher education has started only after the merger of princely state with union of India.This princely state was annexed to Indian Union in 1949 and attained full statehood on January 21, 1972. Since the early 1950's higher education has been diversified and extended its reach and coverage quite significantly. At the time of merger of princely state with union of India, the size of higher education system in terms of number of educational institutions was meagre but since that time there has been an exponential increase in three indicators of higher education, namely the number of educational institutions, students and teachers.The growth pattern of higher education in Tripura is discussed below.

Growth in Term of Number of Institutions

There is expansion of higher education in India after independence. The increase in the Universities during the period 1950-51 to 2010-11 was 19 times. The increase in the colleges for the same period was 47 times. This growth in the Universities and Colleges was due to massive efforts and policy decisions were taken by the central government and the state government (Based on UGC, 2012)[6].

The central government and the state governments are making more provision to promote higher education. While there is a strong case for rapid growth and expansion of higher education in Tripura it is important to see that new colleges and universities are set up after careful consideration and most importantly after ensuring adequate resource support. The growth and expansion should help in improving the quality of higher education. Despite thehurdles, the higher education sector in Tripura has grown at a steady pace and has been able to scale up significantly over decades.

The growth of higher education institutions in Tripura during the period 1950-51 to 2010-11are shown in table-2.1. It appears from the table that the numbers of general degree colleges are increased from 2 in the 1950-51 to 16 colleges in 2010-11. The other higher education institutions include degree level professional and technical colleges. The other higher education institutions has increased to 21 in the year 2010-11 while there was no educational institutions other than general degree colleges in the year 1950-51.

Prior to 1947, there were no degree colleges in Tripura. The Maharaja BirBikram College was set up in 1947 at Agartala. However, After Independence there have been marked increases in the number of establishments of higher education in Tripura. At present in the domain of higher education of Tripura, there are three universities, twenty four general degree colleges and twenty one professional and technical colleges. Out of these, three establishments, namely ICFAI University and Bhawan's College of Science and Technology and Holy cross college are in private management. Despite the increase in the number of establishments of higher studies in Tripura, their performance is not always up to expectation. Before the foundation of Tripura University on 2nd October 1987 all the colleges of Tripura were affiliated to Calcutta University and for ten long years there was a postgraduate wing of the Calcutta University at Agartala. After that all the colleges of Tripura became affiliated to Tripura University (Debroy, 2011)[7].

TABLE 2.1
Higher Education Institutions in Tripura during 1950-51 to 2010-11
(Figure in number)

Year	General Degree Colleges	Other Higher Education Institutions	Total Higher Education Institutions
1950-51	2	0	2
1960-61	2	0	2
1970-71	6	3	9
1980-81	9	6	15
1990-91	14	8	22
2000-01	14	9	23
2010-11	16	21	37

Source: Based on a) Statistical Abstract (2011), Government of Tripura b) Information from Sample Colleges

It is observed that higher education in Tripurais diversifiedand given due importance to technical and professional institutions. The significant growth in the area of engineering, law, music, physical education, medical, etc. is specially found especially during the period 2000-01 to 2010-11. During the said decade 12 professional and technical institutions were established while only 2 general degree colleges were established in that period. The policies of the state government towards the establishment of more professional and technical colleges are encouraging. But the question is the adequacy of funds to maintain such professional and technical colleges. It is reported that many professional and technical colleges of the state are running short of funds and in turn compromising with the quality of the education. Many institutions do not have adequate numbers of faculties even.

The decadal growth of higher education institutions in India and Tripura is depicted in table 2.2 and Fig.2.1.It appearsfrom table 2.2 that there were significant increases of higher education institutions 350% during the period from 1960-61 to 1970-71 and 60.86% during 2000-01 to 2010-11 in Tripura. The decadal growth rate of higher education institutions in Tripura during the period 1960-61 to 1980-81 was higher than the national rate of growth. While the decadal growth rate of higher education institutions in Tripura during the period 1990-91 to 2010-11 was less than the national average.

TABLE 2.2
Decadal Growth of Higher Education Institutions in India and Tripura (Figure in number)

Year	India		Tripura	
	HEIs	Decadal Growth (%)	HEIs	Decadal Growth (%)
1950-51	725	---	2	---
1960-61	1597	120.28	2	Nil
1970-71	3707	132.12	9	350
1980-81	4855	30.97	15	66.67
1990-91	7536	55.22	22	46.67
2000-01	13062	73.33	23	4.5
2010-11	33587	157.14	37	60.86

Sources: a) Statistical Abstract (2011), Government of Tripura b) Economic Review of Tripura, Various Issues, Government of Tripura c) Information from Sample Colleges d) UGC (2012), Higher Education at a Glance; HEIs= Higher Education Institutions

Fig. 2.1: Growth of Higher Education Institutions in during1950-51 to 2010-11

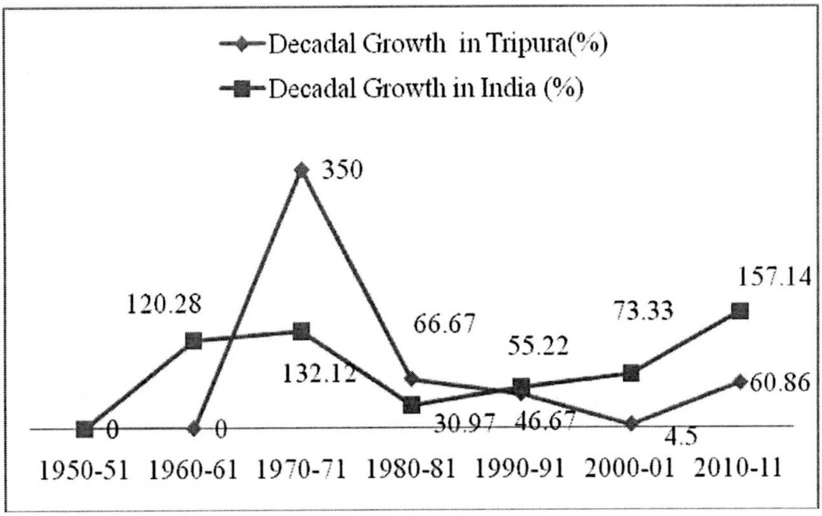

Source: Table-2.2

So far as general degree colleges are concern the significant expansion has taken place during the period 1980-81 to 1990-91.It is also worthwhile to mention that during the decade of 1950-51 to 1960-61 there were only 2 general degree colleges (Table 2.1).

In case of general degree colleges it is also noticed that fund crunch and mismanagement of available funds is a major constraint for running the institutions. The details in this regard are discussed in chapter-3.

To understand the location of the established institutions within the state, district wise data are required.The district wise growth pattern of higher education institutions in Tripura, during the period 1950-51 to 2010-11 are depicted in table 2.3 and fig.2.2. In 1971, the highest concentration of higher education institutes is found to be in the West district alone 7 (seven), and 1 (one) each in the North and South districts while none in Dhalai district. The steady growth of higher education institutes in the West district is also imminent as we find the decadal increase of number of institutions from 1 in 1950-51 to 7 in 1970-71, 10 in 1980-81, 13 in 1990-91 and 28 in 2010-11 which accounts for 75 % of the total higher education institutes of the state of Tripura.

TABLE-2.3

District Wise Higher Education Institutions in Tripura during 1950-51 to 2010-11 (Figure in number)

Year	*West*		*North*		*South*		*Dhalai*		*Tripura*	
	GDCs	*THEIs*	*GDCs*	*THEIs*	*GDCs*	*THEIs*	*GDCs*	*THEIs*	*GDCs*	*THEIs*
1950-51	1	1	1	1	0	0	0	0	2	2
1960-61	1	1	1	1	0	0	0	0	2	2
1970-71	4	7	1	1	1	1	0	0	6	9
1980-81	5	10	2	3	2	2	0	0	9	15
1990-91	6	13	4	5	4	4	0	0	14	22
2000-01	6	14	3	4	4	4	1	1	14	23
2010-11	8	28	3	4	4	4	1	1	16	37

Sources: a) Statistical Abstract (2011), Government of Tripura b) Economic Review of Tripura, Various Issues,Government of Tripura c) Information from Sample Colleges

GDCs= General Degree Colleges, THEIs= Total Higher Education Institutions

It is also observed from table 2.3 that number of general degree colleges in the west district increased from 1 in the year 1950-51 to 8 during the year 2010-11 which was 50% of total general degree colleges in Tripura at that period. In case of south district, there were no general degree collegesduring the period 1950-51 to 1960-61 and 1 college established during the period 1970-71 and also no new colleges were built till 2011 after 1980-81.The students of the state have to make a beeline to the West district for pursuing higher studies as there is a dearth of colleges/institutes in other districts.

Higher education in Tripura was expanded based on urban area, namely Agartala and adjacent areas underSadar subdivision.

Fig. 2.2: District Wise Growth of Higher Education Institutions in Tripura during 1950-51 to 2010-11

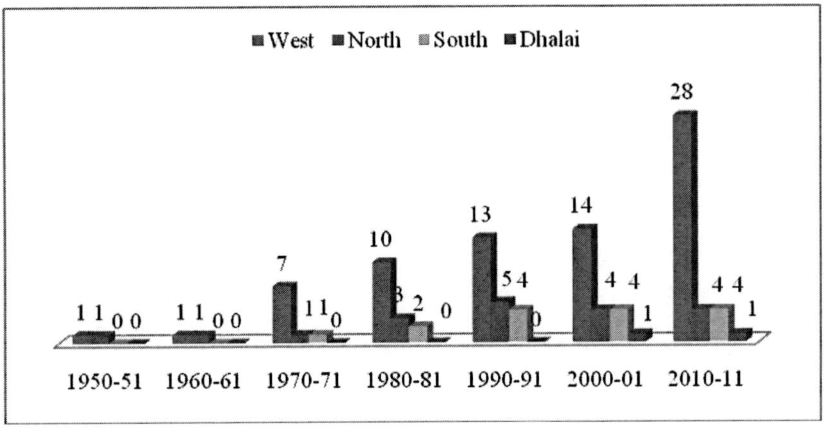

Source: Table-2.3

The process of expansion of higher education base still following the policy of urban based growth. This is evident from the table 2.4. The locations of higher education institutions are classified under the category of sadar subdivision and other subdivisions to understand the location wise disparity in growth of higher education in Tripura.

TABLE -2.4

Higher education institutions in Sadar Subdivision and other Subdivisions of Tripura during 1950-51 to 2010-11 (Figure in number)

Area	*1950-51*	*1960-61*	*1970-71*	*1980-81*	*1990-91*	*2000-01*	*2010-11*
Sadar Subdivision (1)	1	1	6	10	11	12	26
Other sub-divisions of Tripura(16)	1	1	3	5	11	11	11
Tripura	2	2	9	15	22	23	37

Sources: a) Statistical Abstract (2011), Government of Tripura b) Economic Review of Tripura,Various Issues, Government of Tripura c) Information from Sample Colleges

It is evident from the table that there is sub-division wise imbalance in the distribution of higher education institutions. The maximum numbers of higher educational institutions were located in the Sadar sub-division. The data for the period 1950-51 to 2010-11 has revealed that 1 higher educational institutions out of total 2 was established in sadar subdivision during 1950-51 and increased to 26 (70%) out of 37in the year 2010-11.

The imbalance growth in terms of location can be assessed in a better way if we compare the number of institutions with the population of the respective areas. Table2.5shows the population per higher education institutions of each district of Tripura during the period 1950-51 to 2010-11.

TABLE -2.5
District wise Populations per Higher Education Institute in Tripura during 1950-51 to 2010-11 (Figure in number)

District	*1950-51*	*1960-61*	*1970-71*	*1980-81*	*1990-91*	*2000-01*	*2010-11*
West	3,21,775	571329	107372	97625	99528	109499	61,594
North	118103	201956	405009	188173	139466	147728	1,73,320
South	NA	NA	399728	256144	191504	191860	2,18,786
Dhalai	0*	0*	0*	0*	0*	307868	3,77,988
Tripura	3,14,514	571002	172927	136871	125328	139096	99,217

Sources: a) Statistical Abstract (2011), Government of Tripura b) Economic Review of Tripura, VariousIssues, Government of Tripura

NA=Not available * District created after 1991

It can be seen from the table that on an average there was one higher education institution for 3, 14,514populations in the year 1950-51 in Tripura. In the year 2010-11, on an average one institution served for99,217populations which is a positive indication from the standpoint of growth in higher education.

Looking into the district wise figure it is found that there is huge discrimination among the districtsduring the stated period, specially in the year 1970-71 because then in Tripura, there were only 9 higher educational institutions out of which 7 institutions were in the west district only (Table 2.3). As a result, many students are deprived of availing their higher education in institution at other districts. The objective of the government is to provide maximum opportunities within the reach of the students in each sub-division of higher education. But if there is a disparity in setting up higher educational institutions in that area wherethe population is more than it is not possible to achieve this projected goal.

A similar picture is evident inthe case of general degree colleges also. District wise populations per general degree colleges of Tripura during the period 1950-51 to 2010-11 are presented in table 2.6. In case of Dhalai district it is a matter of serious concern. Again during the period 1970-71 a lopsided situation could be observed as there were only 6 general degree colleges in Tripura out of which 4 GDCs were in the west district only (Table 2.3).

TABLE -2.6

District wise Populations per General Degree Colleges during 1950-51 to 2010-11 (Figure in number)

District	*1950-51*	*1960-61*	*1970-71*	*1980-81*	*1990-91*	*2000-01*	*2010-11*
West	321775	571329	1,87,901	1,95,250	2,15,644	2,55,497	2,15,577
North	118103	201956	4,05,009	2,82,259	2,32,443	1,96,971	2,31,094
South	NA	NA	3,99,728	2,56,144	1,91,504	1,91,860	2,18,786
Dhalai	0*	0*	0*	0*	0*	3,07,868	3,77,988
Tripura	314514	571002	2,59,390	2,28,118	2,12,093	2,28,515	2,29,440

Sources: a) Statistical Abstract (2011), Government of Tripura b) Economic Review of Tripura, Various Issues, Government of Tripurac) Information from Sample Colleges.d) Census Report, Government of India

NA=Not available* District created after 1991

Growth in Term of Number of Students

The table-2.7 depicts the total number of students in different higher education institutions of Tripura during 1950-51 to 2010-11. As can be seen from table-2.7 total numbers of students in higher education institutions are increasing. There was remarkable increase of students in other higher educational institutions as well as general degree colleges during the study period.

TABLE-2.7
Number of Students in Higher Education of Tripura during 1950-51 to 2010-11 (Figure in number)

Year	*Students in GDCs*	*Students in OHEIs*	*Total Students in HEIs*	*Decadal Growth in GDCs (%)*	*Decadal Growthin OHEIs (%)*	*Decadal Growthin HEIs (%)*
1950-51	495	---	495	---	---	---
1960-61	1950	---	1950	293.94	---	293.94
1970-71	6769	343	7,112	247.13	---	78.82
1980-81	8166	1208	9,374	20.63	252.19	31.81
1990-91	9650	2591	12,241	18.17	114.49	30.58
2000-01	17371	2831	20,202	80.01	9.26	65.04
2010-11	27388	7789	35,177	57.66	175.13	74.13

Sources: a) Statistical Abstract (2011), Government of Tripura b) Economic Review of Tripura,Various Issues, Government of Tripura c) Information from Sample Colleges

GDCs = General Degree Colleges, HEIs = Higher Education Institutions

Decadal growth of the number of students in General Degree Colleges varies from 18.17% to 293.94%. During 1980-81 to 1990-91 the rate of increase was 18.17%, but during the period 1950-51 to 1960-61 this rate was very high as 293.94%.

In case of other higher education institutions there were significant decadal growth during 1970-71 to 1980-81 which is highest at 252.19% and lowest growth as 9.26% during 1990-91 to 2000-01(Table 2.7).

TABLE 2.8

Number of Students in Higher Education Institutions during 1950-51 to 2010-11 (Figure in number)

Year	*Students in HEIs in India*	*Decadal Growth in India (%)*	*Students in HEIs in Tripura*	*Decadal Growth in Tripura (%)*
1950-51	397000	---	495	---
1960-61	1050000	164.48	1950	293.94
1970-71	1954000	86.1	7,112	78.82
1980-81	2752000	40.84	9,374	31.81
1990-91	4925000	78.96	12,241	30.58
2000-01	8399000	70.54	20,202	65.04
2010-11	16975000	102.11	35,177	74.13

Sources: a) Statistical Abstract (2011), Government of Tripurab) Economic Review of Tripura, Various Issues, Government of Tripurac) Information from Sample Collegesd) UGC (2012), Higher Education at a Glance

Fig. 2.3: Growthof Number of Students in Higher Education during 1950-51 to 2010-11

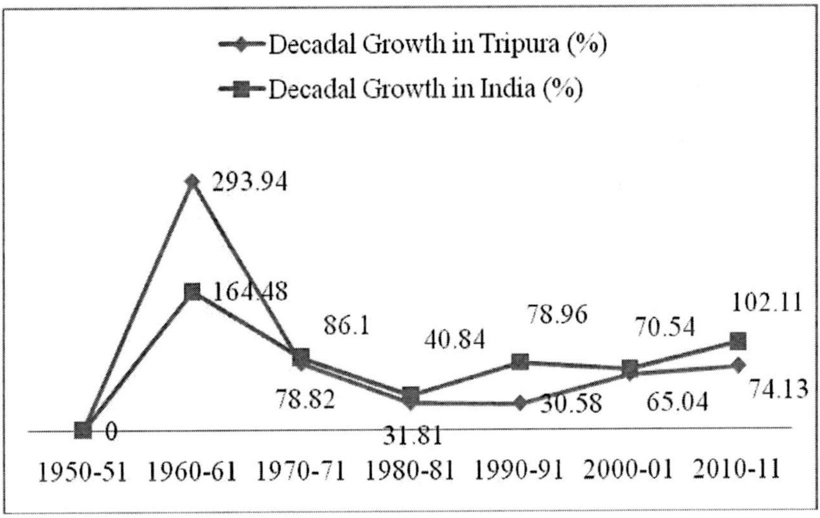

Source: Table-2.8

Number of students in higher education institutions and decadal growth rate in Tripura and India are shown in table 2.8 and fig. 2.3.It is observed from the table that decadal growth of students in higher education in Tripura during 1950-51 to 1960-61 was 293.94 per cent which is very much significant, decline to 31.81 per cent during the period 1980-81, whereas lowest growth rate was 40.84 per cent in India as a whole during same period and again increased to 74.13 per cent in case of Tripura and 102.11 per cent in case of India during2000-01 to 2010-11.It is found that the decadal growth rates of students in Tripura during the period 1970-71 to 2010-11 are less than the national growth rate. But average growth rate is encouraging compared to national average.

TABLE-2.9
District WiseNumber of Students in Higher Education Institutions of Tripura during1950-51 to 2010-11

District	*1950-51*	*1960-61*	*1970-71*	*1980-81*	*1990-91*	*2000-01*	*2010-11*
West	350 (70.71%)	1600 (82.05%)	5529 (77.74%)	7052 (75.23%)	8883 (72.57%)	14103 (69.81%)	24015 (68.27%)
North	145 (29.29%)	350 (17.95%)	845 (11.88%)	1078 (11.50%)	1362 (11.13%)	2249 (11.13%)	4309 (12.25%)
South	Nil	Nil	738 (10.38%)	1244 (13.27%)	1996 (16.31%)	3336 (16.51%)	5724 (16.27%)
Dhalai	Nil	---	---	---	---	514 (2.54%)	1129 (3.21%)
Tripura	495 (100%)	1950 (100%)	7112 (100%)	9374 (100%)	12241 (100%)	20202 (100%)	35177 (100%)

Sources: a) Statistical Abstract (2011), Government of Tripura b) Economic Review of Tripura, Various Issues, Government of Tripurac) Information from Sample Colleges.

District wise numbers of students in higher education institutionsare shown in the table-2.9. The data reveal that the number of students in the West district surpasses all other districts. Regarding the number of students we found that in1950-51 the total number of students in the higher education institutes of the state was 495 and of these 350 were in the West district (70.71%). This trend was maintained all along the decades and even in 2011 we find that out of a total 35,177 students in the entire state, 24,015 were inthe West itself (68.27%).

TABLE 2.10
District wise Number of Students in General Degree Colleges of Tripura during 1950-51 to 2010-11 (Figure in number)

District	*1950-51*	*1960-61*	*1970-71*	*1980-81*	*1990-91*	*2000-01*	*2010-11*	*Average (%)*
West	350	1600	5,186	5,879	6,332	11,458	16,278	66
North	145	350	845	1,043	1,322	2,223	4,257	14
South	Nil	Nil	738	1,244	1,996	3,336	5,724	18
Dhalai	0*	0*	0*	0*	0*	514	1,129	2
Tripura	495	1950	6,769	8,166	9,650	17,371	27,388	100

Sources: a) Statistical Abstract (2011), Government of Tripura, b) Economic Review of Tripura, Various Issues, Government of Tripurac) Information from Sample Colleges

* District created after 1991

Table-2.10 highlights, the district wise number of students in general degree colleges of Tripura during the period 1950-51 to 2010-11.

Thenumber of students in the west district on an average 66%, and rest percent distributed among other three districts. We have observed from the tablethatthe number of students in west district was 350 out of 495 i.e. 70.71 per cent which was higher than those in other districts in 1950-51 and 16,278 out of 27388 i.e. 59.40 per cent during the period 2010-11.

Growth in Terms of Number of Girls Students

Traditionally, education was denied to women in India. However, the constitutional guarantee of equality between sexes, particularly in the context of the promotion of education, was seen as an essential instrument for ensuring their wider involvement in the polity, economic and social transformation. In view of this, sustained efforts to extend education among women were made. Since independence, there has been a phenomenal growth in women's enrollment in higher education. Women enrollment was less than 10 per cent of the total enrollment on the eve of 95 andhas risen to 41.5 per cent in 2010-11. The pace of growth has been particularly faster in the last two decades. It is significant to note that the rise of women enrolment is not confined to a particular stage, but it is consistently rising at all stages viz. graduate, postgraduate and research .Due to the efforts made by the government and the University Grants Commission (UGC), over the years, women education in India has grown both in terms of number of women's colleges and women enrolment (Shodhganga, 2012)[8].

During the post-independence period, there is a significant improvement in women's participation in higher education. Women constitute 43 per cent of the total enrolments in higher education in 2011–12, while there were only 14 women per 100 men in higher education in 1950–51, according to the available UGC statistics (Tilak, 2015)[9].

Table 2.11 depicts the percentage of girl students of total students in higher education. The enrollment of students may be influenced in a wider way by the number of candidates who have successfully completed the preceding public examinations required for entry in different under graduate levels of programmes. Furthermore the data on the number of students, as presented in the above table, for a particular year takes into consideration the total strength of students in particular institutions. These above qualifications apply in case of enrollment of girls' students as well.

TABLE 2.11
Growth of Girl Students in Higher Education during 1950-51 to 2010-11 (Figure in number)

Year	*India*			*Tripura*		
	Students in HEIs	*Girl students*	*Girl students as % of total*	*Students in HEIs*	*Girl students*	*Girl students as % of total*
1950-51	397000	43000	10.83	495	59	11.91
1960-61	1050000	170000	16.19	1950	387	19.85
1970-71	1954000	431000	22.06	7,112	2,083	29.29
1980-81	2752000	749000	27.22	9,374	2,704	28.85
1990-91	4925000	1437000	29.18	12,241	4,550	37.17
2000-01	8399000	3306000	39.36	20,202	8,460	41.88
2010-11	16975000	7049000	41.53	35,177	14,604	41.52

Sources: a) Statistical Abstract (2011), Government of Tripura b) Economic Review of Tripura, Various Issues, Government of Tripurac) Information from Sample Collegesd) UGC (2012), Higher Education at a Glance HEIs = Higher Education Institutions

Based upon the above criteria, it may be observed from the table-2.11 that in absolute terms both the total enrollment and enrollment of girl students shows a somewhat continuous rise located elsewhere in the state Tripura shows a noticeable increase in the girls' enrollment during the period 1950-51 to 2010-11. However, when enrollment of girl students is expressed as a percentage of total enrollment the trend seems to be a decline one during the period 1970-71 to 1980-81 in case of Tripura but it is increasing in case of national level. However, this is not corroborated by the result of the college entry level examination conducted by different Boards/councils. It becomes more surprising since there is actually an increase in the number of candidates passing the above examination.

This discrepancy in an increased number of eligible candidates and decreased level of enrollment in general degree colleges may be explained by the increase of seats in different institutions providing different technical, professional, paramedical and vocational courses.

This phenomenon also supports the near constancy of girl enrollment during the period 1970-71 to 1980-81 in absolute terms and a decline in the same in relative terms in case of Tripura. The establishment of new institutions during the above period catering mostly to the girl students of the stage which included the establishment of other institutions lured away the girl students to pursue professional courses within the state, hence the low enrollment in higher educational institutions as well as general degree colleges. In this way the movement of total enrollment and enrollment of girls students may be explained as this has not been a direct outcome of the number of students passing the higher educational institutions level examination. Lastly, we may conclude that the growth rate of girl enrollment in Tripura is better thanthe national level growth rate.

Gross Enrollment Ratio

There is considerable interstate variation in the level of higher education. By national comparison. GER is lower than the national average in state like Tripura (3.2%), Assam (6.6%), Meghalaya (7.2%), Chattisgarh (7.6%), Orissa (8.2%) ,Jharkand (10.3%),West Bengal (9.7%), Bihar (10%), Sikkim (10.8%), and Rajastan (11%). The enrollment ratio based on eligible student (ERE) is useful estimate as it indicates the access to education to those who have completed the higher secondary stage. In 2003/4 about 59 % of those who completed higher secondary entered into higher education stream. These ratios are higher than the national average by a substantial margin in Mizoram (87.1%), Manipur (87.7%), Nagaland (85.6%), J&K (76.6%) and Kerala (70.6%). By national comparison the ratio is much lower, in Tripura (37.8%),

Chattishgarh (49.6%), Orissa (50.2%), and Arunachal Pradesh (53.5%). In rest of the major states the ratio was around the national average of 59 % (Thorat, 2006)[10].

The expansion in institutional capacity in terms of number of universities and colleges and teachers has provided greater access to the students to post secondary education. The access to higher education is measured in terms of gross enrollment ratio. The estimate of GER is based on data collected from statistical abstract, economic review and also from office of the principal of sample colleges.

TABLE 2.12
Gross Enrolment Ratio in Higher Education of Tripura during 1950-51 to 2010-11

Year	*18-23 Age group Population*	*Students in HEIs*	*GER in HEIs*	*Students in GDCs*	*GER in GDCs*
1950-51	NA	495	NA	495	NA
1960-61	NA	1950	NA	1950	NA
1970-71	1,75,556	7,112	4.05	6,769	3.86
1980-81	2,29,537	9,374	4.08	8,166	3.56
1990-91	3,10,832	12,241	3.94	9,650	3.1
2000-01	3,58,975	20,202	5.63	17,371	4.84
2010-11	4,49,750	35,177	7.82	27,388	6.09

Source: a) Statistical Abstract (2011), Government of Tripura. b) Economic Review of Tripura, Various Issues, Government of Tripura c) Information from Sample Colleges. d) Census Report, Government of India

GDCs = General Degree Colleges, HEIs = Higher Education Institutions, Gross Enrollment Ratio (GER) = Enrolment/Age group population×100, NA = Not Available

Table-2.12 showed the gross enrollment ratio in higher education (Degree Level Institutions) during the period 1950-51 to 2010-11. The access to higher education is measured in terms of gross enrollment ratio. Though GER in Higher Education has improved significantly from 4.05% to 7.82 % w.e.f 1970-71 to 2010 -11, but the GER in degree colleges increased marginally from 3.10 % to 6.09%. During the period 1990-91 the gross enrolment ratio was significantly less than other period of study both the case of higher education and general degree colleges.

Growth in Faculties

Teachers are the key factor for qualitative growth and development of higher education. Without sufficient faculties, educational institutions cannot provide qualitative education. Thus faculties or teachers are the essential component of education. Thedecadal growth of faculty members in higher education institutions of India as well as Tripura presented in the table 2.13 and fig. 2.4.

TABLE 2.13
Growth of Teachers in Higher Education Institutions during 1950-51 to 2010-11

Year	*Teachers in HEIs of India*	*Decadal Growth (%)*	*Teachers in HEIs of Tripura*	*Decadal Growth (%)*
1950-51	23549	---	32	---
1960-61	59673	153.40	95	196.88
1970-71	128876	115.97	447	370.53
1980-81	193341	50.02	520	16.33
1990-91	263125	36.09	668	28.46
2000-01	411628	56.44	958	43.41
2010-11	816966	98.47	1535	60.23

Sources: a) Statistical Abstract (2011), Government of Tripura b) Economic Review of Tripura, Various Issues, Government of Tripura c) Information from Sample Colleges d) UGC (2012), Higher Education at a Glance

Fig. 2.4: Growth of Teachers in Higher Education Institutions during 1950-51 to 2010-11

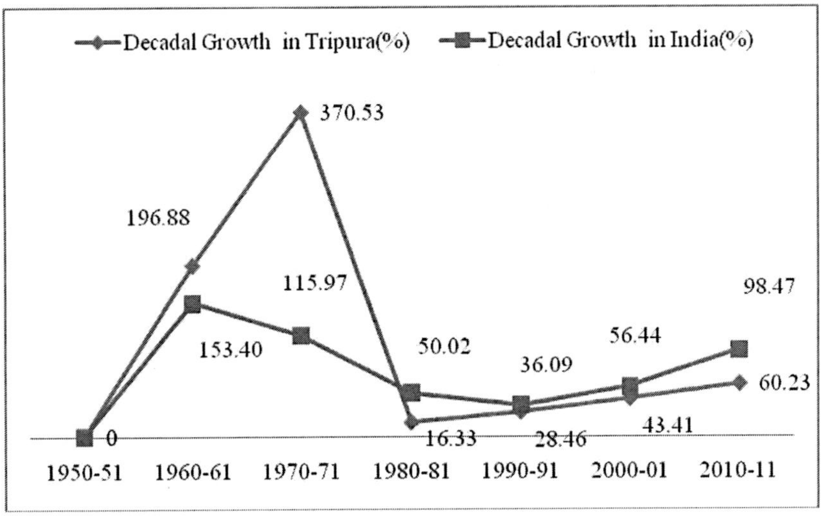

Source: Table 2.13

According to estimates of the association of Indian Universities, there is a shortage of teachers in higher educational institutions. As a result, today, many colleges seem to be running with a larger number of contractual, part-time and guest teachers, also known as teaching assistants in some states and a small number of regular teachers.It is observed from the table that the decadal growth of teachers in higher education institution varies from 36.09 per cent to 153.40 per cent in India.

During 1950-51 to 1960-61 there was the highest growth rate and lowest during the period 1980-81 to 1990-91 at 36.09 per cent. But in Tripura, there was significant growth during 1960-61 to 1970-71 i.e. 370.53 per cent and lowest growth rate during 1970-71 to 1980-81 which stand for 16.33 percent. If we calculate the average decadal growth rate, we can see that 119 per cent growth of teacher in Tripura but in case of India this rate would be 85 per cent.

TABLE 2.14
Teacher-Students Ratio during 1950-51 to 2010-11

Year	*India*			*Tripura*		
	Students in HEIs	*Teachers in HEIs*	*Teacher-Student Ratio*	*Students in HEIs*	*Teachers in HEIs*	*Teacher-Student Ratio*
1950-51	397000	23549	17	495	32	15
1960-61	1050000	59673	18	1950	95	21
1970-71	1954000	128876	15	7,112	447	16
1980-81	2752000	193341	14	9,374	520	18
1990-91	4925000	263125	19	12,241	668	18
2000-01	8399000	411628	20	20,202	958	21
2010-11	16975000	816966	21	35,177	1535	23

Sources: a) Statistical Abstract (2011), Government of Tripura b) Economic Review of Tripura, Various Issues, Government of Tripura c) Information from Sample Collegesd) UGC (2012), Higher Education at a Glance

HEIs = Higher Education Institutions

Conventional norms such as student-faculty ratios or workload may not be very much relevant in higher education as faculty with various specializations are essential. The table-2.14 provides the comparative information about the Teacher-Student ratio of higher educational institutions Tripuraas well as India. UGC considers new norms for Teacher-Student Ratio for the undergraduate courses is as Social Sciences (1:30) and Sciences (1:25) (India Education Review, 2012)[11]. It is observed from the table that though the teacher- student ratio in higher education of Tripura is comparatively less than national average yet encouraging as is reflected in the table-2.14 but distribution of teachers according to subjects and location is not proper and new teacher positions against increased enrollment are not being created at all.

Growth in Term of Academic Programmes

Affiliating colleges are the delivering point of academic programmes prepared by the concerned universities. Thus the sample colleges deliver the academic programme prepared by the Tripura University as affiliating university. In case of sample colleges, academic programme include BA(Pass), BA(Honours), B.Com(Pass), B.Com(Honours), B.Sc(Pass) and B.Sc(Honours). The academic programmes comprise of various subjects like English, Bengali, Accountancy, Physics, Chemistry, Mathematics etc.

TABLE 2.15
Subject Taught in Different Degree Colleges of Tripuraduring 1950-51 to 2010-11

Subjects	*1950-51*	*1960-61*	*1970-71*	*1980-81*	*1990-91*	*2000-01*	*2010-11*
No. of Colleges having subjects between 1 to 5	0	2	0	1	1	0	0
No. of Colleges having subjects between 6 to 10	0	0	6	5	6	5	6
No. of Colleges having subjects between 11 to 15	0	0	0	3	6	8	4
No. of Colleges having subjects more than 15	0	0	0	0	1	1	6
Total No. of Colleges	2	2	6	9	14	14	16

Sources: a) Annual Report (various issues) Tripura University b) Information from Sample Colleges c) Directorate of Higher Education, Government of Tripura

Here we have considered the different courses or subjects (pass &honours) offered in different colleges and this availability of courses increasing day by day since from 1950-51 to the till date (Table-2.15). It is observedthat information collected from sample colleges and secondary sources of information,honours as well as pass courses are not equally introduced in every college. It is also observed that students of Ambedkar College, Govt. Degree College Amarpur, Govt. Degree College Kamalpur, MMD College and Govt. Degree College Kumlung are deprived of availing different subjects as honours course, as well as elective subjects of their own choice. Data from Directorate of Higher Education and Tripura University controller branch reveal that honours courses as well as pass courses are increasing, but science and commerce courses are not available in all the colleges of Tripura. In that respect willing students cannot take science and commerce, subject equally among those colleges.

Disparity

In a democratic society, access to higher education must necessarily be linked to equity. In keeping with this expectation, the National Policy on Education, 1986 (Government of India) emphasized the need to remove disparities so as to equalize educational opportunities, especially for those sections of society that were deprived equality in the past. Diversity in specific policies and programmes of any government often is crucial in forming corrective measures in the development of rural and urban areas. Historically rural areas lag far behind their urban counterparts on multiple indicators of social and economic wellbeing. Disparity reflects not just lower endowments of human and physical capital but also lower returns on them among the SC and ST. There is anecdotal evidence on the lag between urban and rural areas. The government must take the leading role in bridging the rural, urban disparity (Das, Chakraborty and Dey, 2014)[12].

After having assessed the progress atthe aggregate level, we now look at the progress with respect to certain groups or areas and reflect on the situation with respect to inter-group or inter-areas disparities of multiple natures. The present study, however, analyses the disparities between (a) growth in general degree colleges and professional and technical colleges (b) growth in enrolment, number of institutions, deployment of faculties, courses/subjects offered etc. on the basis of rural and urban in the form of state capital and outside state capital, and (c) Inter-District comparisons. In all cases it is found that there are disparities.

Perception of the Respondents

The notion about growth and expansion of higher education in Tripura and its various aspects have been attempted to encapsulate through an opinion survey conducted among Principals / Principal In-charge, DDOs and other faculty members directly or indirectly associated with finance of higher education in Tripura. Perceptions of respondents of general degree colleges of Tripura are shown in Fig. 2.5.

Fig. 2.5: Perception of the Respondents

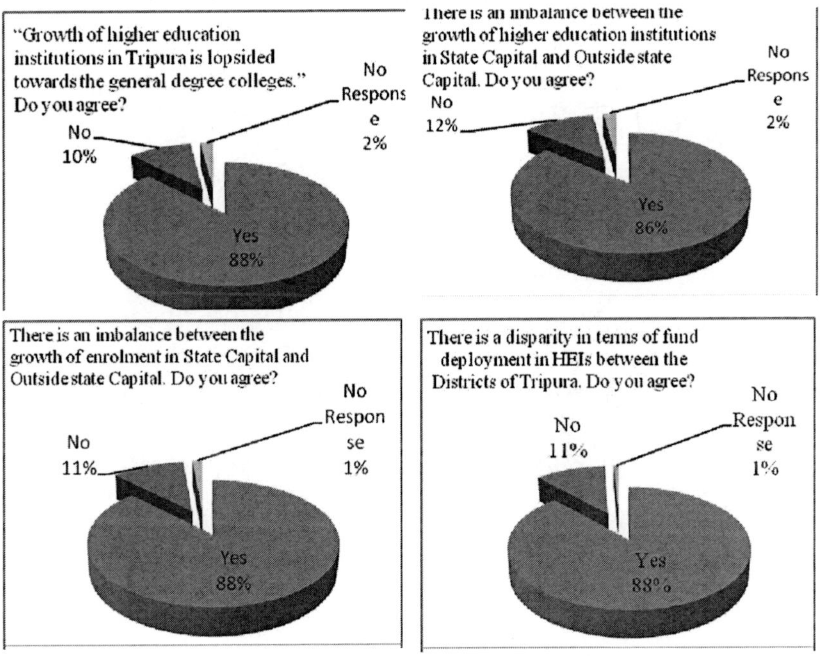

Source: Opinion Survey

Figure 2.5 depicts the responses of the respondents. It was asked to the respondents whether the growth of higher education institutions in Tripura is lopsided towards the general degree colleges. It is found 120 respondents(88%) think that there is a lopsided growth of higher educationtowards the general degree colleges.While discussing the matter further most of the respondents opined that the state government should focus on job oriented technical and professional colleges rather than general degree colleges. It perhaps requires no mention that every year huge number of students are passing out of general degree colleges without any job prospects and the government is spending huge amount for maintaining the system under the constraint of fund crunch.As a result quality of education is compromised.It was also asked whether there is an imbalance between the growth of higher education institutions inthe capital and outside state capital. Most of the respondents confirmed that there is an imbalance between the growth of higher education institutions inthe capital and outside state capital. It is amatter of fact that most of the higher education institutions are concentrated in the state capital, for example, out of 21 technical and professional institutions only one institution are located outside the state capital.

In terms of growth in enrollment the respondents confirm that there is an imbalance between the growth of enrollment in state capital and outside state capital. It is observed during the field study that a large number of school pass out students from all the subdivisions moves to state capital Agartala for higher education due to the following main reasons:

i. Non availability of specific courses/programme

ii. Lack of faculty members even if the courses/programmes are available at sub- division level or district level

iii. Lack of other infrastructure like facility for practical in case science based programmes even if the courses/ programmes are available at sub- division level or district level

While discussing the matter with the respondents it is pointed out by them that lack of funds for building infrastructure as well as for running and maintaining the same are the real problems. Lack of qualified faculty members are another dimension in this issue. They opined these are the main constraints in delivering quality programme.

Whether there is a disparity in terms of fund deployment in HEIs between the Districts of Tripura? This question was put forward to the respondents. Majority of the respondents agreed with the view.

About the finance there is a strong opinion in favour of it being a complex function involving policy making, planning and prudent financial management with sources of finance to be more diversified. About the growth of higher education in Tripura the overwhelming opinion is in favour of it being lopsided towards general degree colleges with disparity in terms of growth, enrollment and course availability existing in the institutions throughout the state. It is clear that maximum number of candidates want to get admitted in the colleges of the capital.

There exists asignificant difference between capital and outside capital in terms of enrollment of students. So it may be deduced that there is infrastructural discrimination in terms of facility among the colleges of capital and outside capital. It has also been observed that the above indices are in favourable condition in the institutions existing in the state capital.

Policy Perspective of State Government

Allocation of inadequate funds and dearth of teaching staff have impacted higher education in Tripura, a report by the Comptroller and Auditor General of India (CAG) said.In its latest report, the CAG said that an absence of an effective monitoring mechanism also prevented ensuring quality education to students in the northeastern state. The University Grants Commission (UGC) has prescribed a norm of 1:30 for the teacher-student ratio in general colleges, but in case of Tripura it is 1: 33 in the year 2011-12(Das, Chakraborty and Dey, 2014)[13]. But the deployment of teachers in different degree colleges is not proportionate resulting concentration of teachers in the state capital.

According to an estimation on an average 13 per cent student passing higher secondary examinations from the Tripura Board have been migrating outside the state to pursue higher education, the CAG report said, adding that this percentage would be higher, if students passing out from the CBSE (Central Board of Secondary Education) and ICSE (Indian Council of Secondary Education) courses are also considered. According to the Union Ministry of Human Resource Development, the percentage of Gross Enrolment Ratio (GER) for higher education in Tripura ranged from 6.16 per cent to 6.83 per cent during the period from 2004-05 to 2006-07 as against the national average of 11.30 per cent during the corresponding period. Despite the Tripura government's assurance to the centre, the state's higher education department neither formulated an action plan nor did it incorporate any policy in the annual action plans to raise GER for higher education up to the national average.The CAG suggested obtaining inputs from the educational institutions before planning its activities and formulating its budget. The Tripura Higher Education Department should take effective action for recruitment of teaching staff in line with UGC norms to ensure quality education.

The Government of Tripura is all set to become an educational hub for the northeastern states and neighboring countries, including Bangladesh. The state government is working on to set-up several technical, medical and educational institutions. Tripura has achieved the remarkable distinction of being the only capital city in the northeastern region to have two medical colleges. The state government has taken up an ambitious plan to set up more technical institutions and degree colleges in each sub-division.

Tripura will set up an Indian Institute of Information Technology (IIIT) in Bodhjungnagar, one of the northeastern region's biggest industrial zones (CAG Report)[14].

Accreditation should be obtained for each College by providing infrastructure and other facilities. B-Grade Colleges should be brought under A-Grading.An Initiative for NAAC accreditation to all Colleges which Strengthen the existing educational institutions and set up new institutions for meeting the requirement of Higher Education of the entire population of the State.

The Colleges having Science or the College proposed to be only a Science College should have leaned on I.T. Mechanism to be drawn to enlighten students for completing the course. In all the Colleges having a Science stream, the laboratories should be well equipped. Colleges to have proper boundaries and proper security system to discourage threat and misuse of classrooms.

The data collected from the sample colleges reveals that on an averageout of 100 students admitted in 1st year only 45 students could complete the 3 year degree course (Das, Chakraborty and Dey, 2014)[15].Thus, there is a huge drop out, resulting wastage of limited government funds available for colleges. To put a check on discontinuation of studies in 2nd year and 3rd year classes it is necessary to evolve a mechanism in each College to find out the reasons for such discontinuation of courses by the students and as far as practicable assistance to be provided.

It has been projected by the Department of Higher Education, Government of Tripura, to achieve the Gross Enrollment Ratio of 15% by 2020. Therefore provision for creation of additional infrastructure to accommodate more students in all the existing General Degree Colleges has been initiated. But the additional funds required for the said purpose are not estimated nor has been sanctioned to any colleges. However to provide higher education facilities in the rural areas for the promotion of tribal, minorities & backward communities living in the sub-divisions, 6 new General Degree Colleges in 6 rural places have been identified and started functioning (Perspective Plan 2010-2020)[16].

Chapter Summary

The present chapter analyses whether the expansion of higher education in terms of number of institutions, enrollments, faculties, programmes offered, etc. has taken place in Tripura during the period 1950-51 to 2010-11 and if so whether this expansion is in balanced direction. The study shows that the expansion has taken place in the area of higher education of Tripura remarkably. After some period of growth the decadal expansion rate was higher than the national rate. However, in most of the study period the decadal growth rate of the state in terms of many parameters was less thanthe national rate of growth.

The next important issue is balance growth across the state. Therefore, one research question was to understand whether disparity or imbalance exists in the process of growth and expansion of higher education in Tripura. At the end of the discussion in this chapter it can be concluded that with the growth of higher education institutions in the state the disparity has also been taken place among the districts or state capital and outside state capital. The study has come up with ample indications that there is a strong disparity in the growth and expansion of the higher education sector. It is revealed in the distribution of establishment of higher educational institutions along the state as emphasis has been given towards the state capital in this regards. The same may be observed in terms of institution to population ratio and its distribution along the state. It is also supported by the fact that institutions of higher education in different fields are also conglomerated around the state capital itself. Thus, it may be observed that with a remarkable growth and expansion of higher education in Tripura it has not been able to be free of bias which indicates a strong disparity in this regards. Besides the secondary data, the selected respondents are also in strong view that disparity in higher education is a matter of concern for the state.

Furthermore, the state government has paid limited attention in this regard. It will not be out of context to mention here that despite the gravity of the issue the state government does not have any policy, for establishing the higher education institution in particular and development of higher education in general. There is no separate cell or desk in the departments of higher education to deal with the expansion and finance related issues. Thus the issue needs the attention of the policy makers.

REFERENCES

1. UGC. (2012).*Higher Education in India at a glance.* New Delhi: UGC.
2. Heggade.O.D. (1998). Finances *and cost of Higher Education in India.* Mohit publication, New Delhi, Pp-34-35.
3. Joshi, S. (2012). Sustainable *Development of the Higher Education Sector in India for Catalyzing Services-Driven Growth* (Working Paper No. 2012/01). Maastricht School of Management. Pp 6-7.
4. Komow,B.,Khanna,R. & Sharma,R.K. (2012).Journey of Higher Education in India: An Analysis of Post Independence Era. *Asian Journal of Multidimensional Research, Vol-I Issue-I,* June.P-8, 9 &12.
5. Sinha,A.&Chakraborty, K.S. (2010). Management of Higher Education Institutions in Tripura. In *Reflection on Economy & Society.* Akansha Publishing House, New Delhi.Pp-104-112.
6. Op.cit. UGC (2012)
7. Debroy, D. (2011). The Advancement of Higher Education in Tripura. *International Journal of Multidisciplinary Research,* Vol. II, No I. April'11 – June 2011, PP 62-65.
8. http://shodhganga.inflibnet.ac.in:8080/jspui/bitstream/10603/40610/9/12_chapter3.pdf accessed on 23.1.2016. Pp-95-96.
9. Tilak,J.B.G. (2015). How Inclusive Is Higher Education in India?*Social Change* .SAGE Publications. 45(2).P-196.
10. Thorat,S. (2006). *Higher Education in India Emerging Issues Related to Access, Inclusiveness and Quality.* Nehru Memorial Lecture, University of Mumbai.P-5.

11. *India Education Review.(2012).*Retrieved 2015, fromhttp://www.indiaeducationreview.com/news/ugc-consider-new-norms-teacher-student-ratio

12. Das, S.,Chakraborty, K.S. &Dey, N.B. (2014). Opportunity of Higher Education in Tripura: A Study With Reference to Disparities among General Degree Colleges. *International Journal of Informative &Fututistic Research, Vol-II,* September. P-61

13. Ibid. P-59.

14. CAG. (2013*). Higher education in Tripura 'ailing'.* Retrieved from. Retrieved from http://www.igovernment.in/site/higher-education-tripura-ailing-cag-373 00 accessed on 6.4.2010.

15. Das,S.,Chakraborty,K.S. &Dey, N.B.(2014). An Analysis of Growth and Development of Higher Education in Tripura: A Review. *Tripura Journal of Social Science, Vol-I,* January-2014, Pp 98.

16. Government of Tripura, *Perspective Plan 2010-20.* Retrieved from http://highereducation.tripura.gov.in/pdf/plan-20.pdf accessed on 6.10.2013.

CHAPTER 3

Sources and Expenditure of Funds

Introduction

Education in India comes under the concurrent list in the Constitution of India. The responsibility of financing higher education is shared by both public and private sectors. Even in the public sector, it's a joint responsibility of Central/Federal government as well as State/Provincial government. About 80 per cent of the public higher education funding has been sourced from State governments and about 20 per cent from the Centre. Of the 80 per cent State government funding about 82 percent goes into non-plan expenditure, i.e. routine administration and maintenance, and hardly in any capacity building (NUEPA, 2009)[1]. The Central government spending is found to be lopsided, more towards Central Universities and Centers of Excellence serving hardly 3 per cent of the total students. While the trend has always been upwards, the total public expenditure on higher education at about 1.25 per cent of the GDP is by any standards certainly insufficient (UGC -2012) [2]. Public expenditure on education should reach the level of 6 per cent of GNP by 1986. Report of the (Punnayya Committee, 1993) [3] pointed out that the existing mechanism of funding for higher education perpetuates inefficiency and suggested that the grant-in-aid system should be suitably modified to reward quality, efficiency and innovativeness. The committee recommended the replacement of the existing practice of negotiated block grants based on historical allocations by policy driven funding based on the unit cost method. There is an urgent need to improve governance by developing expertise in "educational management" and avoid burdening good academics with administrative chores (Yaspal Committee Report, 2008)[4]. An attempt has been made to analyse the financial health of higher education in Tripura in this chapter.

Financing Education

After Independence higher education in India has been largely financed by the government with the social institutions progressively withdrawing. The government's share has steadily increased from 49 per cent in 1950-51 to about 90 per cent today. The government spends about 3.7 per cent of GNP on education of which the share of higher education is about 0.8 per cent.

Amongst the different sectors of education the share of higher education was the highest, at 25 per cent, during the Fourth Five year Plan (1969-74). It remained stable at 22 per cent during the Fifth and Sixth Five Year Plans but declined to only 8 per cent in the Eighth Five Year Plan (1992-97). It was 6 per cent of GNP by the end of the Ninth Five Year Plan (1997-2002). However, the share of higher education is not likely to increase (Gandhi, 2015)[5].

Higher education has generally been recognized as a public good, at least as a quasi-public good. The public good nature of higher education warrants that the state should play a more active role in the financing of higher education. Indeed, the state has been funding higher education since independence. Early on, it was realized that a strong, self-reliant and modern industrial economy could be built only on the foundations of higher education. However, owing to several factors, including the new economic policies adopted since the 1990s, state funding to education in general, and higher education in particular, has been declining in real terms (Prakash, 2007)[6].

Central and state governments have the responsibility of funding higher education – plan expenditure for development and non-plan expenditure for maintenance expenses. The central plan and non-plan expenditure accounts for 20% and state plan and non-plan expenditure accounts for the 80% of public spending to all government managed institutions as well as the segment of private managed institutions. There is of course a segment of private managed institutions which raise their funding from self- financing programmes and do not depend upon government funding. The pattern of public expenditure in higher education can be divided into two important phases. The first phase from 1951 to 1980 saw high growth of public investment and the second, from 1980 to 2004, was a relatively low growth period for public investment in higher education (NUEPA, 2009)[7].

The financing of higher education, however, is often prioritized due to competing demands for budgetary funds from primary and secondary education sectors. As a proportion of GNP in Higher Education was only about 0.19 per cent in 1950-51 of 1980-81 it went up fivefold to 1 per cent but by mid-1990s it again dropped to 0.4 per cent. In the government plan outlay the share of higher education doubled from 9 per cent in the first five year plan to 18 per cent in the second. It increased to 25 per cent in the fourth, but has now come down to 15 per cent in the seventh five year plan. In the eight five year plan it was around 8 per cent. It may be stated that the non-plan expenditure in education is huge compared to plan expenditure. Resource crunch in higher education is being felt in a serious way.

Other sources of financing besides the government have to be developed so that the massive expenditure required for expanding, improving and bringing it to world standards could be carried out. With an expanding middle class and globalization, this is possible provided innovative policies are formulated and implemented (Kaul, 2006)[8].

Two studies by Sudhanshu Bhushan and Ravi Srivastva examined the issues related to financing and brought useful insights on the situation with respect to finances in higher education. Ravi Srivastva's paper worked out the financial requirement of enrollment target of 15% during the 11th Plan. These two papers analyzed the trends in total public expenditure on higher education by the Centre and the states, including the trend in the per student expenditure on higher education.

Of the two levels of government, the bulk of expenditure on education comes from the state governments, although the Centre shares a greater proportion of the expenditure on higher education. The share of the Central government in total expenditure declined from 24.7 per cent during 1970-71 to 1980-81 to 21.1 per cent during 1981-82 to 1991-92 per cent and further to 20.3 per cent during 1992-93 to 2003-04.The rate of growth of expenditure on total as well as higher education was significantly higher than the rate of growth of national income in the first two decades. Total educational expenditure continued to be higher than the growth of national income till the beginning of the reform period. The increase in the public expenditure has also lagged behind the increase in the student enrollment. Enrollment in higher education has been expanding at a rapid pace, even as the tempo of public expenditure has not been maintained. Particularly in the reform phase since 1992-93, the increase in real expenditure has lagged behind the rate of increase in student enrollment in general education. As a result, during this phase, the rate of growth in per student expenditure has been negative. Per student public expenditure has registered a negative rate of growth both for Central as well as State expenditure (Thorat, 2008)[9].

Financing higher education is the key theme in the debate on higher education in the world. With the landscape of higher education changing rapidly, one cannot think of a stable funding structure for higher education. The future of financing higher education cannot be merely an extension of the present, but shaped by new realities, such as massive growth in enrollment, new mechanisms of cost sharing, the appearance of new cross-border suppliers, the emergence and growth of different types of public and private higher education providers, distance education and many other innovations.

Consistent with these realities, new and flexible ways of tackling financing issues in higher education have to be found. This would require alternative policies and mechanisms to provide answers to these challenges (Agarwal, 2006)[10].

Sustainable Financing of Higher Education

Public financing of higher education would fill in the critical gaps. To enable this, public funding has to increase significantly. It is equally important to improve the quality of expenditure by targeting it better. On the basis of the recommendations made by different experts pertaining to sustainable financing and better financial management of higher education in India is mentioned below:

I. There is a need to substantially enhance the level of funding for higher education in the country by both augmenting support from the government and ensuring greater contribution from the households.

II. Funding mechanism needs to facilitate and encourage higher education institutions to raise internal resources, particularly to raise tuition fees to realistic levels.

III. Larger share of public funds, particularly central funds need to be assigned for student-based grants for providing access to students from poor background. This not only ensures better targeting of public funds by guaranteeing equal access opportunities for all, but also would ensure a more efficient and demand driven system of public funding.

IV. Higher education institutions supported by the state governments face acute problems of deteriorating infrastructure and facilities and a large number of vacancies of faculty. Adequate and continuing support is required to bring up the level of these institutions to minimum standards.

V. Public funding, both to individuals and the institutions, may be provided to groups to promote collaboration and cooperation.

To encourage working together, glue funding or mobility grants would be essential. So it may be concluded that public funding for higher education, both at the centre and the state level, need to be increased significantly (Agarwal, 2006)[11].

From the viewpoints of enhancing accountability of the system of education and improving cost efficiency as well as cost effectiveness of investment in higher education, it would be desirable to consider an alternative approach of financing higher education. The prevailing system of financing universities by the centre and the state governments allows for the simultaneous existence of the best or worst performing university departments as a judge from the quality of teaching and research in such departments. Though there are differences in the level of grants received by them in terms of per students' costs, they continue to exist and make increasing claims on government funds and that without improving the quality of education (Ansari, 1988)[12].

Financial Control in Higher Education

Colleges and universities differ not only in how much they spend per student but also in how their resources are allocated. Relative to universities, colleges allocate a significantly larger proportion of their budgets to salaries and allowances and a correspondingly smaller share to non personnel items. On an average, colleges allocate about 93 percent of their budget to salaries and allowances, leaving only seven percent to cover all operational and other instructional costs. A high percentage of personnel expenditure covers the salaries and benefits of nonteaching staff (Bellew and De Stefano, 1991)[13].

TABLE 3.1
Total Budget, Education Budget and Higher Education Budget of Tripura During 2007-08 to 2011-12 (Rupees in Lakh)

Year	*Total Budget (RE)*	*Education. Budget (RE)*	*Higher Education Budget (RE)*	*Education Budget as Per cent of Total Budget**	*Higher Education Budget as Per cent of Total Budget**	*Higher Education Budget as Per cent of Education Budget**
2007-08	427858.79	84369.35	6781	19.72	1.58	8.04
2008-09	512161.28	96421.55	7939	18.83	1.55	8.23
2009-10	655500.21	144833.86	17706	22.10	2.7	12.23
2010-11	629397.96	145210.03	14514	23.07	2.3	10.00
2011-12	705471.8	170441.9	20437	24.16	2.89	11.99

Sources: a) Annual financial statement (various issues), Government of Tripura
b) Finance Department, Expenditure Budget Detailed Account (Relevant years), Government of Tripura

*Result computed

Total budget, education budget and higher education budget of Tripura during the period from 2007-08 to 2011-12 is shown in the table-3.1 & Fig. 3.1. It is observed from the table that higher education budget is fluctuating, as a percentage of the total budget; the figure was 2.89 per cent in the year 2011-12 which has nearly doubled as compared to 1.58 Per cent in the year 2007-08.Higher education budget as percent of the education budget varies from 8.04 per cent to 12.23 per cent. The rate of higher education budget as percent of the education budget is increasing trend during 2007-08 to 2009-10 but thereafter this trend is declining except during 2010-11 to 2011-12. Apart from the compulsion to allot an increased amount of fund in higher education, one can be assured of the fact that there is a percentage of increase in budget expenditure of higher education. Thus a shift in the policy towards more inclusive education can be envisaged in the information contained in the study.

Fig. 3.1: Higher Education Budget as per cent of Total Budget and Education Budget of Tripura during 2007-08 to 2011-12

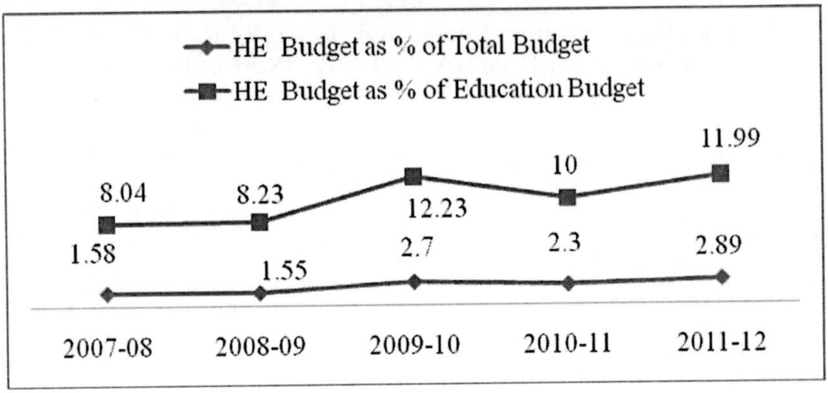

Source: Table-3.1

Adequate resources have always been challenges for higher education. Only about 1 Per cent of India's GDP is spent on higher education, which is lower than that of the country like the U.S.A. per cent U.K. per cent and China per cent (Rayal and Kamble, 2012)[14].Public expenditure (Centre and States) on education is only around 3.6 per cent of GDP. Government funding of higher education is still below 1 per cent of GDP. The percentage expenditure of University and Higher Education to GDP, which was 0.77 per cent in 1990-91 showed a gradual decrease to 0.66 per cent in 2004-2005. Various committees have unanimously recommended that state funding be increased to 6 per cent.

While the Central Advisory Board of Education (CABE) recommends spending 1 percent to higher education and 0.5 per cent to technical education, the proportions in 2004-05 were 0.34 per cent of higher education and 0.03 percent for technical education. India also has one of the lowest public expenditure on higher education per student at 406 US Dollars (Bhatia and Dash, 2010)[15].

Higher education budget as per cent of GSDP of Tripura during 2007-08 to 2011-12 presented in table 3.2 and Fig. 3.2.

TABLE 3.2

Higher Education Budget as per cent of GSDP (Current price) of Tripura during 2007-08 to 2011-12 (Rupees in Lakh)

Year	*GSDP*	*Higher Education Budget*	*Higher Education Budget as per cent of GSDP**
2007-08	1179707	6781	0.57
2008-09	1357264	7939	0.58
2009-10	1534821	17706	1.15
2010-11	1738688	14514	0.83
2011-12	1973096	20437	1.04

Sources: a) Finance Department, Expenditure Budget Detailed Account (Relevant years), Government of Tripura. b) Statistical Abstract (2011), Government of Tripura

*Result computed

Fig. 3.2: Higher Education Budget as per cent of GSDP of Tripura (Current price) during 2007-08 to 2011-12

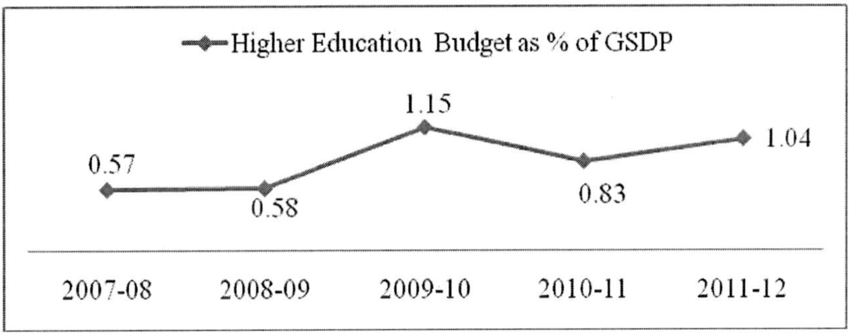

Source: Table-3.2

Since both the information has been provided at current price and idea about the pattern of their movement in absolute terms can easily be observed from the table 3.2. In absolute terms the rise in GSDP during the five year period is almost replicated in the rise of higher education budget of the same period. It may be observed that there has been a substantial rise in GSDP from 0.57

per cent in 2007-08 to 1.04 per cent in 2011-12 with a high of 1.15 per cent in 2009-10. This rising trend in higher education budget during 2009-10 and 2011-12 may be attributed to the following facts:

a) Introduction of revised pay scale for college teachers;

b) Fresh appointment of college teachers necessitated by the introduction of new courses in existing government general degree colleges and fulfillment of posts as vacated due to superannuation of existing college teachers;

c) Providing for infrastructure for the introduction of new courses not only in general degree colleges but also in other areas of higher education.

Plan and Non Plan Expenditure

Plan expenditure is that part of total budget expenditure, which is meant for financing the schemes and programmes, especially framed under the current Five-year plan or the

TABLE 3.3
Growth of Plan and Non Plan Expenditure on Higher Education in Tripura during 2007-08 to 2011-12 (Rupees in Lakh)

Year	*Plan Expenditure*	*Non Plan Expenditure*	*Total*	*AGR in per cent*
2007-08	816	3407	4223	---
2008-09	3595.41	3390	6985.41	65.41
2009-10	5175.25	4607.82	9783.07	40.05
2010-11	7135.75	7190	14325.8	46.43
2011-12	5824.7	6651	12475.7	-12.91
Annual Average Growth Rate				34.75

Sources: a) Finance Department, Expenditure Budget Detailed Account (Relevant years), Government of Tripura. b) Annual Financial Statement (Various Issues), Government of Tripura

AGR = Annual Growth Rate

unfinished tasks of the previous Plans. So the Plan expenditure indicates the direction of changes in the education sector.

Non plan expenditure is the expenditure on operating and maintaining existing education infrastructure. So at the end of a five year plan, the recurring parts of Plan expenditure on different programmes or schemes become part of Non plan expenditure. So the Non plan expenditure is expected to increase steadily over the years. The scope for decreasing this expenditure is very limited, as it involves maintaining the stock of education, infrastructure which has been determined by the policies in the past years and while the savings through introduction of efficiency measures are possible that would be a one-time savings. Another distinction to note is between expenditure on Revenue account, and expenditure on Capital account. Expenditure in Revenue accounts constitutes the bulk of the budget expenditure on education and very little is spent on the Capital account. But this does not imply that there is little or no asset creation in education (Das, Chakraborty and Dey,

TABLE 3.4
Expenditure on Higher Education in Tripura as a % of GSDP during 2007-08 to 2011-12 (Rupees in Lakh)

Year	*GSDP*	*Plan & Non plan Expenditure*	*Plan and Non plan Expenditure as Per cent of GSDP*
2007-08	1179707	4223	0.36
2008-09	1357264	6985.41	0.51
2009-10	1534821	9783.07	0.64
2010-11	1738688	14325.8	0.82
2011-12	1973096	12475.7	0.63

Sources: a) Finance Department, Expenditure Budget Detailed Account (Relevant years), Government of Tripura. b) Annual Financial Statement (Various Issues), Government of Tripura c) Statistical Abstract (2011), Government of Tripura

2014)[16]. Growth of expenditure on higher education in Tripura is presented in the table 3.3.

It is observed from the table that trend of plan and non plan expenditure of higher education in Tripura is declining from 46.43 per cent to (-) 12.91 per cent during the period 2010-11 to 2011-12. Though the annual average growth rate is 34.75 per cent, the annual growth rate of plan and non plan expenditure on higher education is higher during the period 2007-08 to 2008-09 than other periods and negative growth noticed during the period 2010-11 to 2011-12.

Fig. 3.3: Expenditure on Higher Education in Tripura as per cent of GSDP during 2007-08 to 2011-12

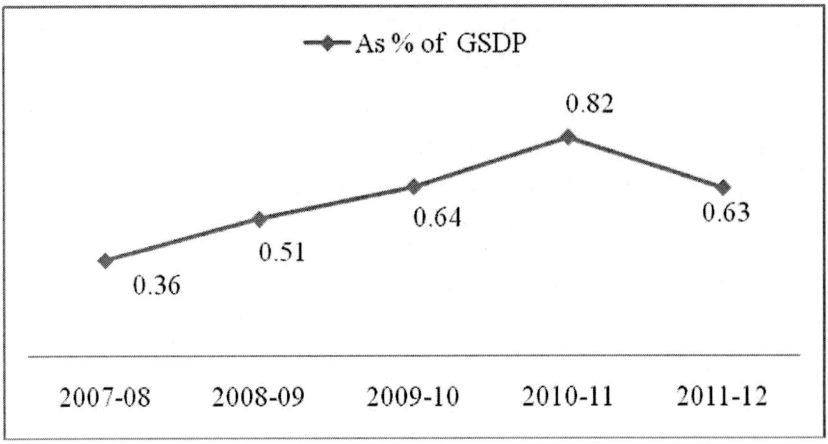

Source: Table 3.4

Table 3.4 and Fig.3.3 depict the expenditure on higher education in Tripura. It is observed that expenditure on higher education as a percent of GSDP varies from 0.36 per cent to 0.82 per cent. During the year 2007-08 this rate was 0.36 per cent, which is the lowest and highest in the year 2010-11. If we consider expenditure on higher education in India we observed that during 2007-08 the rate of expenditure on higher education as a percent of GDP was 1.14 per cent and increased to 1.25 per cent during 2009-10 and decline to 1.22 per cent during 2010-11.

(UGC, 2012 & 2013)[17]. For the growth and expansion of higher education in Tripura government should spend more funds like national average.

Role of Finance in Managing Sample Colleges

Finance is essential for all kinds of academic activities in the college. Therefore, proper management of finance is key to the success of the academic organization, besides other activities. An academic institution is sure to collapse if finance is not supplied adequately. On the other hand the uncontrolled supply of excess fund in any organization cannot ensure the success. The financial management in academic institutions can play a positive role like that of the heart in the human body. Just as the heart gets blood and circulates the same in the body with the help of the brain, in the same way institutions gets finance to circulate it among the various activities under the direction of academics.

As per delegation of financial power vested upon Principal, Drawing and Disbursing Officer and other members of the committees of the colleges must see that the funds are procured and sanctioned properly in a balanced way and there is optimum utilization of funds. It involves the application of general management principles to financial operations (Mahanta, 2013)[18].

It is found that the individual General Degree Colleges in Tripura do not prepare the requirement of fund for their college; rather it is the department of higher education prepares the requirements of funds for all the government colleges as a whole. The Department, in turn, distributes the available funds among the colleges without any proper guidelines or any acceptable mechanism for distribution of such fund. As a result availability of funds as per requirement of the college is not sanctioned by the Department as reported by most of the colleges during field studies. It is also felt by the respondent colleges that inadequate fund in proper head and sub-head wise is one of the important factors responsible for quality education in their institution. It was asked to the respondents what are the most important factors that need immediate attention for providing quality higher education in colleges of Tripura in the light of their experiences. Likert scale method has been used to understand the perception of the respondents.The responses of the respondents were obtained in likert five point scales: strongly agreed, agreed, undecided, disagree, strongly disagree. The results are shown in table 3.5:

TABLE 3.5
What are the most important factors that need immediate attention for providing higher education in your college?

Factors	*SA (5)*	*A (4)*	*U (3)*	*D (2)*	*SD (1)*	*TR=137 (WA)*	*WI*	*Rank*
	NR (Score)	*NR (Score)*	*NR (Score)*	*NR (Score)*	*NR (Score)*			
Availability of adequate finance for running and maintenance of colleges.	130 (650)	3 (12)	1 (3)	2 (4)	1 (1)	670	4.891	1
Availability of funds for purchase of necessary capital items.	126 (630)	8 (32)	0	3 (6)	0	668	4.876	2
Availability of qualified teachers.	100 (500)	28 (112)	2 (6)	1 (2)	6 (6)	626	4.569	3
Availability of classrooms	20 (100)	0	5 (15)	43 (86)	69 (69)	270	1.971	10
Availability of well-equipped laboratory for practical	9(45)	11 (44)	32 (96)	13 (26)	72 (72)	283	2.066	8
Availability of library books	38 (190)	35 (140)	7 (21)	32 (64)	25 (25)	440	3.212	6
Availability of computer lab	13 (65)	15 (60)	9 (27)	25 (50)	75 (75)	277	2.022	9

Availability of academic leadership in management	52 (260)	32 (128)	14 (42)	16 (32)	23 (23)	485	3.540	4
Students participation in academic affairs	38 (190)	29 (116)	5 (15)	21 (42)	44 (44)	407	2.971	7
Over all academic Management of the college	45 (225)	31 (124)	9 (27)	13 (26)	39 (39)	441	3.219	5

Source: Opinion Survey

SA = Strongly Agreed, A = Agreed, U = Undecided, D = Disagreed, SD = Strongly Disagreed, NR = Number of Respondents, TR = Total Respondents, WA = Weighted Aggregate, WI = Weighted Index

Based on the survey a few factors are identified and weighted index computed to find out the ranking of the factor according to their importance to the respondents using weighted index formula. To determine the important factors which need immediate attention for providing quality higher education consideration has been made to arrange those factors on the basis of a rank. Again, this rank has been constructed on the basis of weighted index of each of the factors. This weighted index of each factor has been constructed on the basis of 5 points Likert Scale imposed on the number of responses against each of the factors. For each factor response have been arranged and put on the scale.

This is converted into quantified values of the weighted aggregate ($\sum fiwi$). This weighted aggregate then has been expressed as a weighted index by using the formula $WI = \frac{\sum fi\,wi}{\sum fi}$ Where WI = Weighted Index; fi = frequency of each category; wi = Likert weights. The weighted index of each factor has been arranged and factors, according to rank are as follows:

1. Availability of adequate finance for running and maintenance of colleges.
2. Availability of funds for purchase of necessary capital items.
3. Availability of qualified teachers

These are the most important factors that are able to provide quality higher education in the college.

4. Availability of academic leadership in management
5. Overall academic Management of the college
6. Availability of library books

Factors as per rank 4, 5 and 6 are less important to be considered by the respondents. Last four factors are not considered as factors that are important for quality higher education. On the basis of the above discussion, it may be concluded that to provide quality higher education in general degree colleges of Tripura the prime aspect of consideration is necessary financial involvement which required for both recurring and nonrecurring expenditure. Though there has not been a direct relationship established between fund flows and availability of adequately qualified teachers it may be mentioned that existence of qualified teachers might depend on the financial flow itself.

The factors which have shown that they may be considered less important for the above objective may not be discarded as unnecessary. Rather, this may be viewed as changing attitudes towards quality in higher education for general degree colleges. For example availability of class room has been accorded, as per the above ranking, the least importance, though they might not be considered to be such. This may also be interpreted as dependence on sources other than those available in the institution. All in all the factors identified and ranked as above may provide a strong basis for policy initiative in this respect.

TABLE 3.6
Reliability Statistics

Cronbach's Alpha	*No. of Items*
0.799	10

Again also for identifying the factors affecting quality of higher education in college, we have also used the factor analysis. Before conducting factor analysis, we checked the reliability of the questions asked. The reliability statistic Cronbach's Alpha for the parts came to be 0.799 (table 3.6) shows it quite satisfactory for the further proceedings.

After that we have done factor analysis, it has been carried out using SPSS 17 software for extracting the factors. For avoiding the cross loading among the factors of the variables Eigenvalue criteria (greater than one) and Varimax Rotation criteria has been used respectively. First of all we will present sample adequacy result. Sample adequacy has been checked using KMO and Bartlett's test which is satisfactory it came as more than 0.6 (table 3.7). This shows that number of samples collected is enough for study

TABLE 3.7
KMO and Bartlett's Test

Kaiser-Meyer-Olkin Measure of Sampling Adequacy.	0.686
Approx. Chi-Square	680.552
Df	28
Sig.	0.000

Source: Result calculated on the basis of responses of respondents.

In the second step, summary of the extracted factors and the total variance explained by total number of extracted factors has been presented. Because of cross loading we have omitted one variable (availability of well-equipped laboratory for practical)

and then run the analysis. It is notice that these extracted factors are obtained after avoiding the cross loadings. We found that three factors are loaded and it explains 80.831 per cent variance (table 3.8). This shows that the variables included in the questionnaire are able to explain only 80.831 per cent.of the total variation and reset in unexplained.

TABLE 3.8
Total Variance Explained

Factor	*Eigenvalues*	*Percent of Variance*	*Cumulative Percent*
1	3.189	39.863	39.863
2	1.693	21.166	61.029
3	1.584	19.802	80.831

Source: Result calculated on the basis of responses of respondents.

TABLE 3.9
Varimax rotated loading

Variables	*Factor 1*	*Factor 2*	*Factor 3*
Availability of adequate finance for running and maintenance of colleges	0.943		
Availability of funds for purchase of necessary capital items.	0.926		
Availability of qualified teachers.	0.837		
Availability of classrooms	0.820		
Availability of library books		0.895	
Availability of computer lab		0.853	
Availability of academic leadership in management			0.896
Student participation in academic affairs			0.788

Source: Result calculated on the basis of responses of respondents.

Four variables are loaded under factor 1 and it is explaining 39.863 per cent of the variance out of 80.831 per cent total variance explained. Factor 2 explaining 21.166 per cent and factor 3 explaining 19.802 per cent of the variance out of 80.831per cent total variance explained. Table 3.9 shows the summary result of the factors loaded under each factor.

After conducting the factor analysis with the help of factor score we have conducted a multiple regression analysis (table 3.10) to checks the contribution of each factor to the overall academic management of colleges.

Table 3.10
Result of regression analysis

Variables	Beta	Std. Error	t-statistics	Sig.
(Constant)	2.701	0.091	29.641	0000
Factor 1	0.381	0.091	4.162	000
Factor 2	-0.428	0.091	-4.678	000
Factor 3	-0.331	0.091	-3.617	000
R Square				0.282
Adjusted R Square				0.266
F-statistics				17.428***

Source: Result calculated on the basis of responses of respondents.
Dependent variable: Overall academic Management of the college
Note: *** stands for significant at one percent level.

It is observed from table 3.10 that F-statistics show, the model is fit Adjusted R- square only 0.266 it indicated that the three factors together explaining only 26.6 per cent of the overall academic management of the college. Factor one is positively and other two factors are negatively affecting the overall academic management.

From the above analysis, it is observed that the availability of adequate finance for running and maintenance of colleges and availability of fund for purchase of necessary capital items besides the availability of qualified teachers are the most important factors that need immediate attention for providing quality education in sample colleges. Therefore, it can safely be argued that the crux of all issues is finance.

Sources of Finance

There are multiple sources of finances for education in India. These sources can be broadly classified into external and internal or domestic sources of financing. External sources do not form a significant part of educational finances in India. The domestic sources of funding are broadly divided into public and private sources. The public sources include contributions made by central, state and local governments. The private or non-governmental sources include fees and other household expenditures incurred by the direct beneficiaries (students/parents) of education and endowments and donations made by individuals, trusts, etc. Among the private sources, fees are compulsory payments whereas others are voluntary contributions (Varghese and Tilak, 1991)[19].

Government is the most important financier of higher education. Governments act as financiers because markets cannot provide the required quality of education and maintain it. This pattern of funding by the government is also considered important for equity, efficiency and social control. Therefore, even in market economies, the governments meet substantially the cost of public institutions and sometimes even a portion of the cost of private institutions to the state for help. It is well known that the government and aided colleges are solely relying on government finance, particularly the salary component of the teachers and non-teaching staff. Therefore, the government becomes directly the controller of finance in many undergraduate colleges. Fees realized from the students against admission, tuition fees and other prescribed by universities and colleges go to the university account or government account. Besides registration, examination and other examination related fees are also deposited against development, local fees and other miscellaneous expenditure which is utilized by the college for the welfare of students and staff.

Education in India comes under the concurrent list in the constitution of India. Hence, both centre and state governments are responsible to meet educational expenditure. But about 80 per cent of expenditure on education is met by the respective state governments and only 20 per cent met by the central government. So far as financing higher education is concern the various sources of finances for education in India, excluding the foreign aid, can be classified, as follows: Government sources: i) Central government, ii) State government, iii) UGC iv) AICTE v) Other Governmental agencies; vi) Local bodies. Non-governmental sources: i) Cost recoveries: Tuition fees, Hostel fees, Examination fees, other charges; ii) University sources: Project Grants iii) Other sources; Donation (Das, Chakraborty and Dey, 2014)[20].

Government grants are important and major sources of funds for universities and colleges. The sources of grants include; Central Government, University Grants Commission(UGC) , All India Council for Technical Education(AICTE), other central government agencies, State government and local bodies. Out of these grants, state government grants and grants from UGC are the major sources of income (funds) State government funds provided to state universities while grants from universities are made available to central and deemed to be universities for maintenance and development activities. The UGC also provides grants to universities and colleges for their development activities (Azad, 2008)[21]. The government is the main source of finance for higher education; any other sources of finance have not been tapped. To bring our system to world standards there is a need to identify the additional sources of finance for higher education. This may be in the form of upward revision of fee structure or deregulation of fee structure, education loans, human capital contracts, income contingent loans, graduate tax, education vouchers, and self-financing market determined courses as has been suggested by (Chattopadhyay, 2007)[22].

Higher education in India is characterized by massive public investment, though the investment is still regarded as much below optimum. Such a rapid growth in public financing of higher education in India has been necessary for the following reasons:

(a) Facilities for higher education available at the time of independence were insignificant;

(b) Building up a new socioeconomic system after the end of the colonial rule required large scale manpower with varied skills: so the government could not but expand investment in higher education;

(c) The very development models emphasized high skilled labor force, and building up of huge social infrastructure for excellence in science and technology, and research and development;

(d) Government policies towards equality in education led to the growth in public investment in education, since it involves huge subsidies at all levels of education to a substantial number of students belonging to weaker sections;

(e) The rapid growth of school education naturally pushed the demand for higher education;(Tilak,1993)[23].

Turning to the sample colleges of Tripura, sources of finances during the 2007-08 to 2011-12 are depicted in table 3.11 and relevant chart is shown in figure 3.4. Regarding the sources of funds in general degree colleges of Tripura it may be observed that the state government bears the substantial responsibility of providing funds to the colleges.

TABLE 3.11
Educational Finance by Source in Sample Colleges of Tripura during 2007-08 to 2011-12 (Rupees in Lakh)

Items/Heads	*2007-08*	*2008-09*	*2009-10*	*2010-11*	*2011-12*	*Average of Total*
State Govt.	1,904.81 (87.34)	2,165.02 (84.40)	3,006.12 (85.58)	3,583.43 (88.18)	4,116.76 (85.26)	2955.23 (86.15)
Grants received from the UGC	27.05 (1.24)	90.89 (3.54)	136.94 (3.90)	214.63 (5.28)	202.27 (4.19)	134.36 (3.91)
Grants from other agencies	0	7 (0.27)	29 (0.83)	0	0	7.20 (0.21)
Fees received	23.96 (1.10)	30.12 (1.17)	31.3 (0.89)	39.28 (0.97)	46.65 (0.97)	34.26 (1.00)
Stipend &Scholarship from different sources	223.14 (10.23)	270.22 (10.53)	307.49 (8.75)	222.63 (5.48)	459.24 (9.51)	296.54 (8.65)
Bank Interest	1.84 (0.08)	1.95 (0.08)	1.9 (0.05)	3.82 (0.09)	3.55 (0.07)	2.61 (0.07)
Total	2,180.8 (100)	2,565.2 (100)	3,512.75 (100)	4,063.79 (100)	4,828.47 (100)	3430.20 (100)
Annual Growth Rate per cent	----	17.63	36.94	15.68	18.82	22.27

Source: Collected from Sample General Degree Colleges and computed
Figure in the parenthesis indicate percentage of total

There is a continuous rise in all the sources of funds during the period under the study with the sole exception of the sources under grants from other agencies. Again, this is absent in three years, i.e. 2007-08, 2010-11, and 2011-12 , this source may be identified as coming under a scheme of providing distance education by other universities or institutions. With a rise in the number of students there has been a continuous rise of fund from sources like stipend/scholarship and fees. The fund provided by the source like bank interest also shows an increasing trend reason for which may be explained if we consider the application of funds in the next section.

Fig. 3.4: Educational Finance by Source in sample Colleges of Tripura during 2007-08 to 2011-12 (Average in per cent)

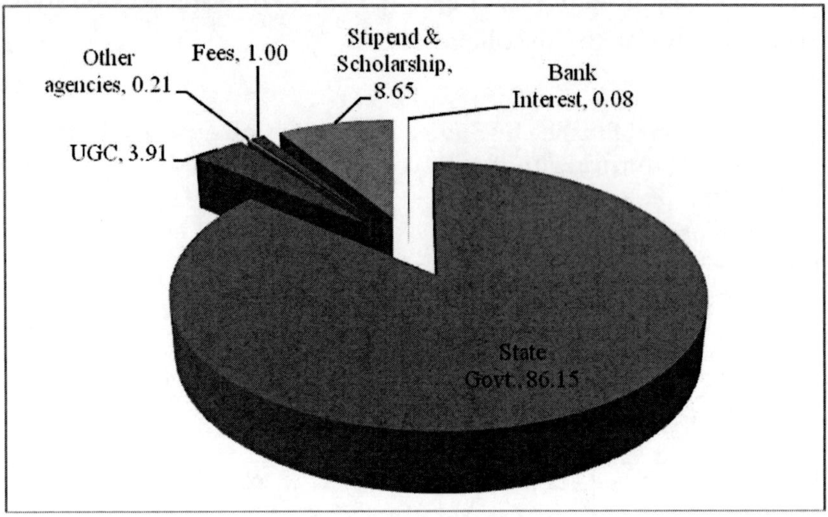

Source: Table 3.11

A look at the pattern of sources of finance for government general degree colleges in Tripura provides different aspect which calls for explanation. During the period of study, it may be observed from table-3.11 that the main source of fund in this case remain the State Government as is very much usual, but it percentage terms, it has remained stable around 86.15 percent. Other sources of funding, which are prominent are, UGC (3.91 percent) and different agencies providing stipend and scholarship to the students (8.65 per cent).

Not only that a closer look may be sufficient to highlight that the dependence on state government might be declining, though at a very small level, in the near future. This aspect is supported by the fact that UGC as a source of fund has been emerging during the period of study. However, it may not be possible for other sources to match the amount still extended by the state government, but these remain in areas which might emerge as the alternative sources of fund in the field of higher education in Tripura.

Besides government sources of income, universities and colleges have to collect resources from non government sources. These sources consist generally of fees from students, (tuition fees, examination fees, hostel fees, etc.), university resources, endowments donations, etc. It is generally accepted that the government contribution for education is very important and non government sources can be utilized for educational development only to supplement the income from governmental sources. Examination fees from students are charged for conduct and management of examination. The expenditure incurred includes: payment of honorarium to examiners, invigilators, paper setters, moderators and evaluators, printing of question papers, answer sheets and meeting computation costs, etc. In case of the state of Tripura all the sample colleges are run by the government and the government decided to remove tuition fees from students' w.e.f. 2008-09. As a result, students are studying in colleges and universities free of cost.

Fig. 3.5: Growth of Educational Finance by Source in Sample Colleges of Tripura during 2007-08 to 2011-12

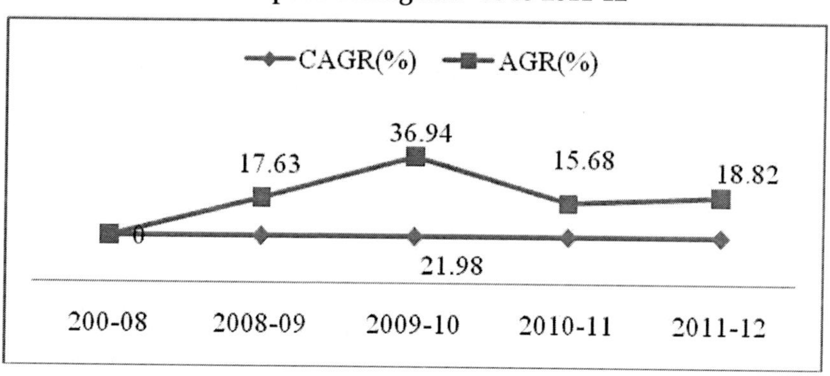

Source: Based on Table 3.11 and Result computed

AGR = Annual Growth Rate; CAGR = Compounded Annual Growth Rate

Figure 3.5 shows the growth of educational finance in sample colleges of Tripura. It is observed from the table that the annual growth rate educational finance varies from 15.68 per cent to 36.94 per cent during the period 2007-08 to 2011-12. The highest annual growth rate noticed during 2008-09 to 2009-10. During the period 2009-10 to 2010-11 the annual growth rate of educational finance is declining to 15.68 per cent and this rate is increased to 18.82 percent during 2010-11 to 2011-12. It is also observed that compounded annual growth rate (CAGR) of educational finance is 21.98 percent over the period of study.

Finance from State Government: Experiences of Sample Colleges

State government is the most important financier of higher education. The state government bears the substantial responsibility of providing funds to the colleges. Funds provided to colleges of Tripura by the state government are shown in the table-3.12 and discussed below:

TABLE 3.12
College wise Finance from State Government during 2007-08 to 2011-12 (Rupees in Lakh)

Name of Colleges	*Year*						
	2007-08	*2008-09*	*2009-10*	*2010-11*	*2011-12*	*AAGR* (%)*	*CAGR* (%)*
MBBC	447.71	442.72	529.97	693.3	711.25	13.00	12.27
BBMC	177.57	163.54	217.85	311.43	324.44	18.11	16.26
WC	244.04	297.73	395.48	482.12	502.14	20.22	19.77
RTC	176.39	231.13	294.33	402.13	446.08	26.48	26.11
ICVC	150.23	176.48	232.42	271.61	343.79	23.15	22.99
NSM	122.36	132.38	220.53	216.86	248.33	21.91	19.36
KNM	52.22	65.17	102.75	117.21	171.23	35.66	34.57
MMDC	37.44	53.43	126.49	95.54	105.09	41.24	29.44
DDMC	90.88	110.53	180.69	185.2	248.9	30.50	28.64
RKM	107.91	139.59	208.14	225.98	274.17	27.09	26.25
Ambedkar College	45.22	56.24	86.15	101.04	137.32	32.69	32.01
GDC Kamalpur	45.72	57.71	64.17	72.46	121.16	29.39	27.54
GDC Amarpur	35.22	48.18	69.02	67.95	91.63	28.34	27.00

GDC Khumlung	29.94	40.74	56.25	71.83	89.22	31.51	31.39
GDC Dharmanagar	141.96	149.45	221.88	268.77	302.01	21.81	20.77
Sample Colleges taken as a whole	1904.81	2165	3006.12	3583.43	4116.76	21.65	21.25

Source: Information from Sample Colleges and Compiled

AAGR = Annual Average Growth Rate, CAGR = Compounded Annual Growth Rate

* = Result Computed

It is observed from the table that funds provided to colleges are increasing significantly. Here the MBB College got more funds than other colleges as its intake capacity of student enrollment, staff position are larger than other colleges and it is the first college in Tripura but annual average growth rate of state government finance is less than other colleges.

The Khumlung College got minimum amount as it is established in the year 2007 as also the students' intake is also minimal. The annual average growth of state government funds differs from college to college. In the above table it is observed that MMDC, RTC, DDMC, GDC, Khumlung, Ambedkar College and KNM got more fund than other colleges as Annual Average Growth Rate of these colleges are more than the Annual Average Growth Rate of the state. The compounded annual growth rate of educational finance also varies among the colleges under the study period.

Grants Received from UGC: Experiences of Sample Colleges

UGC is primarily a disbursing agency; it does not have any fund of its own. What it receives from the government it disburses among universities and other institutions of higher education. The non-plan grants are provided to eligible colleges to enable them to meet recurring expenditure on maintenance of laboratories, libraries and buildings and on a host of other recurring items like internet connectivity charges, stationery, consumable etc. College wise grants received from UGC during the period 2007-08 to 2011-12 are shown in table 3.13.

TABLE 3.13
College wise Grants received from UGC during 2007-08 to 2011-12
(Rupees in Lakh)

Name of College	*Years*					
	2007-08	*2008-09*	*2009-10*	*2010-11*	*2011-12*	*AAGR** *(%)*
MBBC	2.700	7.190	7.940	37.140	1.390	112.06
BBMC	2.100	6.220	13.880	0.000	22.500	54.84
WC	14.000	23.340	17.200	14.550	1.500	-16.17
RTC	2.500	8.280	12.500	1.800	22.500	336.64
ICVC	0.000	22.210	5.280	3.500	35.170	198.73
NSM	2.220	6.650	3.500	29.440	0.000	198.33
KNM	0.000	0.000	3.500	0.000	0.000	-25.00
MMDC	0.000	0.000	3.500	32.470	0.000	181.93
DDMC	0.000	0.000	35.400	52.620	0.000	-12.84
RKM	0.000	0.000	33.290	0.000	0.000	-25.00
Ambedkar Colleges	0.000	0.000	0.000	28.940	20.260	-7.50
GDC Kamalpur	1.660	7.000	0.600	9.170	24.000	455.08
GDC Amarpur	0.000	0.000	0.000	0.000	61.170	0.00
GDC Khumlung	0.000	0.000	0.000	0.000	0.000	0.00
GDC Dharmanagar	1.870	10.000	3.500	5.000	13.780	147.05
Sample Colleges taken as a whole	27.050	90.890	136.940	214.630	202.270	84.41

Source: Information from Sample Colleges and Compiled

AAGR = Annual Average Growth Rate, *= Result Computed

Development grants (plan) on the other hand, are provided for developing infrastructure and basic facilities in colleges and universities for providing teaching and technical manpower, acquiring equipments, books and journals, development of campus, construction of new buildings and providing amenities to students and staff. But often special grants are also given to universities and colleges to meet their specific requirements. Thus UGC has been playing an important role in the maintenance and development of universities, colleges and other institutions of higher education in the country (Azad, 2008)[24]. Table-3.13 provides the information about funds provided by the UGC to the degree colleges in Tripura. It is observed from the table that fund provided to colleges are not equally distributed.

Fund Received from Fees: Experiences of Sample Colleges

The state government does not charge any tuition fees from the students.It is generally accepted that the government contribution for education is very important and non- government sources can be utilized for educational development only to supplement the income from governmental sources. Hence the students are required to pay only for admission and examination purpose which include, library and laboratory charges, certificate fees, etc. College wise fund received from student fees during the period 2007-08 to 2011-12 are presented in table 3.14.

This fee consists of college examination fees, university examination fees. Examination fees from students are charged for conduct and management of examination. The expenditure incurred includes: payment of honorarium to examiners, invigilators, paper setters, moderators, and evaluators, printing of question papers, answer books and meetings, computation costs etc. College examination fees collected from the students are spent on this purpose only. Examination fees generally collected in advance for the year.

This fee has to be paid for the exams, conducting authority in parts at the time of conducting exams or before that. Hence the fees collected can easily be reconciled with the fees paid/ payable to such authority. The examination roll list proves to be a reliable record of the verification of fees paid/ payable. But university examination fees collected from the candidates

TABLE 3.14
College wise Fund Received from Fees during 2007-08 to 2011-12
(Rupees in Lakh)

Name of Colleges	*Year*				
	2007-08	*2008-09*	*2009-10*	*2010-11*	*2011-12*
MBBC	5.19	5.28	9.05	9.98	10.06
BBMC	2.78	3.33	3.08	3.98	5.48
WC	5.02	7.67	5.73	8.93	9.28
RTC	1.26	1.5	1.57	1.91	2.37
ICVC	1.84	2.06	2.07	3.77	3.96
NSM	0.55	0.64	0.8	0.76	0.77
KNM	0.16	0.26	0.25	0.28	0.27
MMDC	0.62	0.92	0.73	1.01	1.06
DDMC	0.56	0.78	0.73	0.78	0.77
RKM	1.1	1.32	1.28	2.33	2.31
Ambedkar College	0.41	1	0.96	1.54	1.65
GDC Kamalpur	1.33	1.7	1.54	2.21	1.25
GDC Amarpur	0.3	0.46	0.38	0.91	1.01
GDC Khumlung	0.14	0.24	0.16	0.31	0.59
GDC Dharmanagar	2.7	2.96	2.97	5.6	5.82
Sample Colleges taken as a whole	23.96	30.12	31.3	39.28	46.65

Source: Information from Sample Colleges and compiled

those who will appear in the examination and filled up form are directly deposited into the university. The university sends the centre fees (a small portion) to the respective colleges, according to their candidate strength and the other part is retained by the university. The college authority can spend only the centre fee by way of remuneration of invigilators and stationary expenses. This money collected as fees deposited to government account through Treasury Challan. The college authority cannot utilize this money. Expenditure on fees and other financial assistance received from various sources was treated as transfer item as fees (student cost) transfer to Government fund or to university.

The admission fee is paid by the students at the time of initial admission to the institution. Generally, admission fees are booked as an income of the year in which it is received, since it does not pertain to a specific academic year but is in the nature of onetime fee paid at the time of admission into the institution. Registration fees are received from the students who wish to apply for admission in the institution and is generally charged to cover the costs involved in taking admission, examination etc.

Regarding tuition fee, generally, received on a period basis in advance as per semester period followed by the institutions. Therefore, at the end of the financial year there is always a portion of the fees which may pertain to the period falling in the next financial year. The fees pertaining to the next financial year should not booked as income during the year, but should not be shown as advanced fees received from students under the head current liabilities and should be charged off to income and expenditure account in the next financial year. Since all the general degree colleges are run by the government and the government decided to give education free of cost so with effect from 2008-09.

Fund Received from Stipend & Scholarship: Experiences of Sample Colleges

A bursary or scholarship is a payment made to a student. These payments are made to students depending on certain criteria, such as the financial position/merit/category etc. of the student determined by the state government or regulatory bodies assigned by the Government.

There are various types of scholarship and stipend given to Girls student, merit scholarship/stipend for all eligible students, scholarship/ stipend for lower income group students, scholarship/

stipend for students belong to Other Backward Community(OBC), scholarship/stipend for students belong to Scheduled Caste (SC), scholarship/stipend for students belong to Schedule Tribe (ST).

There is no income bar for merit scholarship/ stipend and in case of girl students, but in case of students belonging to lower income group the income bar is up to Rs. 60000/- per year, students belong to schedule caste and schedule tribe the income bar Rs. 200000/- per year, and in case of other backward community (OBC) students the income bar is Rs. 100000/- per year as per circular, Government of Tripura, No. F. 3(17-1)-DHE/STIP/89/

TABLE 3.15
College wise Stipend & Scholarship during 2007-08 to 2011-12
(Rupees in Lakh)

Name of Colleges	Year				
	2007-08	2008-09	2009-10	2010-11	2011-12
MBBC	3.62	3.7	5.24	5.69	4.18
BBMC	21.22	28.74	35.34	20.18	54.97
WC	62.07	32.98	75.53	20.51	13.83
RTC	27.8	38.72	27.69	23.11	75.55
ICVC	22.4	15.07	28.6	17.38	49.52
NSM	27.54	18.35	19.25	14.86	40.28
KNM	11.35	15.86	17.15	19.5	36.02
MMDC	4.72	9.75	7.94	12.69	13.54
DDMC	7.02	21.57	---	13.18	23.71
RKM	10.52	16.14	14.1	8.32	34.08
Ambedkar Colleges	2.68	4.89	7.57	1.4	12.62
GDC Kamalpur	---	19.7	22.94	25.75	40.52
GDC Amarpur	4.58	4.95	6.45	6.17	15.54
GDC Khumlung	2.12	6.23	5.5	8.19	14.26
GDC Dharmanagar	15.5	33.57	34.19	25.7	30.62
Sample Colleges taken as a whole	223.14	270.22	307.49	222.63	459.24

Source: Information from Sample Colleges and compiled

642(25) dated 12.06.2009, No 17014-30 F. 5-3/ SCW &OBC/ PLG/06 dated on 14.01.2011 and No. 5231-52 F. 8-13/ SCW & OBC/ PlG/06 dated 26.7.2011 respectively. College wise sanctioned amount of stipend and scholarship are shown in table 3.15.

It is observed that an amount of Rs. 223.14 lakh was sanctioned in the year 2007-08 as a stipend and scholarship for the students of sample colleges and increased to Rs.459.24 lakh in the year 2011-12. But consistency is not maintained in respect of each college for sanctioning the amount of stipend and scholarship.

Fund Received from Bank Interest: Experiences of Sample Colleges

For general degree colleges, the funds are channelized from different sources, the main constituent of which are the state government and developmental assistance grant of UGC. As such funds are not supposed to follow the instant flow input and flow output concept; there arises a possibility of garnering additional fund by management of the same. This can be done by putting reserves in the bank on favorable terms. However, as this is not mandatory for colleges to strictly adhere to proper fund managing system all the colleges may not follow the same procedure. Regarding the fund from bank interest are explained in the following table.

TABLE-3.16
Fund received from Bank Interest during 2007-08 to 2011-12
(Rupees in Lakh)

Name of Colleges	*Year*				
	2007-08	*2008-09*	*2009-10*	*2010-11*	*2011-12*
MBBC	0.12	0.05	0.09	0.18	0.08
BBMC	0.06	0.22	0.35	0.27	0.65
WC	0.13	0.33	0	0.91	0.67
RTC	0.55	0.45	0.31	0.18	0.22
ICVC	0.12	0.15	0.21	0.28	0.35

NSM	0	0	0.1	0.25	0.2
KNM	0	0	0	0	0
MMDC	0	0	0	0	0
DDMC	0.45	0.35	0.29	0.43	0.24
RKM	0.15	0.15	0.25	0.33	0.18
Ambedkar College	0.01	0.05	0.07	0.04	0.01
GDC Kamalpur	0	0	0	0	0
GDC Amarpur	0	0	0	0	0
GDC Khumlung	0	0	0	0	0
GDC Dharmanagar	0.25	0.2	0.23	0.95	0.95
Sample Colleges taken as a whole	1.84	1.95	1.9	3.82	3.55

Source: Information from Sample Colleges and compiled

The table-3.16 gives an indication of procuring additional fund through such management, but as this is not compulsorily adopted by all the institutions, such additional provision of funds has not found a place in the information provided by a few sample colleges. This may also be explained in terms of the stipulation by putting reserves in the current account in the bank with no interest accrued thereon.

However an alternative provision has not been explored so that the reserve may be kept in an account, providing interest with the stipulation that the interest income is to be supported on the head of the account for which the reserve is maintained. This flexibility has given the colleges the opportunity to meet up expenses that might arise in future periods.

Fund from Other Agencies: Evidences of Sample Colleges

There are multiple sources of finances for education. These sources can be broadly classified into external and internal or domestic sources of financing. External sources do not form a significant part of educational finances in India. Sample colleges are not getting funding from other agencies on a regular basis but occasionally they are getting funding for organizing seminar or workshop .For such item analysis have been made in the following table.

TABLE 3.17
Funds received from Other Agencies during 2007-08 to 2011-12
(Rupees in Lakh)

Name of Colleges	*Year*				
	2007-08	*2008-09*	*2009-10*	*2010-11*	*2011-12*
MBBC	0	0	0	0	0
BBMC	0	0	0	0	0
WC	0	0	0	0	0
RTC	0	0	0	0	0
ICVC	0	0	0	0	0
NSM	0	0	0	0	0
KNM	0	0	0	0	0
MMDC	0	0	0	0	0
DDMC	0	0	0	0	0
RKM	0	0	29	0	0
Ambedkar College	0	7	0	0	0
GDC, Kamalpur	0	0	0	0	0
GDC,Amarpur	0	0	0	0	0
GDC,Khumlung	0	0	0	0	0
GDC,Dharmanagar	0	0	0	0	0
Sample Colleges taken as a whole	0	7	29	0	0

Source: Information from Sample Colleges and compiled

Regarding the sources of funds in general degree colleges of Tripura it may be observed that while there is a continuous rise in all the sources of fund during the period under the study with only are sole exception of the sources under grants from other agencies. Again this is absent in three years and this source may be identified as coming under a scheme of providing distance education by other universities or institutions as shown in the table-3.17.

Pattern of Expenditure

An educational institution incurs expenditure on educational and academic expenditure which includes all costs of providing the faculty with the physical supplies for imparting education to students such as stationary, teaching aids, computer rentals laboratories, equipments repair and maintenance, scholarship, medical facilities etc. This section discusses the behavior of expenditure of sample colleges for 2007-08 to 2011-12; the main purpose being to analyze expenditure incurred on various activities. The analysis is expected to reveal the type of activities that are considered important in the working of colleges in terms of financial allocations.

In order to examine the patterns and its changing behavior over the years, expenditure was broken down into recurring and non-recurring components. The recurring expenditure covers direct teaching and non-teaching expenditure, indirect teaching expenditure and students' welfare services.

Nonrecurring expenditure includes expenditure on buildings, furniture, equipments and library books and their maintenance. Expenditure on education can be on recurring items such as salary of teachers, administrative staff, etc., or it can be on capital infrastructure such as school building, libraries, equipment, etc.

Expenditure on recurring items comes under the revenue account, whereas that on non-recurring items constitutes the capital account. Revenue expenditure constitutes major part, around 99 Percent of total expenditure from 1980- 81 to 1999-2000. On the other hand, the capital account forms negligible portion of total spending. So far we have looked into the changing pattern of total public expenditure on education and growth rate pre-and post liberalization. However, one of our primary interests is to analyze the devolution of funds for higher education vis-à-vis the other levels of education. To address this issue, we have looked into the public spending on education at a more disaggregated level (Chakrabarti & Jogleker, 2006)[25].

The pattern of expenditure in higher education may include (a) Recurring Expenditure: i) Direct teaching expenditure, ii) Indirect teaching expenditure, iii) Student welfare activities b) Nonrecurring expenditure: i) Building, ii) Furniture, iii) Library, iv) Laboratory, v) Others;

So far as sample colleges of Tripura are concerned, pattern of expenditure (application of funds) presented in table 3.18.

TABLE 3.18
Applications of Funds in Sample Colleges of Tripura during 2007-08 to 2011-12 (Rupees in Lakh)

Items/Heads	*2007-08*	*2008-09*	*2009-10*	*2010-11*	*2011-12*	*Average*
Salaries &Wages	1,696.21 (77.78)	1,920.77 (74.88)	2,613.54 (74.40)	3,404.11 (83.77)	38,19.85 (79.11)	2690.90 (78.45)
Recurring Expenses out of UGC funds	5.15 (0.24)	15.5 (0.60)	25.75 (0.73)	32.13 (0.79)	35 (0.72)	22.71 (0.66)
Stipend & Scholarship for student	186.82 (8.57)	236.29 (9.21)	253.25 (7.21)	204.86 (5.04)	366.26 (7.59)	249.50 (7.27)
Repair & Maintenance	7.61 (0.35)	19.57 (0.76)	30.6 (0.87)	22.7 (0.56)	6.79 (0.14)	17.45 (0.51)
Electric charges	14.49 (0.66)	15.9 (0.62)	23.56 (0.67)	19.88 (0.49)	24.17 (0.50)	19.60 (0.57)
Furniture	46.43 (2.13)	69.29 (2.70)	61.56 (1.75)	27.72 (0.68)	84.78 (1.76)	57.96 (1.69)
Equipments	94.71 (2.76)	115.28 (3.36)	150.77 (4.40)	183.75 (5.36)	248.77 (7.25)	158.66 (4.63)
Computers	5.88 (0.17)	24.03 (0.70)	47.07 (1.37)	4.75 (0.14)	2.40 (0.07)	16.83 (0.49)

Laboratory Recurring Expenses	20.64 (0.95)	20.76 (0.81)	13.87 (0.39)	14.74 (0.36)	14.61 (0.30)	16.92 (0.49)
Books & Journals	11.72 (0.54)	19.48 (0.76)	15.32 (0.44)	27.51 (0.68)	20.6 (0.43)	18.93 (0.55)
Office Expenses	8.09 (0.37)	9.48 (0.37)	12.85 (0.37)	14.09 (0.35)	18.45 (0.38)	12.59 (0.37)
Refund of Undistributed Stipend	36.32 (1.37)	33.92 (1.32)	51.59 (1.47)	17.76 (0.44)	92.97 (1.93)	46.51 (1.36)
Payment out of fees received from students	23.96 (1.10)	30.12 (1.17)	31.3 (0.89)	39.28 (0.97)	46.65 (0.97)	34.26 (1.00)
Expenses on vehicle	12.13 (0.56)	13.54 (0.53)	14.4 (0.41)	15.4 (0.38)	16.67 (0.35)	14.43 (0.42)
Refund or Unspent amount	10.64 (0.49)	21.27 (0.83)	167.32 (4.76)	35.11 (0.86)	30.5 (0.63)	52.97 (1.54)
Sample Colleges taken as a whole	2,180.8 (100)	2,565.2 (100)	3,512.75 (100)	4,063.79 (100)	4,828.47 (100)	3430.20 (100)
Annual Growth Rate Percent	----	17.63	36.94	15.69	18.82	22.27

Source: Information from Sample Colleges and Result Computed

Figure in the parenthesis indicate percentage of total

Application of funds in general degree colleges of Tripura are shown in table 3.18 and Fig. 3.6. A look into the application of funds in general degree colleges of Tripura shows a prominent aspect that a sizeable amount of fund is disbursed as salary and wages. The other items of expenditure show a continuous rise though they may be relatively lesser in comparison to the expenditure of salary and wages. The year 2009-10 provides a somewhat deviated pattern of expenditure in comparison to other years under the period of study. Introduction of new pay scale may have contributed in this deviation. Undistributed stipends and refund of the same along with the unspent amount of money has also shown a continuous rise. This retention of funds may be taken as an explanation for rising bank interest as shown in table-3.11 and table 3.16.

Fig. 3.6: Average application of funds as per cent of Educational Finance during 2007-08 to 2011-12

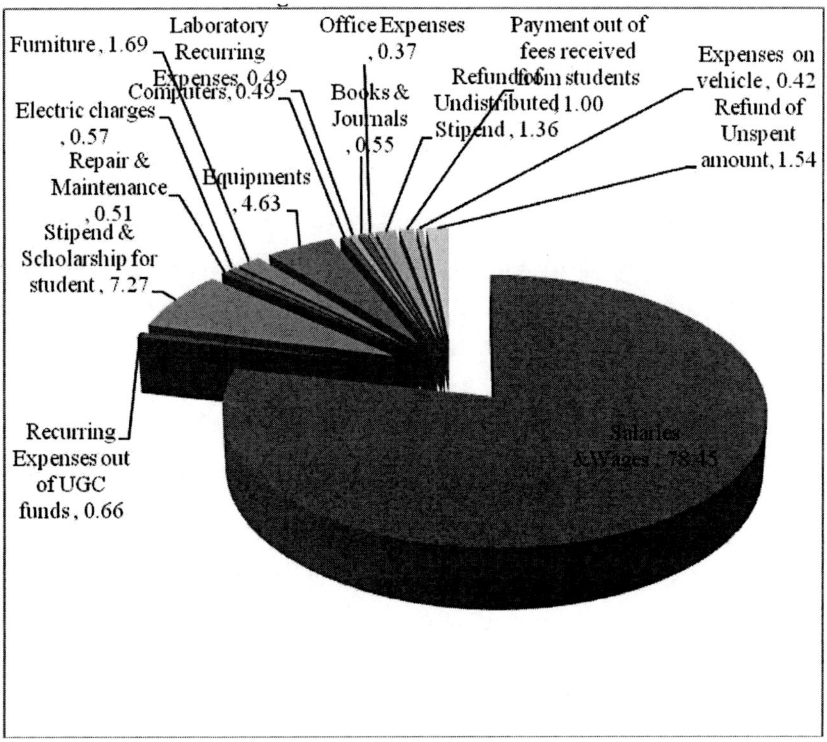

Source: Table 3.18

Regarding recurring expenditure out of UGC funds, fund from UGC is generally received under general development assistance schemes during different plan period. This scheme comprises release of funds for books and journals, instruments and machineries and other education related expenditure. Other than this there are some special projects like establishment of remedial coaching centre, network resource centre and coaching centre for entry into services.

All the above projects are funded by UGC based on criteria as furnished by individual institution. The main component of the fund is nonrecurring in nature like purchase of books and journals, instrument and computer. The only recurring element of this assistance can be viewed in expenditure to run different projects. Normally the college has to search for other agencies or government for running expenditure on items which had been provided by UGC. Thus, in general development assistance fund is provided mainly for purchase of non recurring items and such items required for the establishment of different centre. The only notable recurring items provided by UGC, is in the nature of reimbursement of travelling expenses for faculty members joining in different international and national seminars. Other than this the recurring expenditure as provided by UGC mainly revolves upon the maintenance of different centre established with funds from UGC. However the same expenditure limits of the plan period in which the assistance was provided. Outside the plan period the college has to bear the recurring expenditure of its own funds.

So far as application of funds in the educational institutions under study is concerned a clear idea may be had from the distribution aspect of funds as expressed in percentage terms. Expenditure on salaries and wages 78.45 per cent, as usual, remains the main area where most of the funds are allocated. This is followed by the expenditure on stipend and scholarship 7.27 per cent. However, this area should be viewed with some caution as a sizeable portion remains undistributed and has to be refunded at a later stage. In the present case almost 3 percent funds remain either unspent or unutilized. This area needs to be looked into so that a proper utilization of fund takes place. Since the educational institutions of Tripura are established by the state government, it is not necessary that expenditure of non-recurring nature in a very large scale should appear in every year. Rather expenditure of that type might be present in case of items, like furniture, equipment, computer and library purchase. The information provided in the table-3.18 also confirms this observation.

Expenditure incurred on Salaries & Wages: Evidences of Sample Colleges

Salaries and wages are the main component of institutional costs of higher education. A Substantial portion of educational cost spends on salaries and wages. Expenditure incurred for salaries and wages are shown in the table 3.19.

TABLE 3.19
Expenditure incurred on Salaries & Wages during 2007-08 to 2011-12
(Rupees in Lakh)

Name of Colleges	*Year*				
	2007-08	*2008-09*	*2009-10*	*2010-11*	*2011-12*
MBBC	403.49	414.15	486.12	663.24	688.6
BBMC	171.68	163.45	225.18	322.49	341.19
WC	224.87	252.17	321.55	460.17	386.46
RTC	144.15	189.28	237.99	371.74	363.35
ICVC	122.78	150.18	206.43	263.21	326.78
NSM	115.69	126.43	152.93	186.79	267
KNM	54.58	58.55	98.02	112.34	160.3
MMDC	31.09	44.09	106.98	102.91	100.86
DDMC	81.26	96.52	157.74	175.45	235.05
RKM	86.22	118.92	182	197.16	270.15
Ambedkar College	38.08	45.02	69.07	94.69	120.7
GDC Kamalpur	45.8	52	58.86	63.93	112.4
GDC Amarpur	32.07	40.82	62.04	65.13	88.04
GDC Khumlung	13.34	34.29	49.04	66.74	85.62
GDC Dharmanagar	131.11	134.9	199.59	258.12	273.35
Sample Colleges taken as a whole	1696.21	1920.77	2613.54	3404.11	3819.85

Source: Information from Sample Colleges and Result Computed

AAGR= Annual Average Growth Rate

Table-3.19 provides the information of salaries and wages of teaching and non teaching staff paid by the government. It is observed from the table that expenditure trend on salaries and wages is increasing every year irrespective of all colleges. In the period 2009-10 and 2010-11 we have seen an excessive increase in salaries and wages because of implementation of UGC pay scale and state pay scale. If we compare the figure with total expenditure incurred by the college authority, then we can see that more than 80 per cent of the total expenditure spends on salaries and wages. Remaining little amount spent on all other purposes of running the colleges.

Expenditure incurred on Repair & Maintenance: Evidences of Sample Colleges

The running of an educational institution involves substantial investment in infrastructure such as building, equipments, vehicles, etc. All these items are subject to constant wear and tear and as such expenditure on repair and maintenance a major outflow of funds. The repair and maintenance expenditure may be classified under various group heads in the income and expenditure account in accordance with the functional purpose of the asset in respect of which such expenditure was incurred. The expenditure incurred for repair and maintenance of the college shown in table 3.20.

For repair and maintenance purpose government are not providing money uniformly every year. As a result college authorities are not able to spend money on repair and maintenance though there are urgent needs for maintenance. It is observed from the table that Khumlung College did not spend money for repair and maintenance purpose because the college newly started w.e.f. 2007-08.

TABLE 3.20
Expenditure incurred on Repair & Maintenance during 2007-08 to 2011-12 (Rupees in Lakh)

Name of Colleges	*Year*				
	2007-08	*2008-09*	*2009-10*	*2010-11*	*2011-12*
MBBC	1.75	---	2.5	3.5	---
BBMC	---	0.99	1.38	---	0.75
WC	0.03	0.75	1.15	1	0.67
RTC	---	---	1	0.25	---
ICVC	0.5	1.5	1.99	---	1.05
NSM	0.5	0.8	0.5	---	0.35
KNM	0.15	0.42	---	0.5	---
MMDC	---	2.99	1.03	---	0.85
DDMC	0.2	2.99	---	0.5	---
RKM	2.63	6.56	19.6	14.43	3
Ambedkar College	0.5	---	---	1.6	---
GDC, Kamalpur	0.5	1.27	1	0.5	---
GDC, Amarpur	0.2	0.99	---	0.25	---
GDC, Khumlung	---	---	---	---	---
GDC, Dharmanagar	0.65	0.31	0.45	0.17	0.12
Sample Colleges taken as a whole	7.61	19.57	30.6	22.7	6.79

Source: Information from Sample Colleges and Compiled

Expenditure incurred on Electricity: Evidences of Sample Colleges

Expenditure on electricity in connection with running the institute is necessary. The colleges cannot be run without electricity, be it administrative, laboratory, library or various departments. For running the equipment including computers, electricity is essential components. In table 3.21 presented the expenditure on electricity for sample colleges.

TABLE 3.21
Expenditure on Electricity during 2007-08 to 2011-12 (Rupees in Lakh)

Name of Colleges	*Year*				
	2007-08	*2008-09*	*2009-10*	*2010-11*	*2011-12*
MBBC	6.8	5.2	11.84	10.05	8.89
BBMC	1.7	1.42	1.3	0.92	1.56
WC	0.54	1.95	2.14	1.4	1.49
RTC	0.83	1.04	1.21	1.35	0.9
ICVC	0.85	0.78	2.11	1.39	2.6
NSM	0.85	1	1	0.95	1.1
KNM	0.28	0.39	0.37	0.49	0.85
MMDC	0.19	0.21	0.29	0.13	0.98
DDMC	1.05	1.14	0.85	0.8	1.2
RKM	0.47	0.41	0.56	0.2	0.64
Ambedkar College	0.11	0.21	0.12	0.1	0.45
GDC, Kamalpur	0.45	0.9	0.44	0.53	0.52
GDC, Amarpur	0.04	0.05	0.08	0.12	0.3
GDC, Khumlung	0.18	0.44	0.2	0.21	0.1
GDC, Dharmanagar	0.15	0.76	1.05	1.24	2.59
Sample Colleges taken as a whole	14.49	15.9	23.56	19.88	24.17

Source: Information from Sample Colleges and Compiled

The recurring expenditure for electric bill shown in the table-3.21. It is observed from the table that expenditure on electric bill spent uniformly every year. Total expenditure incurred on the electric bill is 0.50 per cent or more of total expenditure of the institution (Fig. 3.6).

Expenditure Incurred on Furniture: Evidences of Sample Colleges

The table 3.22 depicts the cost of furniture of all the colleges of Tripura. The Furniture is very much essential for such kind of institutions specially benches, Chairs and Tables because every classroom needs these items. About 1.70 per cent of total expenditure spent on furniture. In the year 2010-11 this rate is 0.68 per cent, which is less than the average percentage (Table 3.18)

TABLE 3.22
Expenditure incurred on Furniture during 2007-08 to 2011-12
(Rupees in Lakh)

Name of Colleges	*Year*				
	2007-08	*2008-09*	*2009-10*	*2010-11*	*2011-12*
MBBC	9.82	10.8	11.93	6.95	5.77
BBMC	0.49	3.02	3.63	0.62	13.33
WC	10.59	8.59	5.71	1.35	3.41
RTC	3.18	5.23	5.25	1.02	8.37
ICVC	3.46	18.78	2.52	1.33	8.54
NSM	3.01	2.16	3.56	0.62	1.5
KNM	2.36	3.17	1.96	0	3.1
MMDC	1.15	2.2	2.31	2.2	---
DDMC	1.15	2.2	8.05	4.89	---
RKM	---	1.03	5.45	---	---
Ambedkar College	0.5	2.5	3.21	2.44	3.68
GDC, Kamalpur	0.38	1.75	1.83	5.83	6.76
GDC, Amarpur	0.87	2.62	1	---	11.78
GDC, Khumlung	7.53	2.76	2.61	---	3.12
GDC, Dharmanagar	1.93	2.5	2.54	0.46	15.41
Sample Colleges taken as a whole	46.43	69.29	61.56	27.72	84.78

Source: Information from Sample Colleges and Compiled

Expenditure Incurred on Equipments: Evidences of Sample Colleges

Expenditure on equipment shown in the table-3.23. It is observed that expenditure on equipment incurred by every college. This expenditure mostly required for science departments. In Tripura every college has no science courses, but each college has incurred expenditure on equipments which includes computer and other instruments.

TABLE 3.23
Expenditure incurred on Equipments during 2007-08 to 2011-12
(Rupees in Lakh)

Name of Colleges	*Year*				
	2007-08	*2008-09*	*2009-10*	*2010-11*	*2011-12*
MBBC	10.69	4.91	1.00	25.45	4.48
BBMC	3.15	3.18	9.65	1.16	22.81
WC	9.71	16.52	23.24	27.39	8.36
RTC	5.29	3.70	11.76	8.12	13.64
ICVC	9.48	23.40	9.80	7.50	31.72
NSM	13.62	14.46	22.48	12.77	12.63
KNM	3.74	8.96	9.19	3.00	18.07
MMDC	0.99	2.13	3.55	15.62	0.56
DDMC	14.00	15.25	15.64	38.36	8.50
RKM	13.61	7.08	29.32	3.30	18.30
Ambedkar College	3.61	4.90	5.04	25.31	18.21
GDC Kamalpur	0.68	4.89	4.13	8.55	25.83
GDC Amarpur	4.08	0.86	2.16	2.80	56.25
GDC Khumlung	1.12	0.00	0.00	0.00	0.00
GDC Dharmanagar	0.94	5.05	3.79	4.42	9.41
Sample Colleges taken as a whole	94.71	115.28	150.77	183.75	248.77

Source: Information from Sample Colleges and Compiled

Expenditure incurred on Computers: Evidences of Sample Colleges

Expenditure on computer incurred by every college for which fund provided by UGC as well as State Government. But during the study period this expenditure is not consistent for each and every year and also every college are not able to spend money for that particular item in spite of their requirement. Expenditure incurred on computers during 2007-08- to 2011-12 are shown in table 2.24.

TABLE 3.24
Expenditure incurred on Computers during 2007-08 to 2011-12
(Rupees in Lakh)

Name of Colleges	*Year*				
	2007-08	*2008-09*	*2009-10*	*2010-11*	*2011-12*
MBBC	1	---	5	---	0
BBMC	---	0.9	---	---	1.5
WC	2.5	---	---	---	---
RTC	---		8.08	---	---
ICVC	---	----	8.89	---	---
NSM	---	8.7	0.92	2.25	0.9
KNM	0.99	---	---	---	---
MMDC	---	---	8	---	---
DDMC	---	---	13.03	---	---
RKM	---	5.5	---	---	---
Ambedkar College	0.59	---	1.5	---	---
GDC Kamalpur	0.8	1.67	---	----	---
GDC Amarpur	---	---	0.85	0.5	---
GDC Khumlung	---	---	---	2	---
GDC Dharmanagar	---	7.26	0.8	---	---
Sample Colleges taken as a whole	5.88	24.03	47.07	4.75	2.4

Source: Information from Sample Colleges and Compiled

Expenditure Incurred on Books and Journals: Evidences of Sample Colleges

The table 3.25 depicts the amount of expenditure spent for purchase of books and journals which is an average 0.55 per cent (Fig. 3.6) of the total expenditure incurred by general degree colleges of Tripura during the study period. It is observed from the table that expenditure on books and journal is quite minimum as such item is very much essential to the institution. Books and journals are the one of the parameters for providing quality education. Thus institute as well as concerning department should provide more funds for procuring books and journals for the interest of the students.

TABLE 3.25
Expenditure incurred on Books & Journals during 2007-08 to 2011-12
(Rupees in lakh)

Name of Colleges	*Year*				
	2007-08	*2008-09*	*2009-10*	*2010-11*	*2011-12*
MBBC	0.67	2	1.1	3.95	2.57
BBMC	0.63	0.93	0.85	0.59	2.08
WC	2.34	2.12	1.75	1.85	0.07
RTC	0.63	1.33	0.6	2.5	1.73
ICVC	0.5	2.01	0.72	1.83	2.19
NSM	1.14	1.96	1.52	2.97	3.1
KNM	0.65	0.5	0.65	0.21	---
MMDC	0.25	0.72	0.15	2.7	---
DDMC	0.64	1.01	2.15	5.39	0.5
RKM	0.05	1.36	1.71	0	0.5
Ambedkar College	0.59	1.49	1.44	2.69	2.22
GDC Kamalpur	0.61	0.68	0.52	1.11	1.16
GDC Amarpur	0.4	0.82	1.01	0.25	2.95
GDC Khumlung	2.5	0.7	0.5	0.5	0.5
GDC Dharmanagar	0.12	1.85	0.65	0.96	1.03
Sample Colleges taken as a whole	11.72	19.48	15.32	27.51	20.6

Source: Information from Sample Colleges and Compiled

Office Expenses: Evidences of Sample Colleges

Office expense is one of the components of recurring cost of education. Office is the central point of, an institution where every academic as well as administrative work done. Thus, such type of expenditure incurred by every college of institute, but it is difficult to manage with a minimum amount allotted by the department for running and maintenance the office. Office expenses of sample colleges are presented in table 3.26.

TABLE 3.26

Office Expenses during 2007-08 to 2011-12 (Rupees in lakh)

Name of Colleges	*Year*				
	2007-08	*2008-09*	*2009-10*	*2010-11*	*2011-12*
MBBC	1.6	1.62	1.75	1.8	2.05
BBMC	0.62	0.65	1.1	1.25	1.5
WC	1.02	1.26	1.74	1.89	2.27
RTC	0.6	0.89	1.13	1.37	1.74
ICVC	0.56	0.75	0.95	1.08	2.47
NSM	0.53	0.56	0.87	0.78	1.15
KNM	0.26	0.3	0.45	0.5	0.75
MMDC	0.28	0.29	0.55	0.48	0.53
DDMC	0.4	0.53	0.84	1	1.02
RKM	0.48	0.65	1	0.96	1.25
Ambedkar College	0.25	0.29	0.39	0.55	0.65
GDC, Kamalpur	0.28	0.35	0.39	0.48	0.63
GDC, Amarpur	0.24	0.28	0.35	0.35	0.59
GDC, Khumlung	0.22	0.26	0.32	0.35	0.55
GDC, Dharmanagar	0.75	0.8	1.02	1.25	1.3
Sample Colleges taken as a whole	8.09	9.48	12.85	14.09	18.45

Source: Information from Sample Colleges and Compiled

Expenditure Incurred on Laboratory Recurring Expenses: Evidences of Sample Colleges

The Laboratory is the essential part of the science department. Without laboratory and instruments science students cannot do their practical. To regular practical work it is necessary for incurring recurring expenditure for running and maintenance the laboratory, but due to different constraints institute cannot provide more funds for improvement of those departments. Expenditure on laboratory recurring expenses for the sample colleges are shown in table 3.27.

TABLE 3.27
Expenditure on Laboratory Recurring Expenses during 2007-08 to 2011-12 (Rupees in lakh)

Name of Colleges	*Year*				
	2007-08	*2008-09*	*2009-10*	*2010-11*	*2011-12*
MBBC	1.79	1.65	2.43	2.35	2.62
BBMC	1.33	0.85	0.98	1.02	0.76
WC	1.35	1.26	1.54	1.75	1.85
RTC	0.89	0.93	1.03	1.65	1.01
ICVC	2.49	1.49	1.42	1	1.96
NSM	2	2.5	2	2.25	2.25
KNM	---	6.86	0.8	0.68	0.73
DDMC	1.26	1.22	0.88	0.96	1.33
RKM	8.03	2.55	1.84	1.76	1.25
GDC Dharmanagar	1.5	1.45	0.95	1.32	0.85
Sample Colleges taken as a whole	20.64	20.76	13.87	14.74	14.61

Source: Information from Sample Colleges and Compiled

Expenditure Incurred on Stipend and Scholarship: Evidences of Sample Colleges

Expenditure on stipend, scholarship and other financial assistance received from various sources was treated as transfer items. There are various types of stipend and house rent given to Girls student, merit stipend and house rent for all eligible students, scholarship/stipend for lower income group students, stipend and house rent for students belong to OBC, scholarship/ stipend for students belong to SC, stipend and house rent for students belong to ST.

TABLE 3.28
Expenditure on Stipend and Scholarship during 2007-08 to2011-12
(Rupees in lakh)

Name of Colleges	*Year*				
	2007-08	*2008-09*	*2009-10*	*2010-11*	*2011-12*
MBBC	3.62	3.7	5.24	5.69	4.18
BBMC	16.48	24.26	20.67	18.99	44.19
WC	56.76	36.92	65.7	19.41	10.61
RTC	25.92	30.66	27.69	23.06	72.12
ICVC	18.59	15.01	24.24	17.36	46.24
NSM	21.03	16.2	15.85	14.79	38.79
KNM	9.65	14.99	14.92	19.35	21.41
MMDC	4.72	9.76	7.94	12.69	13.54
DDMC	4.38	20.14	2	12.67	20.25
RKM	8.87	13.67	11.32	12.73	18.96
Ambedkar College	1.99	3.61	5.26	0.81	7.88
GDC, Kamalpur	NIL	18.67	26.93	20.66	24.58
GDC, Amarpur	3.24	3.65	4.61	5.35	13.63
GDC,Khumlung	1.91	6.09	5.33	7.47	12.14
GDC,Dharmanagar	9.66	18.96	15.55	13.83	17.74
Sample Colleges taken as a whole	186.82	236.29	253.25	204.86	366.26

Source: Information from Sample Colleges and Compiled

The table 3.28 shows the increasing trend of expenditure in connection with stipend and house rent. It is observed from the information collected from sample colleges that amount for stipend and scholarship sanctioned by the central or state government (different departments) are not disbursed fully. As a result the amount of stipend and scholarship remain undistributed as 1.36 per cent (Table 3.18).

Expenditure incurred on Recurring expenditure out of UGC fund: Evidences of Sample Colleges

Recurring items provided by UGC, is in the nature of reimbursement of travelling expenses for faculty members joining in different international and national seminars. Other than this the recurring expenditure as provided by UGC mainly revolves upon the maintenance of different centre established with funds from UGC. Outside the plan period the college has to bear the recurring expenditure from its own funds. The non-plan grants are provided to eligible colleges to enable them to meet recurring expenditure on maintenance of laboratories, libraries and buildings and on a host of other recurring items like internet connectivity charges, stationary, consumable etc which is shown in table 3.29.

TABLE 3.29
Recurring Expenditure out of UGC fund during 2007-08 to 2011-12
(Rupees in Lakh)

Name of Colleges	*Years*				
	2007-08	*2008-09*	*2009-10*	*200-11*	*2011-12*
MBBC	0.54	1.27	1.54	6.68	0.26
BBMC	0.42	1.10	2.67	0.00	4.17
WC	2.64	4.12	3.31	2.62	0.28
RTC	0.40	0.92	2.40	0.00	1.86
ICVC	0.00	3.92	1.01	0.63	6.52
NSM	0.44	1.17	0.07	1.20	0.00

KNM	0.00	0.00	0.67	0.00	0.00
MMDC	0.00	0.00	0.67	4.26	0.00
DDMC	0.00	0.00	6.80	9.47	0.00
RKM	0.00	0.00	5.82	0.00	0.00
FatikRoy	0.00	0.00	0.00	4.72	3.55
Kamalpur	0.33	1.23	0.12	1.65	4.45
Amarpur	0.00	0.00	0.00	0.00	11.35
Khumlung	0.00	0.00	0.00	0.00	0.00
Dharmanagar	0.37	1.77	0.67	0.90	2.56
Sample Colleges taken as a whole	5.15	15.50	25.75	32.13	35.00

Source: Information from Sample Colleges and Compiled

Expenditure on Vehicles: Evidences of Sample Colleges

Expenditure on vehicles or consumption of fuel for running the vehicles is essential component of institutional costs. Expenditure on vehicles or fuel shown in table 3.30 below.

TABLE 3.30
Expenditure on vehicle during 2007-08 to 2011-12 (Rs. in Lakh)

Name of Colleges	*Year*				
	2007-08	*2008-09*	*2009-10*	*2010-11*	*2011-12*
MBBC	0.52	0.6	0.65	0.75	0.85
BBMC	0.85	1.08	1.14	1.15	1.25
WC	0.55	0.65	0.75	0.75	0.95
RTC	0.84	0.9	0.95	1.14	1.23
ICVC	0.85	1	1.05	1.1	1.2
NSM	0.85	0.95	1.05	1.1	1.15
KNM	0.75	0.8	0.9	1	1.05
MMDC	0.96	1.02	1.05	1.08	1.2
DDMC	0.9	0.95	0.98	1.02	1.14
RKM	0.92	0.96	1.05	1.14	1.2

FatikRoy	0.96	0.95	0.98	1.02	1.1
Kamalpur	0.84	0.9	0.95	1	1.02
Amarpur	0.9	0.95	0.98	1	1.05
Khumlung	0.49	0.85	0.9	1	1.08
Dharmanagar	0.95	0.98	1.02	1.15	1.2
Sample Colleges taken as a whole	12.13	13.54	14.4	15.4	16.67

Source: Information from Sample Colleges and Compiled

So far as expenditure on vehicles or fuel in the educational institutions under study is concern a clear idea may be had that minimum percentage (0.42%) of total average expenditure (Table 3.18) spend for that particular purpose which is very much negligible amount compare to other components of expenditure. The expenditure on vehicles or fuel for vehicles spent during 2007-08 Rs. 12.13 lakh and increased to Rs. 16.67 lakh during 2011-12.

Payment Out of Fees Received from Students: Evidences of Sample Colleges

This money collected as fees deposited to government account through treasury challan. The college authority cannot utilize this money collected as fees. Expenditure on fees and other financial assistance received from various sources was treated as transfer item as fees (student cost) transfer to Government fund or to University. Payment of fees to Government account is presented in table 3.31.

TABLE 3.31
Payment out of fees received from students during 2007-08 to 2011-12
(Rupees in lakh)

Name of Colleges	*Year*				
	2007-08	*2008-09*	*2009-10*	*2010-11*	*2011-12*
MBBC	5.19	5.28	9.05	9.98	10.06
BBMC	2.78	3.33	3.08	3.98	5.48

WC	5.02	7.67	5.73	8.93	9.28
RTC	1.26	1.5	1.57	1.91	2.37
ICVC	1.84	2.06	2.07	3.77	3.96
NSM	0.55	0.64	0.8	0.76	0.77
KNM	0.16	0.26	0.25	0.28	0.27
MMDC	0.62	0.92	0.73	1.01	1.06
DDMC	0.56	0.78	0.73	0.78	0.77
RKM	1.1	1.32	1.28	2.33	2.31
Ambedkar Colleges	0.41	1	0.96	1.54	1.65
GDC Kamalpur	1.33	1.7	1.54	2.21	1.25
GDC Amarpur	0.3	0.46	0.38	0.91	1.01
GDC Khumlung	0.14	0.24	0.16	0.31	0.59
GDC Dharma nagar	2.7	2.96	2.97	5.6	5.82
Total	**23.96**	**30.12**	**31.3**	**39.28**	**46.65**

Source: Information from Sample Colleges and Compiled

We have seen as a higher education sector, we face formidable challenges over the next decade. Meeting these challenges will require the highest caliber of leaders and managers who are prepared to embrace change through developing management practices and raising the level of strategic thinking within their institutions (Newby, 2003)[26]. Tuning to the sample colleges of Tripura it is observed that the government (central or state)

TABLE 3.32
Unutilized or Balance amount of Fund of Sample College of Tripura during 2007-08 to 2011-12 (Rupees in lakh)

Items/Heads	*2007-08*	*2008-09*	*2009-10*	*2010-11*	*2011-12*
Total fund received	2180.8	2565.2	3512.75	4063.79	4828.47
Total fund utilized	2133.84	2510.01	3293.84	4010.92	4705
Fund unutilized / Refund	46.96 (2.15 %)	55.19 (2.15 %)	218.91 (6.23 %)	52.87 (1.30 %)	123.47 (2.55 %)

Source: Information from Sample Colleges, Compiled and Result Computes

are providing funds for utilizing various purposes, but they (institutes) are unable to spend the full amount of money within stipulated period and table 3.32 and Fig. 3.7 shows the same picture.

Fig. 3.7: Unutilized or Balance amount of Fund of Sample College of Tripura (Rupees in lakh)

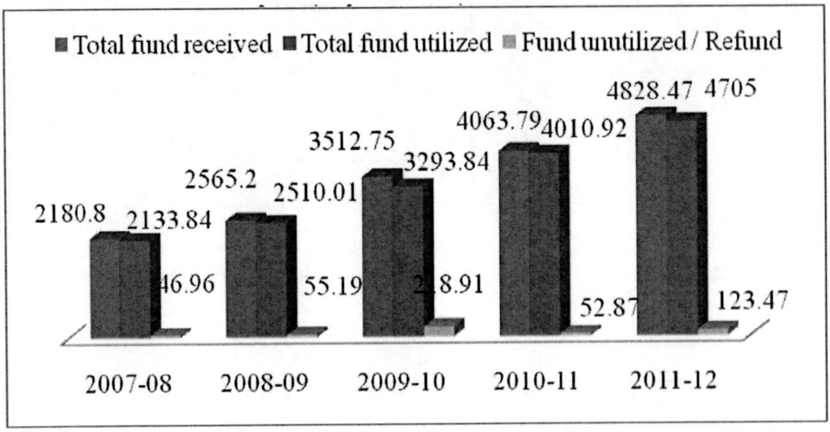

Source: Table-3.31

Table-3.32 and Fig.3.7 shows that total fund allotted for general degree colleges increased significantly during the period of study. It has increased from 2180.8 lakh in the year2007-08 to 4828.47 lakh in 2011-12 resulting Annual Growth Rate of 22.27 per cent (Table 3.11). However fund allotted does not mean the total expenditure incurred by the sample general degree colleges. There are two items / head of expenditure namely refund of undistributed stipend and refund of unspent amount is to be excluded from the total fund allotted to find out total expenditure incurred by the sample degree colleges.

Thus, it is observed that management of finance becomes necessary when funds allotted are not properly expended or remains unutilized. This calls for serious introspection as unspent amount or unutilization of fund blocks the objectives of fund allocation itself. In the present case almost average 3 percent funds remain either unspent or unutilized.

Perception of Respondents

It was asked regarding financing higher education of sample colleges to the respondents. The responses of the respondents are shown with pie chart in Fig. 3.8.

Fig. 3.8: Perception of Respondents

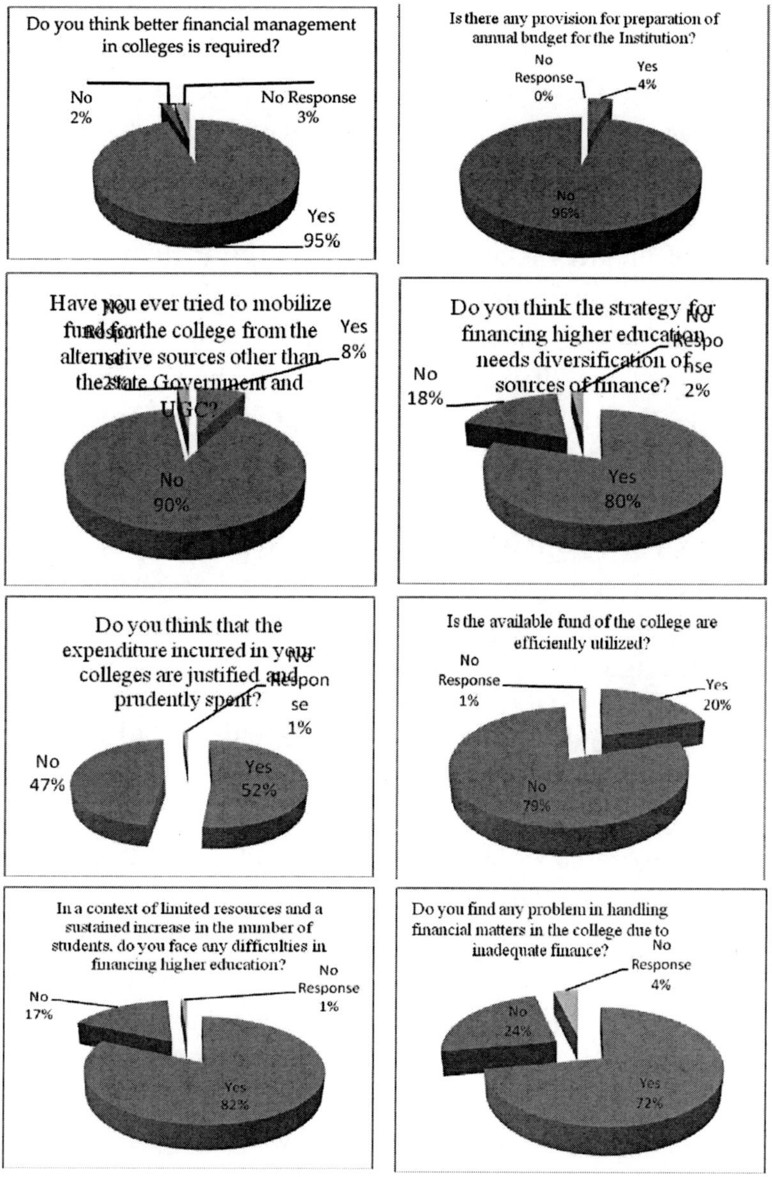

These respondents were asked a few questions regarding alternative sources of fund for maintenance and up keeping of the government degree colleges in the state. It may be observed that 95 per cent of the respondents opined that there is a need for better financial management for smooth running the colleges. A majority of the respondents, 96 Per cent believed that there is no provision for the preparation of the annual budget for the institutions and the colleges only send proposals for their requirement (other than salary head) for running the college. Also 90 Percent respondents knew that the institutions do not mobilize funds from any alternative sources. At the same time 80 per cent respondents are of the opinion that diversification of sources of finances is absolutely necessary for the running the colleges. Quite interestingly, it is found that only 52 per cent finds justification in the expenditure incurred by the colleges and a mere respondents 20 per cent think that the funds for the colleges are efficiently utilized. That means most of the respondents think that the colleges do not efficiently utilize the funds allocated. Hence, we find from the survey that respondents 82 per cent agrees that limited resources and high enrollments lead higher educational institutions to face difficulties and respondents 72 per cent said that they find problems in handling financial matters in the college due to inadequate finances.

The relevant stakeholders in financing and expenditure pattern of the institution do not convey the continuation of the existing pattern. Rather, there is a strong opinion in favour of undertaking reformative reassures in the financing and expenditure pattern of the institution. This reformative measures range from more efficient utilization of fund, prudent and justified expenditure pattern, diversification of sources of finance to maintain a proper and advanced system of financing and expenditure pattern. UGC is regarded as alternative sources of finance have been accepted, though with limited resources and sustained increase in the numbers of student more fund has become necessary.

Chapter Summary

In this chapter the sources of finances and expenditure pattern of general degree colleges in Tripura are examined. Various sources of finance of the colleges have been identified and the category wise amounts received by the sample colleges during the period of study are collected from the respective college. Similarly, head wise expenditures are also collected.

The research question in this chapter was to understand what are the sources and applications of funds in Government General Degree Colleges in Tripura. The State Government plays the most important role in providing finance to the general degree colleges of Tripura as the sample colleges are government colleges. Therefore the state higher education budget is the most important mechanism to finance higher education. As a percentage of the total budget; the higher education budget of the state has increased to 2.89 per cent in the year 2011-12 from 1.58 percent in the year 2007-08. Apart from the compulsion to allot an increased amount of fund in higher education, one can be assured of the fact that there is a percentage of increase in budget expenditure of higher education. Thus a shift in the policy towards more inclusive education can be envisaged in the information contained in the study. Higher education budget as a percentage of GSDP increased from 0.57 per cent in 2007-08 to 1.04 per cent in 2011-12. This rising trend is found mainly due to the following facts: a) Introduction of revised pay scale for college teachers; b) Fresh appointment of college teachers necessitated by the introduction of new courses in existing government general degree colleges and fulfillment of posts as vacated due to superannuation of existing college teachers; c) Providing for infrastructure for the introduction of new courses not only in general degree colleges but also in other areas of higher education.

During the period of study the contribution of the state government in total amount of funding stays at 86.15 (%). Other sources of funding, which are prominent are, UGC (3.91%) and different agencies providing a stipend and scholarship to the students (8.65%). Alternative sources of funding of the GDCs are not found to any noticeable extent. However, it is observed that BCA has been introduced in few government general degree colleges under the scheme of self financing courses.

Regarding the application of funds in general degree colleges of Tripura shows a prominent aspect that a sizeable amount of fund is disbursed as salary and wages and this is followed by the expenditure on a stipend and scholarship. Management of finance becomes necessary when funds allotted are not properly expended or remains unutilized. It is observed that around 3 per cent of funds remains either unspent or unutilized. This area needs to be looked into so that a proper utilization of fund takes place.

It reveals from the perception of the respondents that the finance related factors are the main constraints in delivering quality services to the students as a whole. On the basis of respondents' perception in 5 point scale the following types of factors are identified by using weighted index and factor analysis: availability of adequate finance for running and maintenance of colleges; availability of fund for purchase of necessary capital items; and availability of qualified teachers. Again for identifying the factors responsible we have also used the factor analysis and the same type of factors also have been identified. Therefore, it can safely be argued that the crux of all issues is finance.

REFERENCES

1. NUEPA. (2009). Facing Global and Local Challenges Country Report: India. In Sub-*regional Conference for South, South West and Central Asia on Higher Education.*Feb.25-26, Vigyan Bhawan, New Delhi.P-22.
2. UGC. (2012). *Higher Education at a Glance.* MHRD, New Delhi.
3. Punnayya Committee Report. (1993). *UGC Funding of Institutions of Higher Education.* University Grant Commission, New Delhi.Pp-1-129.

4. Yash Pal Committee. (2008).*Report of The Committee to Advise on Renovation and Rejuvenation of Higher Education.* MHRD, New Delhi. Pp-45-46.

5. Gandhi, M.M.(2015). Financial management of Higher Educational Institutions - with reference to Financing, Pricing, Accounting Standards and Gaps in Practices in Universities and Colleges. *The Business and management Review, Vol-5, No-4,* P-295.

6. Prakash, V.(2007). Trends in Growth and Financing of Higher Education in India. *Economic and Political Weekly, Vol - XLII No. 31*August 4, P-3254.

7. Op.cit. NUEPA. (2009). P-22.

8. Kaul, S. (2006). *Higher Education in India: Seizing and opportunity* (Working Paper No-179). New Delhi: Indian Council for Research on International Economic Relations (ICRIER). Pp-26-27

9. Thorat, S.(2008). Emerging Issues in Higher Education – Approach and Strategy in 11th Plan. In *Higher Education in India - Issues Related to Expansion, Inclusiveness, Quality and Finance.*UGC, New Delhi.Pp-17-19.

10. Agarwal, P. (2006). *Higher Education in India- the Need for change* (Working Paper No. 180). New Delhi: Indian Council for Research on International Economic Relations (ICRIER). P19.

11. Ibid. Pp-32-33

12. Ansari, M.M. (1988). Financial Health of Universities: A Diagnostic Study. *Journal of Higher Education, Vol- 14,* UGC, New Delhi, Pp-84-85.

13. Bellew, R. & Destefano, J. (1991). *Costs and Finance of Higher Education in Pakistan* (WPS-704). Policy, Research and External Affairs, Population and Human Resources Department,World Bank. P-6.

14. Raval, S. K. and Kamble, P.S. (2012). Quality Gaps in Higher Education System in India. *Golden Research thoughts, Vol - I* , ISSUE – VIII.P-4.

15. Bhatia,K.& Dash,M.K. (2010). National Knowledge Commission – A Step towards India's Higher Education Reforms on India's Higher Education. *International Research Journal of Finance and Economics. Issue-53.*Pp-53 -54.

16. Das,S.,Chakraborty,K.S. & Dey, N.B.(2014). Development of Higher Education in North East India: An Analytical Study. *International Journal of Informative & Fututistic Research, Vol-I,* August -2014, P-90.

17. UGC. (2012&2013). *Higher Education at a Glance.* MHRD, New Delhi.

18. Mahanta, D. K. (2013). *Financial Management of Higher Education -A Study on Gauhati University* (unpublished doctoral thesis), Gauhati University. Retrieved from http://shodhganga.inflibnet.ac.in/, P-71.

19. Varghese, N.V. & Tilak,J.B.G. (1991).The Financing of Education in India (XIIIP Research Report No -92). *International Institute for Educational Planning* (UNESCO), Paris. Retrieved from unesdoc. unesco.org/ images /0009 /000902/090282eo.pdf on 15.02.2013. Pp-1-64.

20. Op.cit.Das, S., Chakraborty, K.S. & Dey, N.B. (2014).P-91-92.

21. Azad, J. L. (2008). *Financing and Management of Higher Education in India: The Role of Private Sector*, Gyan Publishing House, New Delhi, Pp- 75-76.

22. Chattopadhyay, S. (2007). Exploring Alternative Sources of Financing Higher Education. *Economic and Political Weekly*, October 20 Pp 4251-59.

23. Tilak,J.B.G.(1993). Financing higher education in India: principles, practice, and policy issues. *Higher Education, Vol. 26, No. 1*, Pp-53-55.

24. Op.cit.Azad, J. L. (2008). Pp- 214-215.

25. Chakrabarti, A. & Jogleker, R. (2006). Determinants of Expenditure on Education: An Empirical Analysis Using State Level Data. *Economic and Political Weekly, VolXLI*, April 15, P-1467.

26. Newby, H. (2003). The Management of Change in Higher Education. *Higher Education Management and Policy , Vol.15, No.1.* P- 17. Paris: OECD.

CHAPTER 4

Analysis of Cost and Expenditure

Introduction

Educational activity had been, for a long time, held as an unproductive sector in an economy and concept of gain or loss was hardly associated with it. Until recently, studies on efficiency and productivity of educational expenditure had not drawn much attention of the economists. Money spent on both capital and revenue accounts constituted total expenditure on education and per capita estimates. Cost analysis can contribute significantly to decision-making, planning, and monitoring in education. The cost of education has much significance as it helps in measuring the internal efficiency of the educational system and sanctioning grants for the maintenance of university and colleges. The educational cost includes institutional cost, private cost and opportunity cost. The institutional cost, which is spent by the institution to provide education, includes recurring and capital cost. Private cost is borne by the student or his/ her guardian. The opportunity cost is earning foregone by the student while receiving education during the working age period (Singh, 2003)[1]. In chapter 4 the cost of higher education in Tripura has been estimated and analyzed on the basis of data collected from the government general degree colleges as sample colleges.

Expenditure and Cost: Conceptual Framework for the Study

At the outset, it is necessary to distinguish between the terms, 'expenditure' on education and 'costs' of education which are often synonymously used. That part of expenditure which has some relationship with the production process and the output only can be referred to as costs; and that part which has no such relationship with the production process and the output is merely expensive. In this sense, expenditure is a broader concept than costs; but the vice-versa is also true, in the sense that while costs can include imputed items like opportunity costs, generally expenditure does not include such items. Expenditure can be expressed only, in monetary terms, while costs can be expressed in monetary as well as in real or physical terms. In this sense, the concept of costs used in economics is quite different from that used by accountants. For example, the concept of shadow prices has never figured in the works of accountants (Tilak, 85)[2].

Expenditure on education and cost of education are not the same. Information on expenditure on education is more easily accessible and available from the budget and accounts of the Central and State governments. There is a tendency to use the term expenditure and cost interchangeably. Cost of education refers to the amount of money spent to acquire or impart education. From the point of view of the individuals, costs refer to the amount of money spent during a particular period (generally a year) to acquire education. From the point of view of the state, it refers to the expenditure incurred on education during a year. The term cost and expenditure are used interchangeably, but more popularly, we use the term 'cost' and refer to cost per student pertaining to a particular level (primary, secondary, higher secondary or university). Similarly, cost per student to the state for a particular course or level is calculated. But cost per student in the state may include expenditures incurred on staff salaries, equipment and buildings, maintenance costs of apparatus, library books, sports, etc. From the point of view of the individual, cost of acquiring education does include expenditure on books and stationery, school fees, travel cost and in case of students making use of hostels, it will also include rent of hostel accommodation, mess charges, etc, Since educational costs are available in current prices, it would be necessary to deflate them by a common deflator with a bench mark, so as to study whether real cost per student or per course is increasing or decreasing over a period of time.

In an educational enterprise, we have to measure the cost incurred by the provider of education and by the consumer of education separately. This necessitates a re-consideration of cost in economics so that it can suitably be applied to education, In fact, when we try to apply the concept of cost to education, three difficulties arise due to the inherent nature of the activity of education. These difficulties are: (a) the definition of production resulting from education; (b) the identification of the economic transactions connected with education; and (c) the fact that education has the character of a public service;

Cost in Economics and Cost in Education

In economics, cost is used when reference is made to the production of goods and services. It implies the cost of resources utilised in the production of goods and services. It can be expressed in monetary terms. In general, the concept of cost comes into play in the production of goods or services. It will be remembered that: (a) cost may be expressed in terms of money or in non-monetary terms; (b) cost affects a specific economic transactor: producer, seller, buyer, consumer, etc. Some economists have carried the distinction between 'real cost' and 'direct production expenditure' a very long way. Literature in economics has distinguished between real costs and money cost. The real cost is said to correspond to the sacrifice of resources or inputs needed to produce goods and services. Therefore, real cost corresponds to opportunity cost; because, as we have noted above, opportunity cost refers to the foregone output that could have been produced had the input been utilized in the next best way. The producer of education may be a government, an institution (public or private), a teacher or a family. The consumers are the students, and their families who are the buyers of education (Hallak, 1969)[3].

Thus, we can speak of cost for both the agencies producing education and the persons consuming education. There can be differences between cost and expenditure because of government subsidies to education, tax relief on institutions, income foregone by students while studying, etc.

Social and Private Cost

The very idea of cost immediately poses the question: cost for whom? Cost can be defined from the supplier's point of view as well as from the consumer's point of view. Moreover, cost can also be of various forms. Social costs concern society, and refer to such costs (or expenditure) as are borne out as a result of all education and training activities in a society at a given point of time. Private costs concern individuals in families and represent costs, which the individuals and the families must bear in return for the education received. Examples of such expenditure are: tuition and examination fees and other such fees; institutional supplies; manuals and books; transport; uniforms; foregone earnings.

Fixed and Variable Cost

Whatever the production level, a firm always bears certain fixed expenses and certain variable expenses which depend on the production level or, in other words, which vary according to the number of units produced. The same distinction can be drawn in the field of education. In the case of a teaching establishment like a school or a university, the fixed expenses include, for example, the capital cost of the building, the equipment and furnishing or their corresponding annual rents, etc. The variable expenses include school books, teaching staff salaries, etc. But for all practical purposes, expenditure on permanent staff salaries (both teaching and non teaching) for permanent staff can be treated as a fixed cost.

Normative and Actual Cost

Very often, it so happens that positive or actual cost prevalent for each level and type of education are different from the normative or expected or planned costs. Such normative costs are generally laid down by the respective public authorities like the Central or State Government or local bodies. There are Cost norms with regard to, for example, salaries. Salary scales of teachers, the number of students per teacher, the total amount of money to be spent per teacher, etc. are planned on expected lines. But these norms may not necessarily match the cost or expenditure actually incurred.

Cost of Education

The cost of education in India varies significantly. Government institutions cost much less than private institutions because it is highly subsidized by the government. India's government maintains laws that educational institutions accredited by the government can only operate under a not for profit status and these institutions of higher education are a way to increase accessibility and educational equality to all citizens of India.

The expenditure on education is an important item of a nation's budget in view of the intimate relationship between the quantum of technical skills and abilities and economic growth. Whether it is capitalistic or socialistic, a country has to devote a sizeable part of its resources towards education. In the two polities' one capitalist and the other socialist, the educational outlays will remain the same if these economies are identical in all other respects of factor endowments and economic goals. The difference between them would however be in the methods of meeting their costs and modes of production (Rao, 1969)[4].

The costs of education will be completely met by the colleges or educational institutions which would engage themselves in the production, purchase and sale of human capital. The cost of education in whichever country incurred, possesses two inseparable attributes-consumption and investment. One can never separate these or categorize these two components as a consumption component of the educational costs and the investment component of education. It is because education is a closely integrated process and does not permit any such segregation. The difficulties of segregation should not lead one to deny the existence of these components.

One of the important purposes of the cost analysis is to enable one to estimate future costs of education. For this purpose, a thorough analysis of the present cost is essential. In analyzing and diagnosing the present situation, the following concepts and techniques are essential.

Determinants of Educational Cost

Knowledge of the major determinants of educational costs is essential for anyone thinking of improving the level of education in the society. The cost of an educational plan or innovation is often expressed in terms of its total cost to indicate the tile value of the total resources devoted to it. But for diagnostic and evaluative purposes, unit cost is more meaningful. Unit cost is the cost per educational unit, e.g. cost per student, cost per school, cost per teacher, etc. But education has multiple outputs measured variously in terms of student achievement; number of graduates passed, and so on. Hence, while estimating unit cost, due care should be taken to avoid ambiguity. For example, costs per student may imply:

a) cost per student enrolled:

b) cost per student successfully completing a given course.

The problem of deciding on the unit cost has to be solved carefully. Choosing the number of students may not always be the right thing to do because all costs do not vary with the number of the students; for instance, the teachers and their salaries, the number of square meters of building space, etc. Hence, cost per teacher or cost per school should also be considered. Educational costs may be divided into three categories: those related to the students; those related to the teachers; and those related to buildings and equipment.

In a normal growing state, a composite unit, including all three could be adopted. Unit cost are likely to rise due to changes in the price level, increase in learner population, rise in the educational standards, the demand for education as well as the pressure for raising the level of school-going age. In making long term forecasts, we have to take note first of the increase in the number of students, teachers and schools and secondly, of the rise in cost per unit.

It is essential to break up the expenditure on education, both by the government and private institutions, into different components like recurring expenditure and capital expenditure. Recurring expenditure (or cost) as the name suggests, takes place regularly at certain intervals. Capital expenditure or costs, on the other hand, are one time investments.

Cost depends on the level and structure of the teachers' salaries; the average pupil-teacher ratio at each level; the non-salary costs of education; and the capital cost of buildings and other equipments. Of course, each of these factors is themselves determined by a number of other factors like availability of funds, teacher, student enrollment, etc. It is because of the variation in these factors that countries or states and districts within the country differ with regard to their educational priorities and the corresponding expenditure.

Behaviour Pattern of Educational Cost

Several behaviour patterns of educational cost are found in the literatures. It may be noted that total cost increases with an increase in the number of students, teachers and institutions. Unit cost, on the other hand, may increase, decrease or remain constant as expansion takes place. In order to study the behaviour of costs of education, we can calculate them along different dimensions: cost by level (like primary, secondary, higher education, etc.); cost by region (like rural and urban); total cost; unit cost; fixed and variable costs; and average and marginal costs. The type of cost analysis will depend upon the purpose for which it is needed. Ideally, the cost per pupil enrolled and the cost per successful student should be the same. This, however, is not usually the case because of the prevalence of dropouts. Therefore, cost per successful student is higher than per student enrolled. The difference is a measure of the efficiency of the system, lower the difference the more efficient the system.

The educational cost includes institutional cost, private cost and opportunity cost. The institutional cost, which is spent by the institution to provide education, includes recurring and capital cost. The recurring cost is incurred every year to keep the courses of education running and it has a relationship with the output. The non-recurring cost includes investment in land, buildings and other infrastructure. It is to create the seat of education. It's also known as capital cost. Private cost is borne by the student or his/ her guardian. It includes tuition fees, funds, examination fees, expenditure on books, stationary, board and lodging, transportation and other incidental expenses. The opportunity cost is earning foregone by the student while receiving education during the working age period. The opportunity cost is high in the countries where employment level is high. The effective cost is the cost per successful student. It considers the effect of wastage and stagnation.

The institutional cost, which is spent by the institution to provide education, includes recurring and non recurring cost.

The recurring cost is incurred every year to keep the courses of education running and it has a relationship with the output. The non-recurring cost includes investment in land, buildings and other infrastructure. It is also known as capital cost. Private cost is borne by the student or his/ her guardian. It includes tuition fees , funds, examination fees, expenditure on books, stationery, boarding and lodging, transport and other incidental expenses (Singh, 2003) [5].

The allocation of resources to the higher professional education demands proper and efficient utilization in all respects. Therefore, an analysis of education cost is highly valuable and a powerful tool in the hands of decision makers to evaluate the efficiency of education institutions in terms of resource allocation and productivity (Vanlalchhawna, 2006) [6]. Another approach to this problem is to conceive of the cost of education as having three different aspects: i) Institutional cost; ii) Students' cost and iii) Opportunity cost (Rao, 1969)[7].

Components of Cost of Education

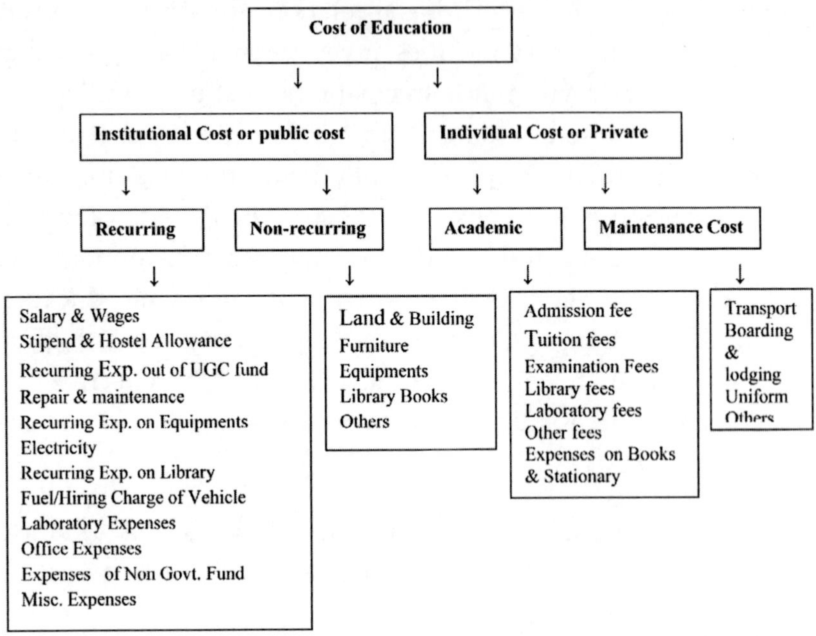

Institutional Cost

Institutional Cost or Public Cost of Education incurred at the institutional level is called institutional cost or public cost of education. Public costs are those that include financing by the government, i.e., all those costs which are needed to create educational facilities or in other words, all those expenditures which are required to establish and run an educational institution. The institutional cost of education is, generally, analyzed using recurring and non-recurring cost of education. As a general rule, those cost which are consumed within a year are included in the Recurring Cost of education. Nonrecurring Cost are those which are incurred almost once for all in the creation of any educational facility. Such type of cost changes with the change in the scale of operation; hence these have also been described as the fixed costs or capital costs (Kalia, 2010)[8].

According to Gurbax Singh (1969)[9] recurring cost can be divided into two parts – non divisible and divisible. The Non divisible cost would comprise those items of expenditure which are incurred for providing common services to all the students of the institution and such as should be equally shared by them from the point of view of the unit cost.

Non divisible Recurring cost covers the following main items: i) salaries and allowances of administrative and establishment staff including library staff. ; ii) gratuity, pension, provident fund contribution and insurance of the entire staff; iii) annual purchase of library books, periodicals, journals, etc. iv) expenditure on extracurricular activities v) rent, interest and administrative charges, vi) rates, taxes and electricity charges and water charges, vii) current repair to building, furniture, etc. viii) contingent expenditure ix) expenditure on organizing examination x) scholarships stipend and xi) miscellaneous recurring charges. Divisible recurring cost on the other hand may be defined as the expenditure which incurred for providing service to a group or part of the student body and as such the expenditure is to be distributed over the members of this group only to calculate the unit cost on this account. The main items under the head of recurring expenditure on consumable stores for the laboratory or other recurring expenditure are i) salaries and allowances of teaching staff, ii) recurring expenditure on science laboratories, iii) expenditure on transport, etc.

Estimation of Institutional Cost: Sample Colleges

In the present study attempt has been taken to estimate the institutional cost of sample colleges i.e. government general degree colleges of Tripura Keeping in mind the limitation of individual scholar ascertainment of private costs, or individual costs are kept out of purview in estimating the cost of education pursued by the general degree colleges of Tripura. The estimated institutional costs are comprised of recurring cost and nonrecurring cost.

Recurring Cost

The measurement of recurring cost is very difficult and involves a large number of issues in the practical situation. Many of the institutions do not maintain the record of costs incurred on various activities under separate heads and accounts. The recording of cost under aggregate heads makes it difficult to account for the cost incurred on the performing of various functions for the supply of education (Kalia, 2010) [10]. Recurring Cost is the aggregation of costs incurred on a number of items. It is found during survey that the sample colleges had incurred 11 types of recurring cost, namely i) salary and wages ii) stipend and scholarship iii) expenses out of UGC fund iv) repair and maintenance v) recurring expenses on equipments vi) electricity vii) laboratory expenses viii) fuel/hiring charge of vehicle ix) expenses on library x) expenses out of non government funds xi) office expenses.

TABLE 4.1
Recurring Cost of Education in Sample Colleges during 2007-08 to 2011-12 (Rupees in Lakh)

Items	*Year*					*Average Cost*	*Percent of Average Total*
	2007-08	*2008-09*	*2009-10*	*2010-11*	*2011-12*		
Salary & Wages	1696.2	1920.8	2613.54	3404.11	3819.85	2690.89	87.35
Stipend &Scholarship	186.82	236.29	253.25	204.86	366.26	249.50	8.10
Portion of Recurring Expenses out of UGC Fund	5.15	15.5	25.75	32.13	35	22.71	0.74
Repair & Maintenance	7.61	19.57	30.60	22.70	6.79	17.45	0.57

Recurring Expenses on Equipments	0.79	0.96	1.50	0.66	0.49	0.88	0.03
Electricity	14.49	15.9	23.56	19.88	24.17	19.60	0.64
Laboratory Expences	20.64	20.76	13.87	14.74	14.61	16.92	0.55
Fuel / Hiring Charges of vehicle	12.13	13.54	14.4	15.4	16.67	14.43	0.47
Recurring Exp. on Library	0.51	0.59	0.59	0.56	0.58	0.56	0.02
Expenses out of Non Govt. fund	23.96	30.12	31.3	39.28	46.65	34.26	1.11
Office expences	8.13	9.94	13.9	14.92	19.51	13.28	0.43
Sample colleges taken as a whole	1976.44	2283.94	3022.26	3769.24	4350.58	3080.49	100.00

Source: On the basis of data Collected from Sample Colleges and compiled.

The recurring cost of sample colleges has been specified for years under the present analysis. It may be observed from the table-4.1 that there is a continuous rise in the recurring cost during the period of study. However, the rise is steep during the period 2009-10 and 2010-11 from the cost incurred in the respective previous years and it is found to be moderate during 2011-12 from that in 2010-11. These substantial increases, as indicated above, may be attributed to a sharp rise in salary and wages in the relevant years. In fact the rise in that category is such that a fall in the other categories of recurring cost has not been able to act as a check on the rise as shown in both salary & wages and recurring cost in relevant years.

Implementation of new pay scale for both teachers and other employees of the institution might have a positive impact on such rise and almost constant or falling recurring expenditure in equipments and a library does not seem to have an impact on maintaining the quality of education as might be expected from a sharp rise in the recurring cost.

Indirect teaching expenditure is an important factor contributing to the teaching-learning process. It consists of expenditure on staff development, libraries, laboratories and computers & equipments, etc. The table-4.1 shows that expenditure on indirect- teaching activities is either negligible or has been declining. The expenditure on libraries is also a negligible percentage.

Although in any academic institutions' libraries occupy a pivotal place, their negligible share in the expenditure shows that the institutions are not receiving importance in the allocation of resources. Also, the low expenditure on laboratories indicates the inadequate priority given to them, although they are significant for colleges' teaching and research functions.

Fig. 4.1: Growth of Recurring Cost of Education in Sample Colleges during 2007-08 to 2011-12

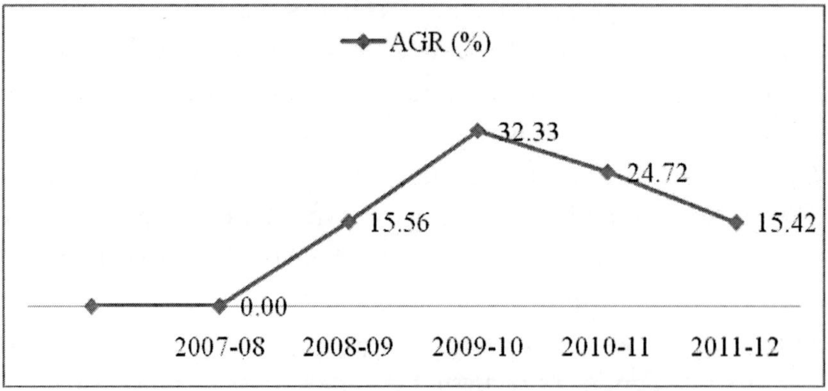

Source: Based on Table 4.1; AGR=Annual Growth Rate

Fig. 4.1 depicts the growth of recurring cost of sample degree colleges during the period 2007-08 to 2011-12. It is observed from the figure that recurring cost of sample colleges' increase from 15.56 percent during 2007-08 to 2008-09 and 32.33 percent during 2008-09 to 2009-10 and declined to 24.72 percent in the year 2010-11 and 15.42 percent during 2011-12. There is a steep rise during the period 2008-09 to 2009-10.

TABLE 4.2
College Wise Recurring Cost of Education during 2007-08 to 2011-12
(Rupees in Lakh)

Name of Colleges	*Year*					*AAGR percent*
	2007-08	*2008-09*	*2009-10*	*2010-11*	*2011-12*	
MBBC	425.55	433.64	521.32	704.15	717.60	14.78
BBMC	195.91	197.23	257.64	349.90	400.93	20.42
WC	292.88	306.91	403.82	498.10	414.98	10.76
RTC	174.93	226.23	275.23	402.67	444.73	26.93
ICVC	148.62	176.80	241.46	289.62	392.88	27.78
NSM	142.53	150.42	175.23	208.76	312.68	22.74
KNM	65.91	82.60	116.47	135.19	185.40	29.89
MMDC	37.89	59.37	119.43	122.61	119.08	39.41
DDMC	90.05	124.40	171.09	202.78	260.90	30.72
RKM	109.01	145.24	224.62	230.80	298.81	30.03
Ambedkar College	42.35	51.11	76.86	105.06	136.01	34.30
GDC Kamalpur	49.57	77.10	90.30	90.98	144.87	33.16
GDC Amarpur	37.01	47.23	68.52	73.16	116.00	34.50
GDC Khumlung	16.30	42.20	55.98	76.14	100.10	64.76
GDC Dharmanagar	147.92	163.46	224.29	284.34	305.61	20.49
Sample colleges taken as a whole	1976.44	2283.94	3022.26	3769.24	4350.57	22.01

Source: On the basis of data Collected from Sample Colleges and compiled.

AAGR = Annual Average Growth Rate

It may be observed from the table-4.2 that there is a continuous rise in the recurring cost of each college. But there is a sharp rise in 2009-10 and 2010-11 from the cost incurred in the respective previous years and there is a moderate rise in 2011-12 from that in 2010-11. This substantial increase, as indicated above, may be attributed to a sharp rise in salary and wages in the relevant years. Implementation of new pay scale for both teachers and other employees of the institution might have a positive impact on such rise.

The annual average growth rate of recurring cost is 22.01 percent, but the annual average growth rate of general degree college; Khumlung is 64.76 percent, where as lowest annual growth rate of Women's College is 10.76 per cent.

The recurring cost in the study consists of the sum total of fourteen different components, viz (1) Teaching Cost ; (2) Office and Administration ; (3) Electricity and Fuels ; (4) Repair and Maintenance ; (5) Conduct of Examinations ; (6) Extra Mural Activities ; (7) Expenditure on Communication ; (8) Purchase of Consumable Items , (9) Transport ; (10) Legal Expenses ; (11) Expenditure on Research and Faculty Improvement ; (12) Publicity ; (13) Scholarships and Fee Concessions ; and (14) Miscellaneous Items .Considering all the components she computed per unit recurring cost of higher professional courses in the case of colleges/institutes affiliated to the Punjab Technical University. On an average it was estimated to be Rs. 22,319 during the period 2006-07(Kalia, 2010)[11]. In government colleges of education in Punjab the per unit recurring cost in correspondence courses department is Rs. 3589 and Rs 98841 in the regular departments for completing the courses. (Singh, 2003)[12]. Turning to Tripura the per unit recurring cost are shown in table 4.3.

Per unit recurring cost shown in the table- 4.3. Per unit recurring cost of general degree colleges of Tripura has been increasing during the period of study except during the period 2007-08 to 2008-09. It has increased from Rs 9260 in the year 2007-08 to Rs.15170 in the year 2011-12. The annual growth rate from during the period 2008-09 to 2009-10 is 41.73 percent, which is highest while 9.70 per cent during the year 2010-11 to 2011-12 which is the lowest among the period of study but The annual average growth rate during the study period is 14.36 percent.

TABLE 4.3

Per unit Recurring Cost of Sample Colleges during 2007-08 to 2011-12

Year	*RC (Rs. in Lakh)*	*No. of Students*	*PURC* (Rs. in Lakh)*	*AGR percent*
2007-08	1976.44	21342	0.0926	----
2008-09	2283.94	26068	0.0876	-5.392
2009-10	3022.26	24338	0.1242	41.73
2010-11	3769.24	27251	0.1383	11.38
2011-12	4350.58	28672	0.1517	9.70
Annual average growth rate (per cent)				14.36

Sources: Table 4.1 and Information from Sample Colleges for number of students

RC = Recurring; PURC = Per Unit Recurring Cost; * = Result calculated; AGR = Annual Growth rate

Colleges and universities differ not only in how much they spend per student but also in how their resources are allocated. Relative to universities, colleges allocate a significantly larger proportion of their budgets to salaries and allowances and a correspondingly smaller share to non personnel items. On average, colleges allocate about 93 percent of their budget to salaries and allowances, leaving only seven percent to cover all operational and other instructional cost. A high percentage of personnel expenditure covers the salaries and benefits of nonteaching staff (Bellew and De Stefano, 1991)[13]. So far as Tripura is concerned salary and wages as a percent of recurring cost of government general degree colleges are presented in the table-4.4 & Fig. 4.2.

The trend of percentage of salary and wages in total recurring cost shows a constant pattern during the years of study. The notable fact is that the constancy stays at a level of around 87 per cent. Whether this can be interpreted in a negative sense or not is open to question. At a purely qualitative level this may be regarded as regressive owing to the fact that all other component stays around 13 %.

TABLE 4.4
Salary & Wages as percentage of Recurring Cost of Education in Sample Colleges during 2007-08 to 2011-12.

Year	*Recurring Cost (Rs. in Lakh)*	*Salary & Wages (Rs. in Lakh)*	*Salary & Wages as percentage of Recurring cost*
2007-08	1976.44	1696.21	85.82
2008-09	2283.94	1920.77	84.10
2009-10	3022.26	2613.54	86.48
2010-11	3769.24	3404.11	90.31
2011-12	4350.58	3819.85	87.80

Source: On the basis of data Collected from Sample Colleges and results computed.

Fig. 4.2: Salary & Wages as percentage of Recurring Cost of Education in Sample Colleges during 2007-08 to 2011-12.

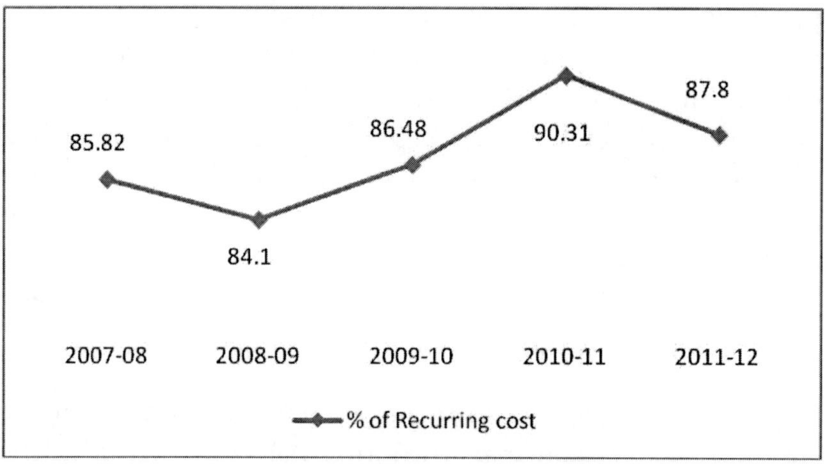

Source: Table 4.4

But the indirect effect of such a high expenditure on salary and wages cannot be taken to be hindering the cause of imparting education. Salary and wages are meant for retaining personnel who are considered to be the real guiding force for imparting education. In this respect this high percentage of salary and wages can be accepted as a positive force in the relevant area under consideration.

TABLE 4.5
College wise Salary & Wages as percentage of Recurring Cost of Education in Sample Colleges during 2007-08 to 2011-12

Name of College	*2007-08*	*2008-09*	*2009-10*	*2010-11*	*2011-12*	*Average percent*
MBBC	94.82	95.51	93.25	94.19	95.96	94.75
Ambedkar College	89.92	88.08	89.86	90.13	88.74	89.35
GDC Dharmanagar	88.63	82.53	88.99	90.78	89.45	88.08
DDMC	90.24	77.59	92.19	86.52	90.09	87.33
BBMC	87.63	82.87	87.4	92.17	85.1	87.03
GDC Amarpur	86.65	86.43	90.54	89.02	75.9	85.71
NSM	81.17	84.05	87.28	89.48	85.39	85.47
ICVC	82.61	84.94	85.49	90.88	83.17	85.42
RTC	82.4	83.67	86.47	92.32	81.7	85.31
WC	76.78	82.16	79.63	92.39	93.13	84.82
GDC Khumlung	81.84	81.26	87.6	87.65	85.53	84.78
RKM	79.09	81.88	81.02	85.42	90.41	83.56
MMDC	82.05	74.26	89.57	83.93	84.7	82.9
KNM	82.81	70.88	84.16	83.1	86.46	81.48
GDC Kamalpur	92.4	67.44	65.19	70.27	77.59	74.57
Average	85.82	84.1	86.48	90.31	87.8	86.9

Source: On the basis of data Collected from Sample Colleges and Result calculated.

The table-4.5 shows the salary and wages as percentage of recurring cost of general degree colleges of Tripura during the period 2007-08 to 2011-12. The notable fact is that the constancy stays at average level of around 87 per cent but in case of GDC Kamalpur the average rate is 74.57 per cent and 81.48 per cent for Kabi Nazrul Mahavidyalay. This rate is less than the overall average rate due to less teaching and non teaching staff is engaged in these particular colleges.

Nonrecurring Cost or Capital Cost

The non-recurring or capital cost is cost incurred on the purchase of land, buildings, furniture, fixtures, equipment, etc. to be used in the production of goods or the rendering of services. In other words, all those costs which are being made in fixed assets in order to bring a project to a commercial operating status fall in the category of capital cost. In a nutshell, the nonrecurring cost include investment in land, building and other physical infrastructural assets. It means the capital costs are inclusive of all the durable items such as the value of land, buildings, furniture and office, laboratory and workshop equipments, library books and all other non-recurring items. Thus, capital cost precisely refer to the cost incurred on the purchase of land, buildings, construction, equipments, books, etc., to be used in the production of goods or the rendering of services.

The capital cost is associated with the investment expenditures on the land, plant, equipment, building, etc. The capital cost is viewed as the set of all of those important items which are capital in nature for which one makes payments for the items that last for a number of years. The important items included in the estimation of capital cost are: (i) value of land & buildings; (ii) furniture items; (iii) equipment (including computer); (iv) library books or, in other words, the non-recurring cost include investment in land, building and other physical infrastructural assets.

In the present study, it may be mentioned that the information might seem to be incomplete as it does not contain expenditure on land & building. The relevant information is found to be, often without the expressed values of those assets or those have been occupied by the government at different period of time. Furthermore the cost of land may not match the existing valuation process of such property as declared by the government in case of private transactions. However an imputed value of those assets might have helped our analysis in a more meaningful way, but paucity of information on this score has restricted us to consider fixed assets like furniture, equipments, computers and library books and journals as the core elements of non recurring cost which is shown in table 4.6.

TABLE 4.6
Nonrecurring Cost of Education in Sample Colleges during 2007-08 to 2011-12 (Rupees in Lakh)

Items	*Balance as on**	*Year*				
	31.3.2007	*2007-08*	*2008-09*	*2009-10*	*2010-11*	*2011-12*
Furniture	216.48	46.43	69.29	61.56	27.72	84.78
Equipments	336.67	94.71	115.28	150.77	183.75	248.77
Computers	4.35	5.88	24.03	47.07	4.75	2.4
Books and Journals	74.13	11.72	19.48	15.32	27.51	20.6
Total	631.63	158.74	228.08	274.72	243.73	356.55

Source: On the basis of data Collected from Sample General Degree Colleges and results computed.

*Estimated by the respective colleges

The above table gives us an idea about the pattern of cost on fixed assets on a non recurring basis. The cost of equipments constitute the substantial portion of total non recurring cost during the study period followed by cost of furniture, cost of books and journal and cost of computer which are essential items for any educational institution.

The above amount of non recurring cost for each year has been restricted to those amounts required for accruing new assets. No cumulative aspects have been attributed in this regard. By the above token, it may be noted that up to 2009-10 there is a moderate rise in the cost, but a sharp fall is noticed in 2010-11 and this is followed by a sharp rise in such cost in 2011-12. This may be attributed to the fact that the share of revenues and taxes along with grants in aid as per recommendation of relevant finance commission may have played a role in the swinging pattern of non recurring cost during the relevant years of study.

TABLE 4.7
College wise Nonrecurring Cost of Education in Sample Colleges during 2007-08 to 2011-12 (Rupees in Lakh)

Name of Colleges	*Balance as on**	*Years*					*AAGR percent*
	31.3.2007	*2007-08*	*2008-09*	*2009-10*	*2010-11*	*2011-12*	
MBBC	97.61	22.18	17.7	19.02	36.35	12.81	3.40
BBMC	17.56	4.27	8.03	14.12	2.37	39.73	414.26
WC	101.14	25.14	27.23	30.7	30.6	11.84	-10.14
RTC	38.41	9.1	10.26	25.69	11.64	23.75	53.12
ICVC	55.62	13.44	44.19	21.94	10.65	42.46	106.42
NSM	65.39	17.78	27.28	28.48	18.6	18.13	5.15
KNM	30.41	7.74	12.63	11.81	3.21	21.17	135.84
MMDC	11.16	2.39	5.05	14.02	20.53	0.56	59.52
DDMC	57.50	15.79	18.46	38.88	48.65	9	17.79
RKM	86.89	13.66	14.97	36.48	3.3	18.8	133.01
Ambedkar College	20.31	5.29	8.89	11.19	30.44	24.11	61.29
GDC Kamalpur	10.69	2.47	8.99	6.47	15.5	33.75	123.31
GDC Amarpur	20.66	5.35	4.3	5.02	3.55	70.97	466.75
GDC Khumlung	00	11.15	3.46	3.11	2.5	3.62	-13.47
GDC Dharmanagar	18.28	3	16.66	7.79	5.85	25.85	179.77
Sample colleges taken as a whole	631.63	158.74	228.09	274.72	243.73	356.55	24.78

Source: On the basis of data Collected from Sample General Degree Colleges and results computed.

*Estimated by the respective colleges

Table 4.7 gives us an idea about the cost of fixed assets (non recurring cost) for general degree colleges of Tripura. The non recurring cost of each year for each college has been restricted to those amounts required for accruing new assets. No cumulative aspects have been attributed in this regard. In most colleges, non-recurring expenditure accounts are very low. This trend of non-recurring expenditure would seem to indicate inadequate attention on the part of colleges to development and up-gradation of infrastructure. In the study the expenditure on land and building has been ignored due to non availability of information about land and building and also the colleges are run by the government. The annual average growth rate of non recurring cost of sample degree colleges during the study period 2007-08 to 2011-12 is 24.78 percent. While in case of Women's college and government degree college, Khumlung we have noticed that this rate is negative and in case of BBM College and government Degree College Amarpur this rate is significantly higher compared to annual average growth rate as a whole.

TABLE 4.8

Per Unit Nonrecurring Cost of Sample Colleges during 2007-08 to 2011-12 (Rupees in Lakh)

Year	*Non Recurring Cost*	*No. of Students*	*Per unit Non Recurring Cost*	*AGR percent*
2007-08	158.74	21342	0.007	----
2008-09	228.08	26068	0.009	28.57
2009-10	274.72	24338	0.011	22.22
2010-11	243.73	27251	0.009	(-) 18.18
2011-12	356.55	28672	0.012	33.33
Annual Average Growth Rate (%)				28.04

Sources: Table 4.6 and Information from Sample Colleges for number of students.

AGR = Annual Growth Rate

Per unit nonrecurring cost shown in the table- 4.8. Per unit non-recurring cost of general degree colleges of Tripura have been fluctuating during the period of study. It has increased from Rs 700 in the year 2007-08 to Rs.1200 in the year 2011-12 whereas per unit non-recurring cost of all the courses affiliated to the Punjab Technical University was Rs. 15,185 per annum during the year 2006-07 (Kalia, 2010)[14].

It is also observed from the table that expenditure on nonrecurring items is gradually increasing except during 2009-10 to 2010-11. Thus, it is evident that institutes /government are conscious about internal infrastructure development. The annual growth rate from during the period 2007-08 to 2008-09 is 28.57 percent decline to 22.22 percent during 2008-09 to 2009-10 and increased to 33.33 percent during 2010-11 to 2011-12, which is highest, while negative growth during the period 2009-10 to 2010-11 but the annual average growth rate during the study period is 28.04 percent.

Chargeable Portion of Nonrecurring Cost (Depreciation)

Depreciation accounting enunciates principles which can also serve as a useful guide in case of nonprofit organizations. It is often seen that the charitable institutions do not charge depreciation in their accounts when the capital expenditure has been considered as application of income. The application of income can be for revenue as capital expenditure. Depreciation on assets is allowed even if the cost of the assets have been fully allowed as application of income under section 11 of accounting standard.

The educational institution may calculate the cost of depreciable assets over its useful life and accordingly charge depreciation to the income and expenditure account. The depreciation rates to be applied may be taken as those specified under the income Tax Act 1961 or that under the companies Act 1956.

The non recurring cost includes the value of capital items of the school or college. The annual depreciation or amortization cost one could take into account to be distributed equally over all the students under instruction in the institution. But since sometimes there is appreciation in the value of capital items in the course of time, it would be better if the rental value of the building is taken into account instead of their annual depreciation. Again, the annual amortization cost of the stock of books and equipment distributed equally over the entire students receiving education during the course of the year.(Singh,1969)[15].

The Depreciation charge on the fixed assets of the university is taken at a rate of 5%for each year. The separate depreciation allocation of one lakh rupees kept apart each year by the university has been added to the depreciation amount of fixed assets. Though this expenditure is not actually incurred on the students, it must be shown as a part of the total expenditure because of the wear and tear that occurs to various fixed and other assets like books, laboratory equipment, etc. of the university (Dash, 1998) [16].

Depreciation cost refers to the diminution in value of an asset due to use and/or the lapse of time. It arises due to the physical wear and tear of an asset on account of the usage of and passage of time. The depreciation cost represents a charge for the usage of capital resources and the cost of the asset has to be recovered from the cost over a lifetime. Capital cost can be spread over time by applying an appropriate depreciation charge to each year, the rate of depreciation varying with the expected and useful life of each item(Kalia, 2010)[17].

A huge amount of money spent on land, building, furniture, equipment and library books. But these assets are not exhausted within one year in the education of a single group of students. An amount of depreciation of a certain percentage according to the life expectancy of each asset included in the revenue account. Rate of depreciation is a much disputed item (Dey, 1969)[18].

A proper assessment of non-recurring expenditure like cost of land and building, furniture, equipment, library books, etc. and calculation of annual depreciation is usually difficult and it is many times ignored in the educational cost calculation (Pandit, 1969)[19].

To calculate the unit cost per year with regard to the fixed costs generally, in most of the studies, it is either ignored, or the rate of depreciation is calculated. But in the absence of definite data on the life expectancy of different assets and definite method of depreciation and rate, we have adopted the reducing balance method and depreciation calculated on furniture @ 7.5%, equipment @ 7.5 %, computer @ 20 % and library books @ 10% as per accounting standard for educational institution issued by ICAI.

TABLE 4.9
Chargeable Portion of Nonrecurring Cost of Education (Depreciation) in Sample Colleges during 2007-08 to 2011-12 (Rupees in Lakh)

Year	*Furniture*	*Equipments*	*Computers*	*Books and Journals*	*Total*	*AGR %*
2007-08	19.72	32.35	2.05	8.59	62.71	---
2008-09	23.44	38.57	6.44	9.67	78.12	24.57
2009-10	26.3	46.99	14.57	10.24	98.10	25.58
2010-11	26.4	57.25	12.6	11.97	108.22	10.32
2011-12	30.78	71.61	10.56	12.83	125.78	16.23

Source: Chargeable Portion of NRC (Depreciation) calculated by the author on the basis of data Collected from Sample Colleges

AGR = Annual Growth Rate

A chargeable portion of nonrecurring cost (Depreciation) for government general degree colleges shown in table 4.9. The pattern of non-recurring cost may be further appreciated if we look at it in real term, i.e. devoid of depreciation for each and every component of the cost. In arriving at their depreciation we have adopted the reducing balance method considering the value of non recurring items as on 30.3.2007.This may be taken into account while analyzing the broader unit cost for the institutions which shall be provided at the end of this analysis. It is also observed from the table that annual growth (increase) rate of depreciation during 2007-08 to 2009-10 remain somewhat constant and during 2009-10 to 2010-11 has a decreasing trend which means that investment for capital items is also decreasing.

TABLE 4.10
Institutional Cost of Education in Sample Colleges during 2007-08 to 2011-12 (Rupees in Lakh)

Year	*Recurring Cost*	*Nonrecurring Cost (Depreciation)*	*Institutional Cost*	*AGR percent*
2007-08	1976.44	62.71	2039.15	----
2008-09	2283.94	78.12	2362.06	15.84
2009-10	3022.26	98.1	3120.36	32.10
2010-11	3769.24	108.22	3877.46	24.26
2011-12	4350.58	125.78	4476.36	15.45
	AAGR (%)			21.91

Source: On the basis of data Collected from Sample General Degree Colleges and results computed.

AGR = Annual Growth Rate; AAGR= Annual Average Growth Rate

Institutional cost consists of recurring and non- recurring cost. The institutional cost of sample colleges is shown in table 4.10 and Fig. 4.3. The recurring cost during the said period Rs 1976.44 in the year 2007-08, Rs 2283.94 in 2008-09, Rs.3022.26 in 2009-10, Rs. 3769.24 in 2010-11 and Rs 4350.58 during the period 2011-12 respectively.

Fig. 4.3: Institutional Cost of education in Sample Colleges during 2007-08 to 2011-12

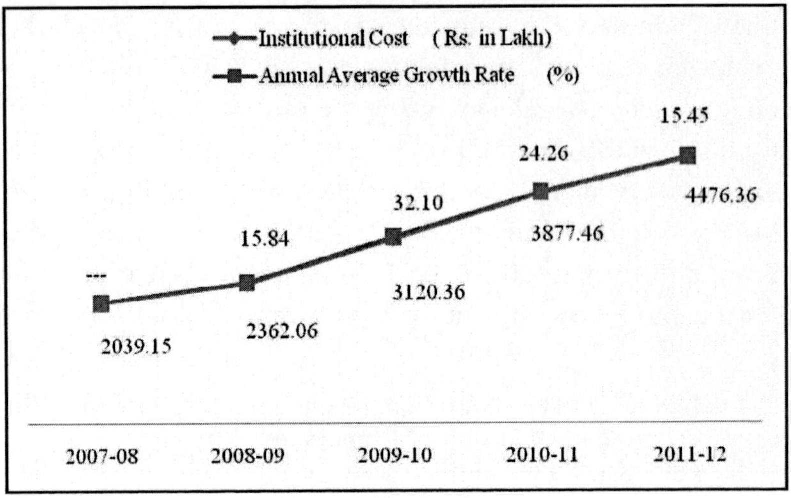

Source: Table 4.10

And the portion of non-recurring cost (Depreciation) calculated for the colleges of Tripura are Rs.62.71 lakhs in 2007-08 , 78.12 in 2008-09, 98.1 in 2009-10, Rs. 108.22 lakhs and 125.78 lakh in 2010-11 and 2011-12 receptively. Therefore, we can say that total expenditure have been increased from Rs. 2039.15 to Rs. 4476.36 lakh during the period from 2007-08 to 2011-12.

In case of non-recurring cost, as stated above only the portion of depreciation has been considered in view of the fact that the assets as a result of such cost in every year has the long term value which may not be included as a cost element for the said year. The institutional cost, in the above table have been showing a rising trend over the years and this trend may be attributed to the continuous rising recurring cost in the relevant years. The emergence of growing recurring cost, particularly from 2009-10 to 2011-12 calls for a close scrutiny. The underlying facts concerning the management of institutions may be considered for such items suitable for the said scrutiny.

It is found from the table-4.10 and Fig. 4.3 that the institutional cost of sample degree colleges of Tripura have been increasing gradually during the period of study. It has increased from Rs 2039.15 lakh in the year 2007-08 to 4476.36 lakh in the year 2011-12. The annual growth rate for the period 2010-11 to 2011-12 is 15.45 percent, which is lowest during the period of study while 32.10 percent was during the year 2008-09 to 2009-10 which is the highest among the period of study. The Annual Average Growth Rate (AAGR) during study period is 21.91 percent.

TABLE 4.11
College wise Institutional Cost of Education in Sample Colleges during 2007-08 to 2011-12 (Rupees in Lakh)

Name of College	*Year*					*AAGR percent*
	2007-08	*2008-09*	*2009-10*	*2010-11*	*2011-12*	
MBBC	435.07	443.75	532.68	717.30	730.62	14.64
BBMC	197.66	199.57	260.85	353.03	407.02	20.58
WC	303.10	318.34	416.63	512.20	428.83	10.64
RTC	178.63	230.44	282.06	409.71	452.88	26.80
ICVC	154.09	185.18	251.95	299.91	405.43	27.61
NSM	148.94	159.52	185.69	219.97	324.36	22.36
KNM	69.07	86.43	120.88	139.48	190.92	29.31
MMDC	38.97	60.76	122.77	127.10	123.10	39.58
DDMC	95.71	131.03	181.80	216.13	273.64	30.29
RKM	116.71	154.19	235.52	241.00	309.56	28.91
Ambedkar College	44.50	53.77	80.35	110.57	142.90	34.28
GDC Kamalpur	50.83	79.12	92.58	94.22	150.37	33.51
GDC Amarpur	39.04	49.45	71.07	75.82	123.81	35.09
GDC Khumlung	17.21	43.30	57.24	77.75	101.81	62.64
GDC Dharmanagar	149.62	167.22	228.28	288.31	311.10	20.62
Sample Colleges taken as a whole	2039.15	2362.06	3120.36	3877.46	4476.36	21.91

Source: Information collected from Sample colleges and Result calculated.

AAGR = Annual Average Growth Rate

It is pertinent to mention it here that the price index of India during the said period has increased 82.2918 to 120.147. In terms of average annual inflation rate during the year 2007 to 2012 is 9.94 per cent. Therefore, it can be inferred that the growth in the annual average cost of education in general degree colleges is higher than the annual average inflation rate. It is also appears that the cost of education in general degree colleges are increasing rapidly over the years during the period of study.

The table-4.11 depicts the college wise institutional cost of general degree colleges in Tripura during the period 2007-08 to 2011-12. The institutional cost of each college have been showing a rising trend over the year. This trend may be attributed to the continuous rising recurring cost in the relevant years for every college, which is most important component of institutional cost.

Correlation is a statistical measure that indicates the extent to which two or more variables fluctuate together. A positive correlation indicates the extent to which those variables increase or decrease in parallel; a negative correlation indicates the extent to which one variable increases as the other decreases. Datt (1969)[20] used Pearson correlation test in his study and opined that correlation analysis suggests that while association of all the variables with the institutional cost or unit cost in case of all colleges; it is not so in the case of private colleges.

Since the objective is to predict a relation between institutional cost of all the colleges and recurring as well as non-recurring cost, accordingly simple correlation test is used for study purpose. To achieve the objective Pearson Correlation has been calculated and its significance has been tested. Positive correlation indicates that both variables increase or decrease together, whereas negative correlation indicates that as one variable increases, so the other decreases, and vice versa.

This test is used to measure the strength of a linear association between two variables, where the value r = 1 means a perfect positive correlation and the value r = -1 means a perfect negative correlation. The value of r is calculated by using the Pearson correlation formula:

$$r = \frac{\sum_i (x_i - \overline{x})(y_i - \overline{y})}{\sqrt{\sum_i (x_i - \overline{x})^2} \sqrt{\sum_i (y_i - \overline{y})^2}}$$

Identifying the Variables: Recurring cost includes Salary& Wages, Stipend & Scholarship, Repair & Maintenance, Electricity charges, Laboratory expenditure, Fuel & hiring charges of vehicles, recurring expenditure on library, expenses out of Non-Government funds and office expenses. A Chargeable portion of nonrecurring cost includes Furniture, Equipments, Computers, Books & journal.

Steps of using Correlation Test: There are some costs which are included in the recurring cost and there are some costs which are included in the non-recurring cost. All the variables are taken together and then run the correlation test.The variables which have high correlation with institutional cost and significant at 1 percent level and 5 percent level, these variables are taken into consideration and run the correlation test. The variables which have a low correlation with institutional cost and are not significant at 1 per cent and 5 per cent level, are excluded from the test.

Considering the correlation between institutional cost and recurring cost it is found that some of the variables of recurring cost like as Salary and wages, portion of recurring expenditure out of UGC fund, fuel and hiring charges of vehicles, expenses out of non government funds , office expenses have high correlation with institutional cost.

Other variables like stipend and scholarship, repair and maintenance, recurring expenditure on equipment, laboratory expenditure, and recurring expenditure on library have no any correlation with institutional cost. But there is a moderate correlation between institutional cost and expenditure on electricity. In case of the chargeable portion of non-recurring cost, i.e. the depreciation on furniture, equipment, computers and library books have high correlation with institutional cost.

TABLE 4.12
Correlation of different Variables with Institutional Cost (IC)

Variables	*r- value*	*Level of Significance*
IC and Salary & Wages	0.998	Significant at 1 % level
IC & Stipend &Scholarship	0.707	Significant at 10 % level
IC &RC out of UGC fund	0.969	Significant at 1 % level
IC & Repair & Maintenance	-0.419	Not significant
IC & RC on Equipments	-0.425	Not significant
IC & Electricity	0.828	Significant at 10 % level
IC & RC on Laboratory	-0.809	Significant at 10 % level
IC & Fuel & hiring charge of vehicles	0.986	Significant at 1 % level
IC & RC on Library	0.416	Not significant
IC & RC on Non Govt.Fund	0.976	Significant at 1 % level
IC & Office Expenses	0.973	Significant at 1 % level
IC & Non Recurring Cost	0.987	Significant at 1 % level

IC = Institutional Cost

RC = Recurring Cost

It is evident from the table-4.12 that the correlation between institutional cost and expenditure on salaries and wages of all the colleges is positive. The correlation value (r=0.998) is significant at 1 per cent level. There is a moderate correlation between institutional cost and stipend and scholarship. The value of R is 0.707 which means that high X variable scores go with high Y variable scores (and vice versa).The correlation between institutional cost and the portion of recurring expenditure out of UGC fund is 0.960, which is significant at 1 per cent level. A positive correlation value r=0.982 is found in between institutional cost and fuel charges or hiring charges of vehicle. The correlation value is significant at 1 per cent level. Institutional costs have a direct relationship with office expenses. The correlation value = 0.973 and is significant at 1 per cent level. The correlation between institutional cost and expenses out of the non government fund is strongly positive. The value of R is 0.969.The Correlation between institutional cost and a chargeable portion of non-recurring cost i.e. depreciation on furniture, equipment and library books of all the colleges is positive and the value is 0.987. The correlation value is significant at 1 per cent level. It is concluded that as expenditure on salaries and wages, portion of recurring cost out of UGC fund, fuel charges, office expenses, a chargeable portion of non recurring cost increases, and the institutional cost is also increasing.

TABLE 4.13

Recurring Cost as a percent of Institutional Cost during the 2007-08 to 2011-12

Year	*Institutional Cost (Rs. in Lakh)*	*Recurring Cost (Rs. in Lakh)*	*Recurring Cost as % of Institutional Cost*
2007-08	2039.15	1976.44	96.92
2008-09	2362.058	2283.94	96.69
2009-10	3120.361	3022.26	96.86
2010-11	3877.46	3769.24	97.21
2011-12	4476.36	4350.58	97.19
Average			**96.97**

Source: On the basis of data Collected from Sample Colleges and results computed.

Fig. 4.4: Recurring Cost as percent of Institutional Cost during 2007-08 to 2011-12

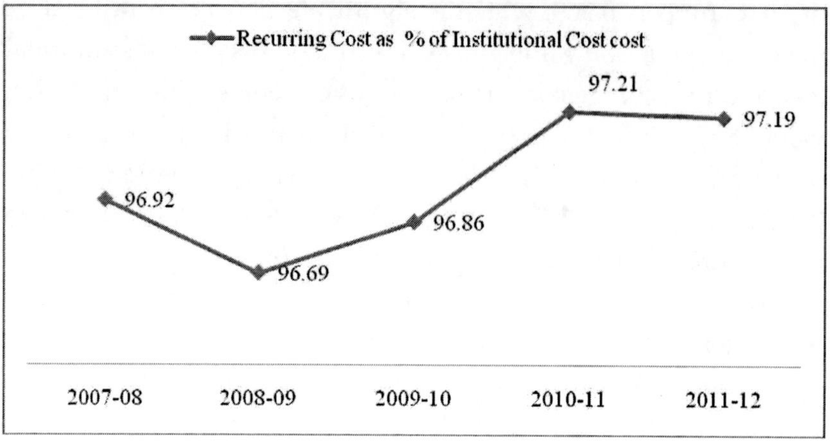

Source: Table 4.13

The table-4.13 & Fig. 4.4 shows the picture of recurring cost as percent of total institutional cost. Be it the colleges taken individually or taken collectively the percentage hovers around 97 per cent. This phenomenon is present in each institution and expenditure on salary and wages may be attributed as a major

TABLE 4.14
Nonrecurring Cost (Depreciation) as percent of Institutional Cost during 2007-08 to 2011-12

Year	*Institutional Cost (Rs. in Lakh)*	*Nonrecurring Cost (Depreciation) (Rs. in Lakh)*	*Non Recurring Cost as % of Institutional Cost*
2007-08	2039.15	62.71	3.08
2008-09	2362.058	78.12	3.31
2009-10	3120.361	98.1	3.14
2010-11	3877.46	108.22	2.79
2011-12	4476.36	125.78	2.81

Source: On the basis of data Collected from Sample Colleges and results computed.

instrument in this respect. However the colleges individually or collectively this percentage has been showing a downward trend 96.92 per cent to 96.69 per cent during 2007-08 to 2008-09. This trend may not be remarkable, but may be considered as an improvement in the management of finance. But after 2008-09 this trend is increasing upto 2010-11 and again decaling to 97.19 percent during 2011-12.

Fig. 4.5: Nonrecurring Cost (Depreciation) as percent of Institutional Cost during 2007-08 to 2011-12

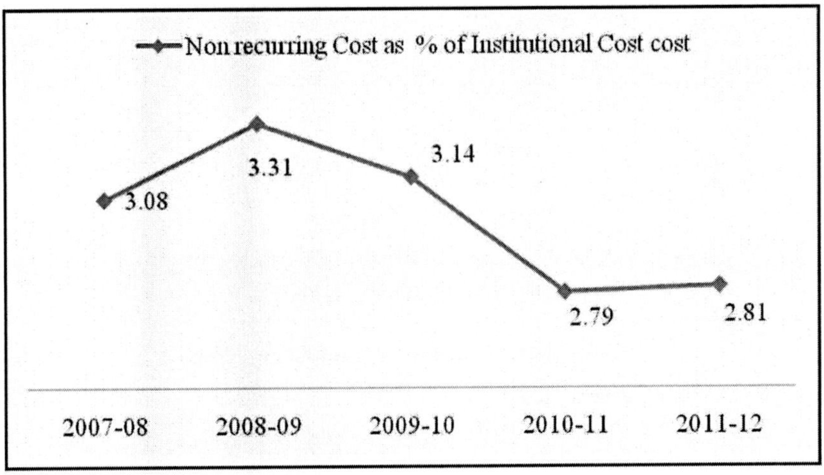

Source: Table 4.14

The table-4.14 & Fig. 4.5 shows the picture of nonrecurring cost as per cent of total institutional cost. Non recurring cost during 2007-08 is 3.08 percent of institutional cost, 3.31 percent in 2008-09, 3.14 percent in 2009-10, 2.79 percent in 2010-11 and increased to 2.81 percent in 2011-12. However the colleges individually or collectively this percentage has been showing downward trend from 2008-09 during the period of study. This trend may not be remarkable as management of institution or government give attention for internal infrastructural development.

TABLE 4.15
Salary & Wages as percent of Institutional Cost during 2007-08 to 2011-12

Year	*Institutional Cost (Rs. in Lakh)*	*Salary & Wages (Rs. in Lakh)*	*Salary & Wages as percent of Institutional Cost*
2007-08	2039.15	1696.21	83.18
2008-09	2362.06	1920.77	81.32
2009-10	3120.36	2613.54	83.76
2010-11	3877.46	3404.11	87.79
2011-12	4476.36	3819.85	85.33
Average			84.28

Source: On the basis of data Collected from Sample Colleges and results computed.

Fig. 4.6: Salary & Wages as percent of Institutional Cost during 2007-08 to 2011-12

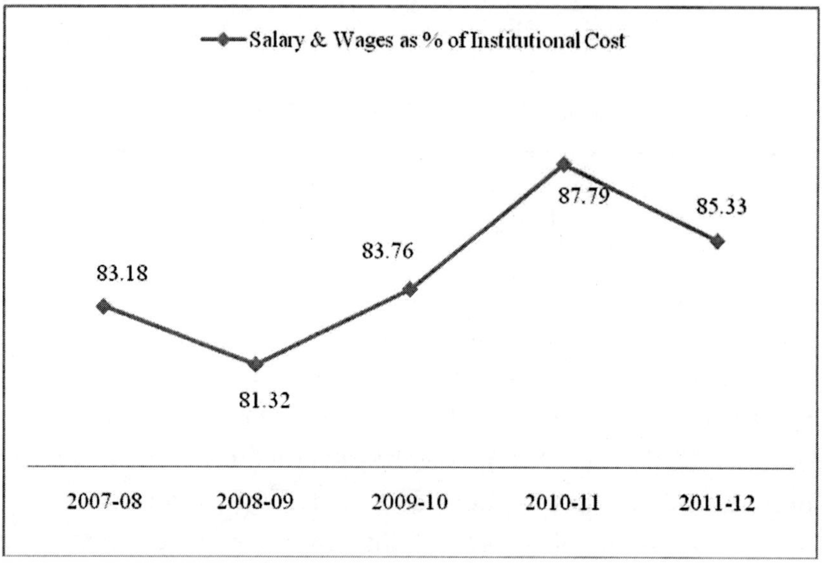

Source: Table 4.15

The predominance of running cost in the institutional cost finds more substance in the table-4.15 & Fig. 4.6 as the running cost concentrates upon a single item i.e. salary and wages to institutional cost hovers around 84 per cent. Implementation of new pay scale for both teachers and other employees of the institution might have a positive impact on such rise in the year 2010-11.

It is worthwhile to note that any viable institution can be said to be properly managed if the percentage as exemplified above stays around 85 per cent (ICRIER, 2007)[21] and 90 per cent(Agarwal, 2006) [22].

TABLE 4.16
College wise Salary & Wages as percentage of Institutional Cost during 2007-08 to 2011-12

Name of College	*2007-08*	*2008-09*	*2009-10*	*2010-11*	*2011-12*	*Average*
MBBC	92.74	93.33	91.26	92.46	94.25	92.81
BBMC	86.86	81.90	86.33	91.35	83.83	86.05
WC	74.19	79.21	77.18	89.84	90.12	82.11
RTC	80.70	82.14	84.37	90.73	80.23	83.63
ICVC	79.68	81.10	81.93	87.76	80.60	82.22
NSM	77.67	79.26	82.36	84.92	82.32	81.30
KNM	79.02	67.74	81.09	80.54	83.96	78.47
MMDC	79.77	72.56	87.14	80.97	81.94	80.48
DDMC	84.90	73.66	86.76	81.18	85.90	82.48
RKM	73.88	77.13	77.27	81.81	87.27	79.47
Ambedkar College	85.57	83.73	85.96	85.64	84.46	85.07
GDC Kamalpur	90.11	65.72	63.58	67.85	74.75	72.40
GDC Amarpur	82.14	82.55	87.30	85.90	71.11	81.80
GDC Khumlung	77.51	79.19	85.68	85.84	84.10	82.46
GDC Dharmanagar	87.63	80.67	87.43	89.53	87.87	86.63
Sample Colleges taken as a whole	83.18	81.32	83.76	87.79	85.33	84.28

Source: On the basis of data Collected from Sample Colleges and results computed.

College wise Salary & Wages as a percent of Institutional Cost during the period 2007-08 to 2011-12 shows in the table-4.16.The table depicts that the average percentage of salary and wages as a per cent of institutional cost is 84.28. The highest per cent is 92.81 for the MBB College while the lowest is 72.40 per cent for general degree college, Kamalpur which is below average.

Unit Cost of Education

Cost of education have no meaning if they do not refer to a unit, in which case the same statistics can be called the unit cost of education. Unit cost should be defined as the cost of an educational unit. Then the question that arises is: what is an educational unit? Ideally, educational unit can be defined as "the ability acquired by the educated to participate in the development of the economy and of civilization. Sometimes it is also being suggested that unit cost of education should be calculated per child of the relevant age-group population. But unit cost is simply the total expenditure incurred by an educational enterprise in a given period either for the whole system or more likely, a particular part of it, divided by the number of students in the same educational category.

This may indicate to some extent the 'efficiency' of the education system, efficiency being measured in terms of the coverage of the relevant age-group population by the education system. For certain purposes of comparison, cost of education per capita, taking the whole population of the concerned region into account, are also computed. Unit cost of education are of particular importance in educational planning. They are most essential for educational planning in general and planning the resources in particular. Certain concepts of Unit cost are also efficiency indicators. The inverse of unit cost based on the output of the system, is after all, an index of total factor productivity in the production process. (Tilak, 1985)[23].

The need of complete knowledge about various types of unit cost for different disciplines and different level of education in the planning process cannot be over emphasized. The unit cost are needed: i) for working out financial allocations and costing of educational programme, ii) for studying the level of efficiency at which the educational plant is run, iii) to estimate optimum utilization and to improve the efficiency of resources invested in education through their analysis and consideration of various alternative combinations of their components; and iv) to measure the cost of inputs in the education industry in determining the returns to education and productivity of the process (Sharma, 1969)[24].

The unit cost of education simply means average cost per student per year. The unit institutional recurring cost is per student cost incurred by the institution during the academic session. The Unit cost is simply the total expenditure incurred by an educational Institution in a given period divided by the number of students in the same educational institution / category.

Generally, unit in unit cost means the total number of students enrolled in a course in a particular year. Sometimes, it is said that the number of learners actually attending the classes should be taken for the purpose of calculation of unit cost and not the total number of learner enrolls. Alternatively, unit cost refer to the unit of output, i.e. successful learner or graduate. This is called effective cost of education. This type of cost calculation education takes care of wastage in education too. The difference between the effective cost and the normal cost of education reveals the efficiency of the given level of the educational system. Thus, we can calculate alternative forms of unit cost of education. These are: (a) Unit cost per student = Total Expenditure/Total enrollment, (b) Unit cost per successful learner = Total Expenditure/Number of Pass-out learner.

TABLE 4.17

Unit Cost of Sample Colleges of Tripura during 2007-08 to 2011-12

Year	*Institutional Cost (Rs. in Lakh)*	*Number of Students*	*Per Unit Cost (Rs. in Lakh)*	*Annual Growth Rate (percent)*
2007-08	2039.15	21342	0.096	---
2008-09	2362.06	26068	0.091	-5.16
2009-10	3120.36	24338	0.128	41.49
2010-11	3877.46	27251	0.142	10.98
2011-12	4476.36	28672	0.156	9.72
Annual Average Growth Rate (per cent)				14.26

Source: Table 4.10 and information from Sample Colleges for number of students

Fig. 4.7: Unit Cost of Sample Colleges of Tripura during 2007-08 to 2011-12 (Rupees in Lakh)

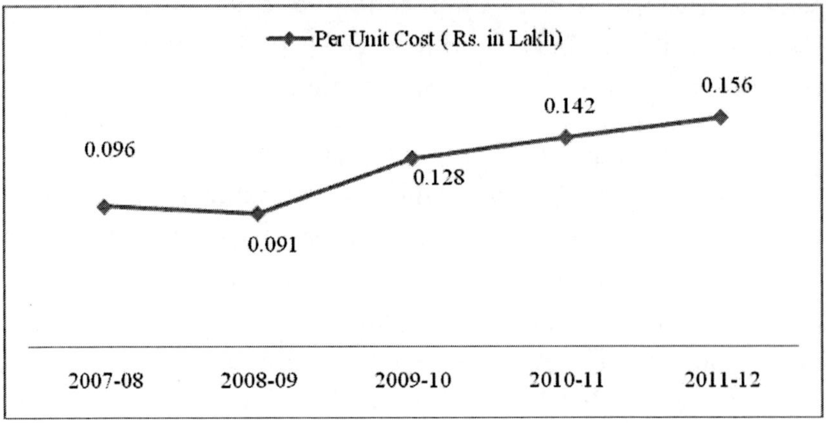

Source: Table 4.17

Table-4.17 and Fig. 4.7 considers the trend of unit cost of general degree colleges in Tripura. A look into the table may be sufficient to ascertain that the unit cost has been showing a slow rise during the period of study if it is considered in terms of the expression of per unit cost. However a detail look into that cost which is expressed in rupees may help us to understand that the slow rise is more intense. But a proper analysis of unit cost cannot be complete without taking account of the elements involved in building up the unit cost. The pattern of student enrollment has got a definite bearing on the per unit cost is evident by the above figure & table. At the same time the pattern of cost has an impact on the student enrollment takes a back seat. What is important in this respect is the fact that both institutional cost and student enrollment are entwined in a cause-and-effect relationship. For this reason, even if there is a rise in student enrollment in 2008-09 corresponding to 2007-08 the per unit cost in absolute term has actually come down.

It is found from the table that the unit cost per year of general degree colleges of Tripura have been increasing gradually during the period of study except during the period 2007-08 to 2008-09. It has increased from Rs 9600 in the year 2007-08 to Rs.15600 in the year 2011-12. The annual growth rate for from the period 2010-11 to 2011-12 is 9.72 per cent which is lowest during the period of study while 41.49 percent was during the year 2008-09 to 2009-10 which is the highest among the period of study. The annual average growth rate during study period is 14.26 percent.

It is pertinent to mention it here that the price index of India during the said period has increased 82.2918 to 120.147. In terms of average annual inflation rate during the year 2007 to 2012 is 9.94 per cent. Therefore, it can be inferred that though the growth in annual average cost of education per year in the general degree college has been on the rise, this rise may not be considered an absolute term. If it is deflated with the help of the annual rate of inflation, then the real cost of education may not be considered to be increasing at such a rapid rate.

Table-4.18 shows the College wise unit cost during the period 2007-08 to 2011-12. The annual average growth rate of unit cost of the students of general degree colleges of Tripura is 14.15 per

TABLE 4.18
College wise Unit Cost during 2007-08 to 2011-12 (Rupees in Lakh)

Name of colleges	*Year*					*AAGR percent*
	2007-08	*2008-09*	*2009-10*	*2010-11*	*2011-12*	
MBBC	0.129	0.116	0.137	0.162	0.170	7.78
BBMC	0.084	0.070	0.113	0.138	0.114	12.52
WC	0.108	0.098	0.137	0.165	0.154	11.09
RTC	0.074	0.085	0.102	0.132	0.142	18.14
ICVC	0.088	0.091	0.123	0.124	0.157	16.50
NSM	0.071	0.073	0.092	0.094	0.130	17.12
KNM	0.094	0.092	0.135	0.118	0.173	19.43
MMDC	0.114	0.132	0.277	0.266	0.248	28.72
DDMC	0.070	0.065	0.127	0.114	0.156	28.87
RKM	0.112	0.083	0.168	0.160	0.206	25.08
Ambedkar College	0.145	0.127	0.209	0.235	0.305	23.63
GDC Kamalpur	0.094	0.123	0.104	0.101	0.130	10.28
GDC Amarpur	0.183	0.172	0.217	0.155	0.257	14.27
GDC Khumlung	0.148	0.234	0.556	0.420	0.283	34.53
GDC Dharmanagar	0.080	0.071	0.095	0.134	0.128	14.96
Sample Colleges taken as a whole	0.096	0.091	0.128	0.142	0.156	14.15

Source: On the basis of data Collected from Sample Colleges and results computed.

AAGR = Annual Average Growth Rate

cent where as lowest annual average growth rate of unit cost is 7.78 percent of MBB College and highest annual average growth rate of unit cost is 34.53 percent for GDC Khumlung. The sudden rise in the unit cost of this college calls for explanation as the college established during 2007-08. Another very notable aspect may be the fact that the institutions became eligible for receiving funds from UGC during the said period. Per unit cost of MMDC,

Ambedkar College, and GDC Khumlung may be a case in the point. The information as stated particularly in the period 2009-10 to 2011-12 may lead us to believe that the number of students might have decreased remarkably causing and upshot in the per unit cost.

But the real picture is not such. In fact this variation may only be explain if it is considered that funds from UGC has started pouring during the said period as those colleges were covered for the first time under section 2(f) and 12(b) of UGC Act. Furthermore this also provided the colleges in question to ask for funds from UGC as new college. To examine the increase in unit cost in connection with growth and expansion of higher education in Tripura it is required to find out how much there is a variation in the magnitude of unit cost due to the variation in the magnitude of other variables, i.e. how much there is a degree of association between unit cost and other variables.

The average cost per graduate, is arrived at by taking a notional group of pupils or students, assessing the total cost of educating them until they have all quit the education sector. The average cost per graduate, is the ratio of the total cost to the number of graduates. In practice, the theoretical cost and the real cost indicate the volume of economic wastage from drop-out and repeating. It is, however, interesting to note that the assignment of the whole financial burden to graduates alone has the effect of substantially increasing the cost per graduate, since it disregards the other pupils who quit the education system after attaining a certain level (Hallak,1969)[25].

After higher secondary school, a student can become a graduate on completing a course of three years of study. For completion of the study an institution has to incur expenditure as institutional cost as a whole. As a unit of expenditure can be obtained by dividing the number of successful students. Per unit cost of a graduated student of sample colleges are shown in table 4.19 and Fig. 4.8.

TABLE 4.19
Per unit Graduating Cost in Sample Colleges of Tripura during 2007-08 to 2011-12 (Rupees in Lakh)

Year	*Institutional Cost (Rs. in Lakh)*	*No. of Successfully Passing out Students**	*Per unit Graduating Cost (Rs. in Lakh)*
2007-08	2039.15	4473	0.4559
2008-09	2362.06	4015	0.5883
2009-10	3120.36	4350	0.7173
2010-11	3877.46	4933	0.7860
2011-12	4476.36	4956	0.9032

Source: Table 4.10 and On the basis of data Collected from Sample Colleges and results computed.

* = a) Number of successfully passing out students means students admitted in 1st year and graduated after completion of 3 years of study in the colleges.

b) The pass out figure is obtained from the respective colleges as well as from the Tripura University as affiliating university.

Fig. 4.8: Per unit Graduating Cost in Sample Colleges of Tripura during 2007-08 to 2011-12 (Rupees in Lakh)

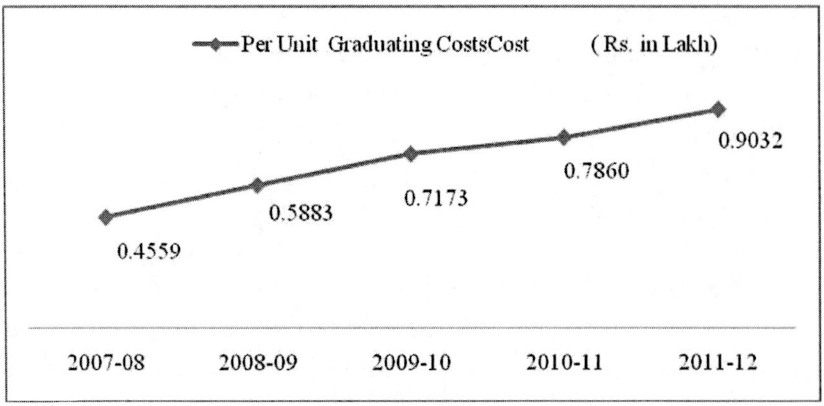

Source: Table 4.19

It is observed from the table that per unit graduating cost is increasing from rupees 45590 during the period 2007-08 to rupees 90320 during 2011-12. Per unit graduating cost calculated by dividing the number of successful students to institutional cost. Here it is mentioned that number of successfully passing out students' means students admitted in 1st year and graduated after completion of 3 years of study in the colleges. Compare to the net per student effective cost in correspondence courses is Rs. 6281, while it was Rs. 98841 in the regular departments under Punjab University, Patiala (Singh, 2003)[26].

TABLE 4.20
Correlation of different variables with Unit Cost (UC)

Variables	*r- value*	*Level of Significance*
UC and Salary & Wages	0.978	Significant at 1 % level
UC & Stipend &Scholarship	0.644	Significant at 10 % level
UC &RC out of UGC fund	0.936	Significant at 5 % level
UC & Repair & Maintenance	0.025	Not Significant
UC & RC on Equipments	-0.310	Not Significant
UC & Electricity	0.875	Significant at 10 % level
UC & RC on Laboratory	-0.910	Significant at 5 % level
UC & Fuel & hiring charge of vehicles	0.930	Significant at 5 % level
UC & RC on Library	0.332	Not Significant
UC & RC on Non Govt. Fund	0.900	Significant at 5% level
UC & Office Expenses	0.960	Significant at 1 % level
UC & Non Recurring Cost	0.955	Significant at 5% level

UC = Unit Cost; RC= Recurring Cost

The table-4.20 shows that there are correlation in between unit cost, salary, recurring cost out of UGC fund, fuel charges, office expenses, expenses on equipment, the chargeable portion of non-recurring cost, i.e. (depreciation cost on furniture, equipment, computer, and books and journal).

The correlation between unit cost and salary and wages is positive. The correlation value (r=0.978) is significant at 1 per cent level. The correlation between unit cost and recurring cost out of UGC fund is 0.936, which is significant at 5 per cent level. The correlation between unit cost and fuel charges is positive and the value is 0.930, which is significant at 5 per cent level. The unit cost has a positive relation with office expenses. The value of correlation is 0.960, which is significant at 1 per cent level. The correlation value r = 0.955 between unit cost and nonrecurring cost (depreciation on furniture, equipment, computers and depreciation cost on books and journal). The correlation value is significant at 5 per cent level.

Perception of Respondents

To understand the issues dealt in the present study perception of the Principals / Principals in charge, Drawing and Disbursing Officers and Academics associated with finance related activities of the sample colleges were also taken. A set questionnaire was designed to gather response. The responses are analysed in the context of higher education of Tripura.

Fig. 4.9 depicts the perception of respondents regarding different aspects of the colleges. From the point of view of the stakeholders (mainly students) expenditure of collegiate education can best be understood by the unit cost of different years for the period under study. The expenditure on collegiate education may be viewed in terms of the overall institutional cost as well as in terms of unit cost. This diverging view is kept in this analysis so that the expenditure of collegiate education can be accessed from the point of view of either the fund provider (mainly government) or stakeholders (mainly students).

On the assumption that all the stakeholders are directly or indirectly involved in the maintenance /running the higher education institutions the researcher put forward a very pertinent

Fig. 4.9: Perception of Respondents

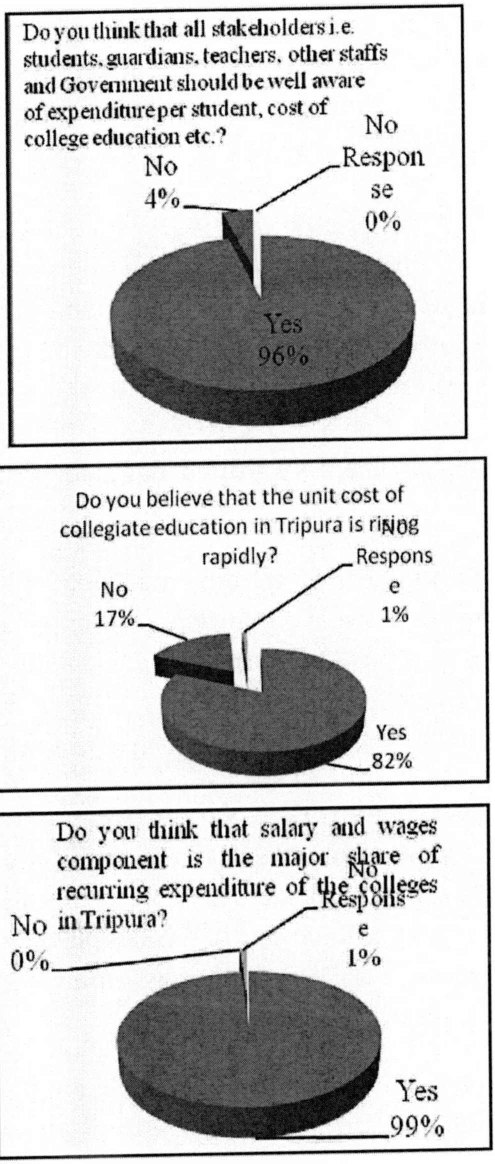

Source: Opinion Survey

question—whether all stakeholders (students, guardians, teachers, staff, government, etc., should be well aware of the expenditure incurred per student/ cost of college education, a majority of the respondents, (96%) gave a positive response. (99 %) respondents were well aware that a salary/wage component is the major share of recurring expenditure of the colleges in Tripura and also (82%) respondents have realized that the unit cost of collegiate education is rising rapidly.

Chapter Summary

This chapter attempts to analyse the institutional cost, unit cost and expenditure of collegiate education in Tripura based on relevant information during the study period from 2007-08 to 2011-2012. Therefore the components of institutional cost / unit cost in Government General Degree Colleges in Tripura were the focus of analysis in the background of established theory and practices.

The institutional cost covers both recurring and nonrecurring cost for the maintenance of institutions and imparting education to the students. It is found that the contribution of recurring cost in institutional cost of sample colleges is 96.97 percent. Only around 3 percent is spent for expenditure of capital nature.

Again out of different heads of recurring cost, the expenditure on salary and wages comprises of 87 percent of recurring cost or 84.28 per cent of institutional cost. Thus it reveals that around 84.28 per cent of institutional cost of the sample colleges are spent on only one head, i.e. salary and wages, while a little portion is spent to upkeep the system.

However the institutional cost has been showing a rising trend over the years from Rs. 2039.15 to Rs. 4476.36 during the period from 2007-08 to 2011-12 registering 21.91 percent annual average growth. This increase may be attributed to the continuous rising recurring cost in the relevant years. In case of individual colleges, institutional cost of GDC, Khumlung, MMDC, Ambedkar College, DDMC and KNM (62.64, 39.58, 34.28, 30.29 and 29.31 percent, respectively) are much higher than the annual average growth rate of Tripura.

Per unit recurring cost of education of general degree colleges of Tripura has been found increasing trend during the period of study. It has increased from Rs 9260 in the year 2007-08 to Rs.15170 in the year 2011-12.

Per unit cost of education in general degree colleges of Tripura per year has been showing an upward trend Rs 9600 in 2007-08 to Rs 15600 in 2011-12 which may be taken to be normal and realistic in consideration with the pattern of expenditure evident in the institutions under study.

The annual average growth rate of unit cost of the students of general degree colleges in Tripura is 14.26 % whereas lowest annual average growth rate of unit cost is 7.78% for MBB College and highest annual average growth rate of unit cost is 34.53% for GDC, Khumlung. The sudden rise in the unit cost of this college calls for review by the government as the college established during 2007-08.

Per unit graduating cost of sample colleges is also estimated. It is found that the per unit graduating cost of sample colleges has been increased from Rs. 45590 in 2007-08 to rupees 90320 in the year 2011-12.

The correlation between institutional cost /unit cost and components like expenditure on salaries and wages, portion of recurring expenditure out of UGC fund, fuel charges or hiring charges of vehicle, office expenses, expenses out of non government funds, a chargeable portion of non-recurring cost (depreciation of furniture, equipment and on books and journal) of all the colleges are found positive. But there are negative correlation observed between institutional /unit cost and repair

& maintenance, recurring cost on equipments, recurring cost of laboratory and recurring cost of the library.

Regarding the perception of respondents whether all stakeholders, should be well aware of the expenditure incurred per student/ cost of college education, a majority of the respondents, (96%) gave a positive response. (99 %) respondents were well aware that a salary/wage component is the major share of recurring expenditure of the colleges in Tripura and also (82 %) respondents have realized that the unit cost of collegiate education is rising rapidly.

REFERENCES

1. Singh, J. (2003). Unit Recurring Cost for Regular and Correspondence Course in Punjabi University. *Journal of Distance Education.* P- 144.
2. Tilak, J.B.G. (1985). Analysis of Cost of Education in India (*Occasional Paper 10*) National Institute of Education, Planning and Administration (NIEPA), New Delhi, Pp-9-10.
3. Hallack, J. (1969). *The Analysis of Educational Cost and Expenditure,* IIEP, UNESCO, Paris.Pp-13-14.
4. Rao, H. V. (1969). Educational Cost: Concepts and Issues. in Pandit, H. N. (ed) *Measurement of Cost Productivity and Efficiency of Education,* NCERT, Madras. Pp -48.
5. Op.cit.Singh, J. (2003). P- 144-45.
6. Vanlalchhawna.(2006). *Higher Education in North-East India -Unit Cost Analysis,* Mittal Publication. New Delhi, Pp- 13-14.
7. Op.cit.Rao, H. V. (1969).Pp -49.
8. Kalia, S. (2010). *Cost of Higher Education and Financing Practices among Students in Punjab: A Study of Professional Education.* Unpublished Doctoral Thesis, Punjab Technical University. Retrieved 5.5.2012from http:// shodhganga.inflibnet.ac.in /bitstream/10603 /2094/7/ 07_absract. pdf P-36.
9. Singh, G. (1969).Concept in and Methodology of measuring Unit Cost in Education. In Pandit, H.N. (ed), *Measurement of Cost Productivity and Efficiency of Education,*NCERT, Madras. Pp- 44-45.
10. Op.cit. Kalia, S. (2010). P-156.
11. Ibid. P-168.

12. Op.cit. Singh, J. (2003). P- 150.
13. Bellew, R. & Destefano, J. (1991). *Costs and Finance of Higher Education in Pakistan* (WPS-704). Policy, Research and External Affairs, Population and Human Resources Department, World Bank.P-6.
14. Op.cit. Kalia, S. (2010). P-174.
15. Op.cit. Singh, G. (1969). Pp- 44.
16. Dash, M. K.(1998).*Formulating a Unit-Cost Approach for Restructuring the Financing Pattern of Central Universities: A Comparative Study of University of Delhi and Jawaharlal Nehru University* (unpublished doctoral thesis), Jawaharlal Nehru University. Retrieved from http://shodhganga.inflibnet.ac.in/ P-113,127.
17. Op.cit. Kalia, S. (2010). P-33.
18. Day, B. (1969). On Costing of Education. In Pandit, H.N. (ed.), *Measurement of Cost, Productivity and Efficiency of Education.* National Council for Educational Research and Training (NCERT), New Delhi. Pp -18.
19. Pandit. H.N. (1969). A Study in Unit Cost at the school stage in India: A Design of the Research Project. In *Measurement of Cost Productivity and Efficiency of Education.* NCERT, Madras, P- 9.
20. Datt, R. (1969). Unit cost of Education- A case study of Haryana College. In Pandit,H. N. (ed), *Measurement of Cost Productivity and Efficiency of Education.* NCERT, Madras.P-106.
21. ICRIER. (2007). *Towards Excellence Higher Education in India (*WP-179). Based on Pawan Agarwal entitled Higher Education in India: The Need for a Change, P-6.
22. Agarwal, P. (2006). *Higher Education in India- the Need for change* (Working Paper No.-180). New Delhi: Indian Council for Research on International Economic Relations (ICRIER). P-23.
23. Op.cit. Tilak, J.B.G. (1985). Pp-15-17.
24. Sharma, D.L. (1969). Unit cost of educations, our knowledge, gaps and our need. In Pandit, H.N. (ed), *Measurement of Cost Productivity and Efficiency of Education.* Pp 27-28.
25. Op.cit. Hallack, J. (1969). Pp-41-42.
26. Op.cit. Singh, J. (2003). P- 151.

CHAPTER 5

Accounting and Auditing

Introduction

Maintenance of Accounts is one of the important functions of any organization. The question is how far the accounting system adopted by the organization is effective. In chapter 5, attempts have been made to explore and analyse the provisions and general practices of accounting system adopted by government general degree colleges of Tripura. Colleges and universities are non-profit organizations with missions in the fields of instruction, research, and public service. As such, institutions of higher education have unique obligations for accounting and financial reporting according to the sources of funds received and their subsequent uses rather than to report net income to investors. The different constituencies that have special interests in the ways educational institutions use their funds include state and local governments, funding organizations, and other stakeholders.

In recent years, with an increase in government expenditure to educational institutions, particularly in the form of concessions and incentives, the greater need is being felt for accountability of the financial resources used by the educational institutions. Moreover, the present system of accounting and financial reporting followed by educational institution does not meet the accountability concerns of the stakeholders, including government as educational institutions in India follow not only diverse accounting practices but also different basis of accounting. Due to these factors, the financial statements of various educational institutions are incomparable. A need is, therefore, being felt for improved accountability of the financial resources used by the educational institution. A sound accounting and financial reporting framework acts as an important ingredient for promoting accountability and for development of the education sector.

Accounting for Educational Institutions: Concepts and Terminologies

Financial accounting enables an organization to have better control and management of finance. It is often argued that since profit is not the objective of educational institutions, the accounting framework, which is relevant for business entities, is not appropriate for educational institutions. The concepts aim to identify the items that should be considered as income, expenses, assets and liabilities by educational institutions, for the purpose of including the same in the financial statements by defining the aforesaid terms. Assets are resources controlled by an entity from which future economic benefits or service potential is expected to flow to the entity. Therefore the definition of 'asset' would remain the same whether an entity is a business enterprise or an educational institution, in so far as expectation of the future economic benefits is concerned. In other words, what is considered as an asset by a commercial entity, e.g., Land, Building, Furniture and Equipment, etc., would be considered as an asset by an educational institution also. However, in case of an educational institution, certain items which may not have future economic benefits, but have service potential would also be considered as assets. The other elements of financial statements, viz., income, expenses and liabilities, will also remain the same for educational institutions as in commercial entities. There is no difference in the application of the recognition principles to commercial entities and educational institutions. For example, the timing of the recognition of a grant as an income in the financial statements of an organisation does not depend upon the purpose for which the organisation is run.

Academic Institutions receive grants from different sources. A grant is recognised as income in the financial statements, under the accrual basis of accounting, when it becomes reasonably certain that the grant will be received and that the organisation will fulfill the conditions attached to it. Thus, a commercial entity and an educational institution would both follow the aforesaid criteria for recognition of grant as income. Similarly, principles for recognition of other incomes, expenses, assets and liabilities would be the same for commercial entities and educational institutions.

So far as the measurement principles are concerned, the same principles are relevant to a not-for-profit organisation as well as to a commercial entity. For example, depreciation of an asset represents primarily the extent to which the asset is used during an accounting period by an organisation.

Thus, whether an asset, such as a photocopying machine, is used by an educational institution or a commercial entity, the measure of charge by way of depreciation depends primarily upon the use of the asset rather than the purpose for which the organisation is run, i.e., profit or not-for-profit motive (ICAI, 2012)[1].

Accordingly, the measurement principles for income, assets and liabilities should be the same for commercial entities and not for- profit organizations such as educational institutions. So far as a financial statement is concerned, educational institution generally follows what is known as 'fund based accounting' whereas the commercial entities do not follow this system. This is because educational institution may be funded by numerous grants, donations or similar contributions, which may or may not impose conditions on their usage.

In other words, the use of any funds may be restricted by an outside agency such as a donor or self-imposed by the organisation. It, therefore, follows that the financial statements of educational institution should reflect income, expenses, assets and liabilities in respect of such funds separately so as to enable the users of financial statements such as the contributors, to assess the usage of the funds contributed by them. However, it may be noted that fund based accounting is relevant primarily for the purpose of presentation of financial statements and not for the purpose of identification, recognition and measurement of various items of income, expenses, assets and liabilities. It may be concluded from the above paragraphs that while the identification, recognition and measurement of elements of financial statements are sector neutral, the presentation of financial statements may differ between the two sectors, viz., for profit sector and not-for-profit sector. Similarly, disclosure principles may also differ.

Needless to mention that certain fundamental accounting assumptions underlie the preparation and presentation of financial statements. The following have been generally accepted as fundamental accounting assumptions which are also relevant for Higher Educational Institutions; a) Going Concern: The enterprise is normally viewed as a going concern, that is, as continuing in operation for the foreseeable future. It is assumed that the enterprise has neither the intention nor the necessity of liquidating or of curtailing materially the scale of the operations. b) Consistency: It is assumed that accounting policies are consistent from one period to another. c) Accrual: Revenues and costs are accrued, that is, recognised as they are earned or incurred (and not as money is received or paid) and recorded in the financial statements of the periods to which they relate. If the fundamental accounting assumptions are followed by financial statements, specific disclosure is not required. If a fundamental accounting assumption is not followed, the fact should be disclosed (ICAI, 2012)[2].

The accounting policies refer to the specific accounting principles and the methods of applying those principles adopted by the institutions in the preparation and presentation of financial statements. There is no single list of accounting policies which are applicable to all circumstances. The differing circumstances in which enterprises operate in a situation of diverse and complex economic activity make alternative accounting principles and methods of applying those principles acceptable. The choice of the appropriate accounting principles and the methods of applying those principles in the specific circumstances call for considerable judgment by the organization concerned.

Accordingly the Institute of Chartered Accountants of India (ICAI) has set up a standard format for higher educational institutes of the country. As per the body, all higher education institutes will have to report their financial information in that standard format set by the ICAI. As per the format, the institutes will now have to disclose their balance sheet and the income and expenditure account. The new format will be helpful for presenting general purpose financial statements to ensure proper accountability, financial discipline, end-use of funds and to meet the needs of stakeholders. It will define transparently the revenue earned through various sources – tuition fee and other charges, income from consultancy or from intellectual property owned by the institution.

The proposed new system is a shift from the present cash basis of accounting to accrual-based system. While the balance sheet will include sources and applications of funds along with liabilities and assets, the income and expenditure statement would reflect the academic receipts, grants and donations. With education being a not for profit activity, the MHRD wants to enforce these standards in order to check how much profit the educational institutes are making.

Government Accounting System

As the present study deals with government general degree colleges of Tripura, it is necessary to understand the government accounting system. Government accounting is the process of recording, analyzing, classifying, summarizing communicating and interpreting financial information about government in aggregate and in detail reflecting transactions and other economic events involving the receipt, spending, transfer, usability and disposition of assets and liabilities. The purposes of government accounting are:

1. To carry out the financial business of government in a timely, efficient and reliable manner (e.g. to make payments, settle liabilities, collect sums due, buy and sell assets, etc.) subject to necessary financial controls.
2. To keep systematic, easily accessible accounting and documentary records as evidence of past transactions and current financial status, so that detailed transactions can be identified and traced and all aggregates can be conveniently broken down into their constituent parts.
3. To provide periodic financial statements, containing appropriately classified financial information, as a basis for (a) stewardship and accountability and (b) decision-making.
4. To maintain financial records suitable for budgetary control, internal control and the needs of auditors.
5. To provide means for effective management of government assets, liabilities, expenditures and revenues.

On the basis of these purposes the government accounting system has to be; relatively uniform, well-documented, simple to operate and easy to consolidate. The mass of government transactions is cash based; hence the cash system of accounting is followed. However, for certain transactions for which Government acts as banker, remitter, borrower or lender, accrual System of Accounting is followed. There are three pillars viz., elements (expense, revenue, receipt, disbursements, liabilities, cash balance), measurement and recognition.

The methods or systems of preparing government accounts can be classified into four broad categories:

i. Cash basis

ii. Modified Cash basis

iii. Accrual basis

iv. Modified Accrual basis

i) Cash basis of accounting is a system of accounting in which only transactions involving increases or decreases of the entity's cash are recorded. Under the cash basis of Accounting, transactions are recorded when the related cash receipts or cash payments take place. Thus, the revenue of educational Institutions, such as donations, grants, etc. is recognised when funds are actually received. The primary advantage of the cash basis of accounting is to record and summarize transactions. In addition, the financial statements are easy to prepare and the net income is the same as the cash flows from operating activities. Similarly, expenses of acquisition and maintenance of assets used for rendering services as well as for employee remuneration and other items are recorded when the related payments are made. The end-product of cash basis of accounting is a statement of Receipts and Payments that classifies cash receipts and cash payments under different heads. In cash basis of accounting, no account is taken of whether the asset is still in use, has reached the end of its useful life, or has been sold. Thus, cash based information fails to show a proper picture of the financial position and performance for the accounting period (ICAI, 2012)[3].

According to Wagh, Ashok (2014)[4] some colleges follow Cash Basis of Accounting System whereas a few follow Accrual Basis of Accounting. Even some colleges follow the hybrid or mixed system of accounting for maintaining their accounts. It was found in his study that there are 86.67% of Mumbai City District colleges follow cash basis accounting system and 06.66% follow accrual basis of accounting system, whereas 06.67% of the follow hybrid (combination of both bases of accounting) basis of accounting system. Thus it was concluded that majority of colleges prefer a cash basis accounting system.

ii) The modified cash accounting recognises transactions and events that have occurred by year-end and are normally expected to result in a cash receipt and/or disbursement within a specific period after year-end. Under this system, the accounting period includes a complementary period for payments (e.g., one or two months) after the close of the fiscal year. Receipts or payments over the complementary period that are related to the transactions of the previous fiscal year incurred during the fiscal year are reported as the revenue or expenditure of the previous fiscal year. Usually, this is achieved by keeping the books open during the complementary period. This aims at ensuring a greater conformity between the annual commitments made during a fiscal year and the payments that are reported as budgetary expenditures.

iii) Accrual basis of accounting is a system of accounting in which revenue is recorded as it is earned and expenses are recorded when they generate revenue. It is the method of recording transactions by which revenue; expenses, assets and liabilities are reflected in the accounts in the period in which they accrue. The accrual basis of accounting includes considerations relating to accrual of income, provisioning of expenses, deferral, allocations like depreciation and amortization. This basis is also referred to as 'Mercantile Basis of Accounting'.

Accrual basis of accounting records the financial effects of the transactions and other events of an enterprise in the period in which they occur rather than recording them in the period(s) in which cash is received or paid. Accrual basis recognizes the economic events that affect an enterprise's performance often do not coincide with the cash receipts and payments.

The goal of accrual basis of accounting is to relate the accomplishments (measured in the form of revenue) and the efforts (measured in terms of costs) so that the reported net income measures an enterprise's performance during a period rather than merely listing its cash receipts and payments.

According to Schaik (2004)[5] the use of accrual accounting compared with traditional cash accounting seems more desirable, since in accrual accounting, expenditures are compared with the performance objectives not with budgets that have already been agreed. Essence of presenting accrual basis may make understanding what it plans to present difficulties, it shows a kind of reality that is considered by developers of accounting standards opined by Nesbakk (2010)[6]. Thomas (2007)[7] states that accrual accounting possesses advantages for the public sector, such as: better facilitation of planning and management of financial resources, performance evaluation, presenting financial position and its evaluation, and also, assessment of financial flexibility and providing required conditions for implementation of operational budgeting.

Thus the accrual basis is the superior method of accounting for the economic resources of any organisation. It results in accounting measurement based on the substance of transactions and events, and thus enhances their relevance, neutrality, timelines, completeness and comparability. Under accrual accounting, entries are made on the dates when revenue or expenses fall due and not on the date when they are paid or received. The accrual basis of accounting is a scientific system for reporting income and also for preparation of financial statements. It is based on two basic accounting principles namely revenue recognition principle and matching principle.

According to the Revenue Recognition Principle, revenue is reported in the financial statements in the accounting period in which cash representing that revenue is actually received. According to Matching Principle, all expenses associated with the generation of revenue must be matched against that revenue in the same period in which revenue was actually earned. Consequently under the accrual basis of accounting, cash received in advance for services to be rendered in future is not recognized as revenues at all and are treated as deferred revenue and shown as liability in Balance Sheet.

Similarly, expenses paid in advance are not matched against the revenue of current year and treated as prepaid expenses and shown as an asset in the Balance Sheet. Likewise, income earned, but not received in cash is taken as accrued income, and is treated as income of the current year and shown as an asset in the Balance Sheet. Expenses incurred but not paid for is provided for and charged against revenue of current year and shown as a liability in the Balance Sheet. The adjustments made on an accrual basis ensure better financial statements. Accrual basis is the most widely accepted basis of accounting. The accrual basis of accounting is a scientific method. It emphasizes on proper recognition of income & expenses to have a clear picture of receivables and payable without inflating/deflating income or expenses.

The financial statements produced under a full accrual accounting system cover revenues; expenses (including depreciation); assets (financial and physical). Under the full accrual system the three statements that are normally prepared include, Operating Statement, Balance Sheet, and the Statement of Cash Flows. The number of the statements and the nomenclature by which these are called may differ from country to country.

iv) The modified accrual accounting (sometimes also called as expenditure basis) recognizes transactions and events when they occur, irrespective of when cash is paid or received. However, there is no deferral of costs that will be consumed in future periods. Physical assets that will provide services in the future are written -off (or expensed) in the period of acquisition. Modified accrual and full accrual accounting (discussed subsequently) have the same accounting framework. The major difference, however, lies in the time between the acquisition of goods and assets and their utilization. Under modified accrual accounting, supplies are considered consumed and assets are written off as soon as they are acquired. Under full accrual accounting, changes in inventories are recognized and assets are progressively depreciated according to their useful life.

Government Accounting and Financial Reporting is based on a cash based system of accounting which in consonance with the basis followed for the formulation of the budget of the Government. Cash Basis of accounting denotes that the transactions in Government accounts represent the actual cash receipts and disbursements during a financial year as distinguished from amounts due to or by the Government during the same period. However, certain books, adjustments may be specifically authorized by the Central Government on the advice of the Comptroller and Auditor General of India, as exceptions to the cash basis of accounting.

The basis of accounting being cash, the depreciation of physical assets and impairment losses are not recognized or expensed. The losses or write-offs of the physical assets at the end of their life are also not recognized or expensed in the accounts. Under Cash Basis of accounting transactions are recorded when there is an actual flow of cash. Revenue is recognized only when it is actually received. Expenditure is recognized only on the outflow of cash. No consideration is given to the 'accrual' fact of the transaction. All cash received or spent during the year are taken into account even though some part of these may relate to a different period.

Under this system the liabilities are not accrued for and there is no charge for the use of the capital asset and no distinction is made between the capital and non- capital expenditure. Each department of the government prepares an appropriation account showing how much was voted for that department by the Parliament for a given year and how much was spent under each head, showing explanatory notes for any major variances between estimates and actual. This system of accounting is noted for its simplicity, certainty and the linkage to the direct movement of the funds and as such needs less skill on the part of the accountant. Its whole focus is on cash management. The recognition trigger is simply the flow of cash. Budgetary and legislative compliance is easier under this system. It does not take cognizance of performance and output.

Books of Account Maintained by the Educational Institutions

Higher educational institutions in India are considered as service entities under non-corporate sector, for which no suitable accounting guidelines are available. The method of presentation of accounts of these institutions is totally dismal and is not in keeping with the requirement of transparency and exposure of professional skills of these institutions.

Most of these institutions are public institutions with power to regulate academic activities on their campuses as well as in their area of jurisdiction through the affiliating system. Most of them are funded by the State Government or Government of India and all are governed by the rules and regulations framed by the government from time to time.

No initiative has been taken by the regulating authorities to bring out guidelines for uniform financial reporting practices for these institutions.

For proper reflection of the financial health of an organization, adopting an adequate accounting system is necessary. The accounts should be prepared in such a way that one can radically find the fund-wise position of income, function-wise classification of expenditure and can help to analyze and interpret the financial data generated during the process of record keeping. Conceptual framework of accounting helps to examine the accounting system of an organization.

As a general principle, the accounts and financial records are maintained in prescribed forms and registers. Indian universities maintain their accounting records on the single entry system or double entry system. There is no uniformity in the maintenance and preparation of accounts in university institutions in India. Irrespective of the system of accounting followed, most of the university institutions of India prepare receipts and payment account, income and expenditure account and balance Sheet for every financial year to report their financial results and financial position on a particular date (Mahanta, 2013)[8].

There are different ways to format or display an account, but the most common way is by using T-accounts. T-accounts format account balances by keeping the debits on the left side and the credits on the right. The overall account balance is then calculated at the bottom. T-accounts also have a title or heading that displays the name and number of the account. Accounts can also be displayed as a listing of transactions in the general ledger.

In other words, the cash account might just have a list of all the transactions that affected the cash account during that period. Although the list format ultimately works, T-accounts and similar reports are much easier to read and use. T-accounts are also helpful in the accounting cycle before preparing trial balances.

Books of account may be maintained following the rules of Double Entry Book Keeping System and generally accepted accounting practices prevailing in India. Every educational institution should maintain proper books of account with respect to:

(a) all sums received by the educational institution and the matters in respect of which receipts, take place, showing distinctly the amounts received from income generating activities and through grants and donations;

(b) all sums of money expended by the educational institution and the matters in respect of which expenditure takes place;

(c) all assets and liabilities of the educational institution.

The educational institutions generally maintain the following books of account: 1. Receipt Book; 2. Journal; 3. Cash Book / Bank Book; and 4. Ledger. The books of account of educational institutions may be structured in a manner that is suited to its needs and requirements, viz., a separate set of books and records may be maintained for foreign and Indian contributions, as per the requirements of the Foreign Contribution (Regulation) Act, 1976. Similarly, separate sets of books and records may be maintained for the various projects, etc. that the educational institutions may have for implementing its programmes. Separate ledgers, accounts and records may also be maintained with regard to the various funds representing the grants received from various sources, received with or without stipulations and restrictions. This may also be referred to as Fund Based Accounting, which is discussed in detail in the following paragraphs. Educational institution with reference to specific requirements may maintain the following additional books of account, as considered necessary for maintenance of proper books of accounts: Purchase Book; Sales Book / Bill Book; Inventory Register; Other Books as deemed necessary.

Moreover, following registers and other records like vouchers should also be maintained so as to give information in relation to:

1. Fees received from students (in respect of admission fee, tuition fee, library fee, examination fee, etc.)
2. Grants-in-aid received from various sources.
3. Scholarship and special stipends.
4. Funds such as building, library, laboratory, sports, furniture, equipments, endowment, provident fund, poor students fund, deposits, etc.
5. Immovable properties and other fixed assets.
6. Investments.
7. Minutes of the meetings of the Managing Committee of the educational institution.
8. Stock (for books, stationery, uniform, etc.)
9. Caution money received from students.

The above list is illustrative only and not exhaustive. Proper books of account would not be deemed to be kept with respect to the matters specified therein:

(a) if such books are not kept as are necessary to give a true and fair view of the state of affairs, income and expenditure and cash flows of the educational institution, and to explain its transactions;

(b) if such books are not kept on the accrual basis and according to the double entry system of accounting (ICAI, 2012)[9] & (Mahanta, 2013)[10].

Accounting Standards in Higher Educational Institutions

Accounting Standards remove variations in the treatment of several accounting aspects and to bring about standardization in presentation. They intent to harmonize the diverse accounting policies followed in the preparation and presentation of financial statements by different reporting enterprises to facilitate intra-organization and inter-organization comparison. An accounting system that presents a true and correct picture of the state of affairs of an educational institution is a necessary requirement for transparency and accountability and enables less intrusive but more effective regulation of the education sector besides assisting in the prevention of malpractices that presently plague the sector.

Accounting Standards (AS) is Written Policy Documents Issued by Expert Accounting Body or by Government or other Regulatory Body covering the aspects of recognition, measurement, treatment, presentation and disclosure of accounting transactions in the financial statements.

The Accounting Standards as laid down by the Institute of Chartered Accountants of India are set of neutral principles for drawing up the financial statements so that there is the minimum possible ambiguity and uncertainty about the figures contained in those statements. The objective of Accounting Standards is, therefore, to reduce the accounting alternatives in the preparation of financial statements within the bounds of rationality, thereby ensuring comparability of financial statements of different enterprises with a view to provide meaningful information to various users of financial statements to enable them to make informed economic decisions.

In order to ensure transparency, consistency, comparability, adequacy and reliability of financial reporting, it is essential to standardize the accounting principles and policies. Accounting Standards provide the framework and standard accounting policies so that the financial statements of different enterprises become comparable.

The Accounting Standards reduce the accounting alternatives in the preparation of rational financial statements, thereby ensuring comparability of financial statements of different enterprises. The Accounting Standards deal with the issues of: i) recognition of events and transactions in the financial statements, ii) measurement of these transactions and events, iii) presentation of these transactions and events in the financial statements in a manner that is meaningful and understandable to the reader, and iv) the disclosure requirements which should be there to enable the public at large and the stakeholders and the potential investors in particular, to get an insight into these financial statements which helps the users to take prudent and informed business decisions.

The objective of Accounting Standards is to standardize diverse accounting policies with a view to eliminate, to the maximum possible extent, a) the non-comparability of financial statements and thereby improving the reliability of financial statements, and b) to provide a set of standard accounting policies, valuation norms and disclosure requirements (ICAI ,2012)[11].

Admittedly, accounting is a language of a college or university, It speaks about the state of the financial management whether an institution is appearing well or not as the institutions have been financed by the Government, UGC, industries, business houses, donors, general public, so on and so far. What is required is complete transparency in accounting methods and standards. Accounting standards setting exercise have been initiated and persuaded by accounting bodies all over the world, during the past three decades. In India the Accounting Standard Board constituted by ICAI shoulders the responsibility of formulating the accounting standards for various organizations in general and for business and industries in particulars. It is necessary to understand the major users and their requirements with reference to education institutions. A set of standards for accounting information and guidelines for its communication depends upon an examination of who are the major users of accounting information and for what purpose they require such information. Following are the stakeholders, who have every right to the access of accounting information:

***State Government*:** The State Government provides a maintenance grant for salary and non-salary expenses to colleges and universities. The Government through its Regional Joint Director, Office carries out yearly assessment and periodical audit.

Therefore, the state government requires information about the receipts of tuition fee, other fees, etc. and salary and non-salary expenses with reference to grantable criteria as laid down in grant-in-aid code, and the utilization of other fees such as library fees, gymkhana fees, magazine fees, extension activity fees etc.

***UGC and other Funding Agencies*:** UGC and other agencies provide financial assistance for the development of undergraduate education and post-graduation departments which satisfy the conditions laid down by UGC & such funding agencies. The UGC and such funding agencies require information as per their requirements about the grants sanctioned, released and utilization thereof, compliance of terms & conditions, completion of work, target etc.

***Trustees, members of the Society, Donors, etc.*:** They provide initial finance for the establishment of colleges and fulfilling deficit in running the colleges. They require information about receipt of funds, donations, utilization thereof, and reasons of deficit.

Industries, Business houses, Alumni associations, NRIs, etc.: With a view to mobilize external resources for various development plans and projects through participation, contributions from individual Indians or non-resident Indians, Alumni Associations, public and family trusts, industries, business houses, co-operatives, professional associations, employees' unions /associations, Municipalities, municipal corporations, are often contacted and funds are raised. This category of funding persons/agencies require information about the beneficiary of project/plans, funds raised and received utilization thereof and achievement of goals, targets,etc.

Employees' and Teachers' Organisation: Employees and Teachers are concern with the financial stability and sound financial management of the educational institutions. It indicates the scope for possible wage and fringe benefit increases and security of employment and retirement benefits, etc.

Parents, Students: They are the backbone of every educational institution. Students pay tuition fees and other fees for college; and eligibility fee, examination fee etc. to universalities. They are concerned with the effective utilization of their fees and returns thereof with reference to quality teaching, good extension activities, souvenir/magazines, seminars, cultural activities, conduct of examination, timely declaration of eligibility and examination results, timely issue of mark lists and degree certificates and counseling guidance and placement services, if possible.

Society at Large: As higher education is main instrument of social transformation and the government funds are given to educational institutions out of taxes paid by the society at large, it is concerned with the effective and proper utilization of funds and scarce resources by the educational institutions, universities and colleges (Gandhi, 2015)[12].

There are defiantly gaps in accounting practices in mainly educational institutions, universities and colleges. It is unfortunate to state that there is no transparency in financial management and accounting practices in educational institutions. It is also unfortunate that there is no mechanism to detect such gaps, misappropriation of funds and changes in utilization of funds.

The main aim of setting the accounting Standard is to bring about uniformity in financial reporting and to ensure consistency and comparability in the data submitted by educational institutions. Standards for accounting information ought to be attended by an accounting system in providing information needed by the aforesaid seven types of users. The standards determine the quality of information. Hence the usefulness of accounting data is to be ensured.

While standards are closely related to accounting theory, there is a difference between the two in that accounting theory is concerned with the attributes of the accounting system itself, whereas accounting standards are concerned with the quality of the information generated by that system.

As there are gaps in accounting standards laid down by the Institute of Chartered Accountants of India, standards may be set either by the government, university and/or management of the colleges or educational institutions. The concepts and standard underlying accounting for financial reporting purpose are called generally accepted accounting principles. There may be a number of approaches. The determination of certification of current major practice: a common law approach, i.e. case by case as a distillation of experience and the use of an implicit or explicit conceptual framework is needed (Gandhi, 2015)[13].

Thus, all educational institutions should follow a common format for presentation of its general purpose financial statements to ensure proper accountability, financial discipline, end-use of funds and to meet the needs of stakeholders.

The accounting standards should enable the society, the student and the citizen:-

i. to define transparently the revenue earned through various sources – tuition fees and other charges, income from consultancy or from intellectual property owned by the institution (for higher educational institutions) etc;

ii. to recognize segment reporting of accounts (each school under the same institution being considered as a separate segment for accounting purposes);

iii. to recognize costs and revenue separately for UG and PG programmes and for research and teaching activities;

iv. to define relevant financial ratios derived from the accounts for inter the comparison on research to total expenditure, income from fees to total income, salary expenditure to total expenditure etc). These ratios could enable greater understanding of funding needs, especially in respect of government funding.

v. to identify if surpluses are being generated and the manner in which the surpluses are utilized or invested;

vi. to disclose related party transactions;

Accounting Practices in General Degree Colleges of Tripura

All the sample colleges maintain books and accounts conventionally which do not follow the statuary provisions and general practices followed by all other educational institutions in India. Though Government of India is trying to introduce a uniform accounting system all over the country, but it is observed that general degree colleges of Tripura are not at all aware of the uniform accounting system or procedure what is to be followed.

Accountant of the general degree colleges is responsible for maintaining all types of books and records, registers and accounts. It is revealed from the study that most of the employees work as accountants have no accounting background. They perform the function of accountant only have consolidated training programmes of 15 days or like this. As a result, they generally follow what their seniors have done or make the records as they are getting readily available.

Though there is a general practice of maintaining books and accounts as per government accounting rules and accounting standard for educational institutions but the accounts of degree colleges are not maintained in the way as instructed or advised. In most of the cases matters with less importance are ignored while preparing books and accounts, which is contrary to the statutory provision.

As per the prevailing accounting system in government degree colleges in Tripura they record only cash receipts and payments only in the cash books i.e. only receipts and payment accounts are prepared where as there are provisions of preparing income and expenditure statement and balance sheet which are not prepared even by a single sample college. The accountant of the colleges' record cash receipts and cash payment only in the cash books, i.e. they prepare only Receipts and Payments Account though there is a provision to prepare income and expenditure statement, balance sheet at the end of every financial year. But no college in Tripura prepares an income and expenditure statement and balance sheet.

As per statutory provisions and general practices for accounting procedure, reconciliation statement is mandatory, but no college prepares reconciliation statement regularly. They prepare reconciliation as an when asked for. While there is a provision of keeping registers for various items of assets and stores, but the sample institutions keep few registers only like stock register, GPF register for Gr. D employee. They do not keep register for consumable items and other important items.

As a whole general degree colleges of Tripura do not maintain proper books and accounts as per statutory provisions and also as general practices followed by other educational institutions in India. So there is need to give more attention to develop the existing accounting system followed so as to maintain a parity with the national level, which will obviously support the efforts taken by the government of India in executing uniform accounting system in educational institution throughout the country. ICAI, Government of India recommended accrual basis of accounting system, but the study shows that all the degree colleges maintain their books of accounts using the cash basis of accounting which is almost obsolete. Under cash basis, the actual position of fund

TABLE 5.1
Maintenance of Register by the Sample Colleges

Types of registers	Maintain Register Percentage of colleges
Bill Register	100
Stock Register	100
Stipend and Scholarship Register	47
Fees Register	30
GPF Register	60
Telephone Register	0
Expenditure Register	0
Register of Valuables	0
Conveyance Register	0
LTC Register	100
Purchase Order Register	53

Sources; Information from sample Colleges and percent calculated receivable, expenditure payable, value of assets and liabilities is not included and disclosed to stakeholders. So the accrual basis of accounting should be followed by the government degree colleges so that the actual position of the institution can be brought to the view of the stakeholders as well as government.

It is mentioned earlier that the maintenance of documents and financial information is the key area of effective financial management system. As per Government of Tripura circulars and directions issued from time to time every government general degree colleges are supposed to maintain registers of various nature. Therefore, it was investigated during the field survey what kind of registers the colleges maintained. The list of registers maintained in sample colleges is provided by the respective colleges in the prescribed proforma designed for this study. The said list of registers provided by the respective colleges is checked and verified during the personal visit to the colleges during the study period.

Bill register is one of the important registers maintained by the sample colleges. In colleges' different kinds of bills are raised for making payments. The bills are processed through the account section of the college checked and verified by the drawing and disbursement officer and necessary payment are made with the approval of the competent authority. The summary of such bill is recorded in a register called Bill Register. It is found that all the sample colleges maintain bill register properly, but it is also observed that the proforma of bill register is different in a few colleges.

Similarly, stock register is another important record maintained by the sample collees. There are two kinds of stock registers; one is stock register for consumable goods and another for non-consumable goods. All kinds of goods procured, consumable or non -consumable, are recorded in the respective stock register.

If consumable goods are issued, this also needs to be recorded in the register of consumable goods. Precisely the detail of procurement of consumable goods (quantity, price, quality, supplier's name, date of delivery, etc.) and the details issue of consumable goods (to whom issued, quantity, date of issue etc.) are recorded in the stock register for consumable goods. On the other hand, stock register for non consumable goods are maintained for recording the summary of purchase of capital items. In this register the nature of capital goods, price, quality, name of supplier, bill register reference etc. are recorded. It is observed that all the sample colleges maintain both the register. On checking the registers it is found that the registers are properly maintained. In many cases it is seen that all the entries are not filled up as per requirement. In case of the register of consumable stock it is often found that the name of the person to whom it is issued is not recorded or the purpose of issuing bulk quantity is also not reported. While discussing this matter with the concern drawing and disbursing officer it is reported that the dealing assistant finalizes the register only before the audit team visit or at the end of the financial year.

Register of valuables is one of the important registers usually maintained by all organizations. The demand draft, cheque, etc. received by the colleges are recorded in the register of valuables. It is unfortunate to note that no government general degree colleges (sample colleges) maintain a register of valuables. In a few cases it is also observed that the concern official does not even aware of maintaining registers of valuables. At the same time it is also found that the internal and external audit has raised the issue of maintenance of register of valuable in a few cases.

Another important aspect is that no sample colleges maintain telephone register and conveyance register. The objective of maintaining registers for telephone bills and conveyance is to put a check on misutilization from the standpoint of accounting control. However, it may be mentioned here that proper bill and vouchers are maintained by the colleges and the transaction are recorded in the cash book.

It is also found that around 53 percent of the sample colleges maintained Purchase Orders Register. Purchase Order Register is maintained to record the summary of purchase orders issued by the college authority. The nature of goods, price, expected time of delivery, advanced payment, etc. is recorded date wise in the register of purchase order.

It is reported by the sample colleges who does not maintain this register that they do not maintain the register because their quantity or value of price is very less in comparison or other large government degree colleges in Tripura.

There are several kinds of stipends and scholarships that are disbursed among the students of sample degree colleges. It is mandatory for every sample college to maintain stipend and scholarship register for each financial year. But it is surprising to note that 50 per cent of the sample colleges maintained stipend and scholarship register during the period of study. While maximum number of students of sample colleges avails benefit of different kind of stipends and scholarship therefore, it seems that maintenance of a register for the stipend and scholarship is most essential in terms of prudent financial management. In this connection the CAG audit raised several objections against most of the colleges regarding the non compliance of government directives and specific guidelines in this regard. It may be stated that an amount of Rs. 223.14 lakh was sanctioned in the year 2007-08 as a stipend and scholarship among the students of sample colleges and the amount increased to Rs.459.24 lakh in the year 2011-12.

TABLE 5.2
Maintenance of Books of Accounts by the Sample Colleges

Types of Books of Accounts	*Maintain Books of Accounts Percentage of colleges*
Cash Book	100
Petty Cash Book	15
Journal	0
Ledger for Capital Assets	30
Ledger for Miscellaneous Payments	0
Ledger for Fees UGC Fund	100
Ledger for Non Government Fund	100
Any Others Books of Account	15

Sources; Information from sample Colleges and percent calculated

Maintenance of cash book is perhaps the most important book of accounts maintain by any organization. Proper maintenance of this book of account is considered as the barometer for any organization. All sorts of financial activities of the organization are reflected in cash book.

It is found that all the sample colleges maintain a cash book to record all financial transactions. As the accounting of the sample colleges is maintained under a cash basis system of accounting, maintenance of cash book, is, thus, inevitable. However the following issues relating to maintenance of cash book is observed:

a) There is no uniformity in the proforma of cash book maintain by the sample colleges.

b) Double column or triple column cash book is used by the different sample colleges as per their convenience due to lack of any specific guidelines from the state government.

c) Cash books are not updated regularly. Even sometimes it is observed that recording of cash transaction in cash book is pending for more than a year in a few cases.

d) Cash books are not always properly signed and verified by the competent officials of the college authority.

e) There is no regular procedure for verification of cash book balance with actual cash.

f) Balances of cash column are not tallied with the balances of bank column.

g) Cash book is also considered as a journal. But it is found that no details of the transaction are recorded in cash book.

h) While recording received of cheque and demand draft or making payment through cross cheque, the details of cheque of demand draft (Cheque No, DD No, Date of issue, issuing bank etc.) are not recorded.

Petty cash book is maintained to record the petty transactions under different heads or sub heads. In managing the sample college, it is observed that many transactions are incurred which is petty in nature. But surprisingly, no colleges maintained any cash book of such kind. Non maintenance of petty cash book may lead to misappropriation of funds and embezzlement of cash as opined by many drawings and disbursing officer of the sample colleges.

The Journal needs to be prepared by all organization as it is primary books of account. It is to be stated here sample colleges do not maintain any journal for recording the financial transaction.

Any transaction in connection with purchase of capital items is recorded in the cash book. Correspondingly the entry should also be made in ledger against the respective capital items.

Sale of old capital items, charging depreciation, and declaration of obsolete also needs to be recorded in the ledger against the respective capital items for the purpose of proper and sound financial management. It reveals from the table that sample colleges do not maintain this kind of ledger. Similarly, sample colleges do not maintain any ledger for miscellaneous payments like electrical charges, telephone bills etc.

Colleges received grants from the UGC under different heads. Therefore the colleges' needs to maintain the records of all transactions incurred out of UGC funds separately following the UGC guidelines in this regard. It is found that all the sample colleges maintain a separate ledger for UGC transactions.

Fees collected from the students under different heads are kept and maintain separately under the heading 'Non Government Fund'. A separate ledger is also maintained by all the sample colleges in connection with the said fund.

TABLE 5.3

Preparation of Annual Accounts

Preparation of Accounts and Statement	*Maintained Percentage of Colleges*
Preparation of Annual Bank Reconciliation Statement	20
Preparation of Annual Receipts & Payment A/C	100
Preparation of Annual Income & Expenditure Statement	0
Preparation of Balance Sheet	0

Sources: Information from sample Colleges and percent calculated

Keeping books of accounts and maintaining leads to preparation of annual accounts. The government financial year ends on 31st March every year. Therefore, as per provision of the financial rules every government degree colleges (sample colleges) are required to prepare annual accounts. Once the annual accounts are prepared it is being audited internally and externally.

Bank reconciliation statement is one of the important statements required for scrutiny of the transactions. It is found that only 20 per cent of the sample colleges prepare bank reconciliation statement.

While discussing the matter with the Drawing and Disbursing Officers of the sample colleges it has come to knowledge that audit team always raises the issue of non availability of bank reconciliation statement. In some cases they themselves prepare the bank reconciliation statement for test checking purpose.

Receipts and payments account is essential in case of sample colleges as the accounts are maintained under cash basis system of accounting. All the sample colleges are found that they prepare annual receipts and payments account in compliance with department's instruction in this regard.

Income and expenditure statement is essential if the accrual basis of accounting system is followed. No sample colleges thus prepare income and expenditure statement. Similarly balance sheet is also not prepared by the sample colleges.

However if the MHRD's proposed guidelines regarding the uniform accounting system for higher education institutions are implemented, than both income and expenditure account as well balance sheet have to be prepared under new scheme.

In examining the pattern of maintenance of registers and accounts in general degree colleges of Tripura (Table 5.1 , 5.2 and 5.3), it has been found that there are explicit ways of maintaining the same in each college. To take the case of maintenance of records first it may be observed that the different goods acquired by the college for its use are categorized in same given pattern. This may not be conforming to practice as is follows in other institutions but it readily serves it purpose. In some cases there may not be some specified registers, but records are maintained in a chronological way in connection with different assets, consumable goods and such other things.

There is some prefix pattern to maintain accounts in an institution. Though the colleges in question do not follow the pattern in an exact way, but a clear idea can be had as cash book, bill register, payroll, fees register etc are maintained regularly. However, strict accounting principle may be absent in the maintenance of such accounts. But still an idea about the receipts and payment can clearly be made from the books of account maintained by the college.

Audit of Accounts in General Degree Colleges of Tripura

Audit of Accounts discloses the strength and weakness of the financial system of the organization. Audit is a systematic and independent examination of data, statements, records, operations and performances (financial or otherwise) of an enterprise for a stated purpose. Generally two types of audit practices are being prevailed in the institutions ,i.e. internal audit and statutory audit or concurrent audit. Internal audit is the independent appraisal of activities within an organization for the review of accounting, financial and other business practices as a protective and a conductive arm of management. The purpose of the audit is to: 1) provide comfort to management that operations are well managed; 2) identify weakness in the management system and recommend improvements; 3) suggest opportunities to reduce expenditure, increase revenues and better project government assets; 4) analyse the differences between actual and expected performance; 5) report gap between actual and expected performance; and 6) make recommendations to support management in minimizing risk.

It is generally accepted rules to perform the audit function at a regular time gap, i.e. after the completion of every financial year. It is surprisingly followed in both internal and external audit that no such span of time or the periodicity concept is maintained. Besides this the audit function is restricted only in finding out the mathematical mistake and utilization of fund received from various sources. No advisory activities regarding maintenance of prescribed accounting system or development of accounting procedure on the part of both internal and external auditors are noticed.

It is often noticed that two agencies like government auditor and internal auditor carry out their responsibility without any preset accounting standards. The entire task of auditing the accounts and financial management of educational institutions is taken very lightly. The control over effective utilization of scarce resources is often diluted.

Therefore, it is, high time to define the role and responsibilities of auditors of educational institutions and the accounting standards and practices. No doubt the interest of all the aforesaid users of educational institutions must be safeguarded. Internal audit system must be implemented with quality and seriousness; management control system must be perfect and effective. Misappropriation, frauds, misrepresentations must be detected and curbed at their initial stage. Auditions must see whether the accounting standard have been strictly followed by the educational institutions or not (Gandhi, 2015)[14].

During the period under study, year wise audit report of all general degree colleges are not available. On scrutiny, it is observed that out of 15 (fifteen) colleges 10 (ten) colleges have not made any audit by the Directorate of Audit, Government of Tripura during the study period. Remaining 5(five) colleges covered under audit only once during the study period. On examination of available audit report of general degree colleges of Tripura during the study period following observations are summarized.

TABLE 5.4
Observation of Internal Audit conducted by Directorate of Audit, Government of Tripura during 2007-08 to 2011-12

Sl. No.	*Observations*	*Percentage of Colleges*
1	Bank reconciliation statement was not done.	20
2	Undisbursed amount not deposit to Govt. A/c immediately on expiry of 3 months of its drawl.	80
3	Collection of non government fund (students fees) not entered in the daily collection register and non government cash book	20
4	No VAT was deducted from the gross amount of bills at the of making payments to the parties concerned.	60
5	Undisbursed stipend not refunded or deposited to government account in due time.	60
6	Non Recordance of office materials in the general stock book or stock register.	20
7	Requisite details like cheque no., challan no, name of parties etc. Had not been found to be recorded for clear identification and future reference.	40
8	Payment entries had not been found to be attested by the DDO of the establishment.	20
9	Cash book maintained in the establishment did not exhibit the correct position of cash balance.	20
10	Physical verification of library books not conducted and value of the library books so issued had not been recorded in the issue register of the library.	20
11	A good number of officials did not sign / were reluctant to sign on the acquaintance Roll register with revenue stamp.	20
12	Using correction fluid were noticed which is against the provision of Rule 77 of CTR	20
13	There is wide variation between bank balance as per bank statement that of cash book.	0
14	Regarding UGC fund, utilization certificate not furnished at the end of the financial year.	0
15	Assets register not maintained properly.	20

Source: Internal Audit Report, Government of Tripura

Directorate of Audit, Government of Tripura is entrusted with the audit of all the government departments while the external audit is done by the Accountant General, Tripura. Accordingly the audit of general degree colleges is performed as a part of government departments. It has been observed from the audit report that during 2007-08 to 2011-12, MBB College, BBM College, Womens College, Ramthakur College and GDC, Kamalpur covered under audit of accounts. It is observed from table 5.4 that:

1. Bank reconciliation statement is one of the important statements required for scrutiny of the transactions. It is found that 80 percent audited colleges prepared bank reconciliation statement properly.
2. Undisbursed amount not deposited to Govt. A/c immediately on expiry of 3 months of its drawl by 80 percent colleges.
3. Fees collected from the students under different heads are kept and maintain separately under the heading 'Non Government Fund' but not entered in the daily collection register and non government cash book of 20 percent colleges.
4. 60 percent colleges not deducted VAT from the gross amount of bills at the of making payments to the parties concerned.
5. 60 percent colleges not refunded or deposited undisbursed stipend to Government Account in due time.
6. Office materials purchased by General Degree College are recorded in the general stock book or stock register by 80 percent colleges.
7. For clear identification and future reference 60 percent colleges keep record or detail like cheque no., challan no, name of parties etc.

8. Cash books are not always properly signed and verified by the competent officials of the college authority. Payment entries had not been found to be attested by 20 percent DDO of government general degree colleges.
9. 20 percent colleges maintained cash book did not exhibit the correct position of cash balance.
10. Physical verification of library books conducted 80 percent colleges.
11. Value of the library books so issued had not been recorded in the issue register of the library by 20 percent colleges.
12. About 80 percent of officials of staffs signed on the acquaintance Roll register with revenue stamp.
13. Only 20 percent colleges used correction fluid for rectification which is against the provision of Rule 77 of CTR.
14. There is no variation between bank balances as per bank statement that of cash book among all the colleges.
15. Regarding UGC fund, utilization certificate furnished by every college at the end of the financial year.
16. 20 percent colleges not maintained assets register properly but records are maintained in a chronological way in connection with different assets, consumable goods and such other things.

Thus unaudited colleges cannot take opportunity for correcting their mistakes which will identify by the audit team assigned by the Directorate of Audit, Government of Tripura.

Accounting Practices in General Degree Colleges of Tripura: Perception of Respondents

It was asked to the respondents regarding accounting practices and audit of accounts in general degree colleges of Tripura and their responses are presented in table 5.4.

TABLE 5.5
Perception of Respondents

Question	*No. of Respondents (%)*		
	Yes	*No*	*No Response*
Is there any standardized accounting procedure followed across the GDCs in Tripura?	0	99	1
Whether verification of accounts is done on a day to day basis?	1	99	0
Is there is any provision for annual internal audit?	4	95	1
The institution has any Monitoring mechanism policy to assure the proper functioning of the Schemes?	6	93	1
Are you satisfied with the accounting system followed in your college?	2	83	15
Do you think that standardized accounting procedure across the GDCs may help in strengthening the MIS system pertaining to finance matter?	79	18	3
"Maintenance and documentation of records in GDCs of Tripura are proper and adequate" Do you agree?	9	89	2
"It is felt necessary to introduce both internal and external audit mechanism at a particular interval regularly in GDCs" Do you agree?	96	4	0
Do you think academic audit apart from financial audit across the GDCs is the need of the hour?	57	40	3

Source: Opinion Survey

That the colleges do not follow a sound accounting procedure seemed to be a point of concern for the respondents (99%). Almost all of them think that no verification is done on the accounts on a day to day basis. Quite surprisingly, there is no regular annual internal audit carried out, neither do the institutions have any monitoring mechanism to assure proper functioning of the schemes. They also opined that both internal and external audits along with academic audit be carried out for smooth running of the colleges.

At the same time the opinion is also in favour of undertaking reformative measure in this regard so that it leads to a gradual approach to accept and practice the standard procedure of accounts as followed in the government institutions. Overall, it has been found that with some difficulties the accounting system and its various aspects will not seem to face a change in the near future.

Approaches Towards Cost Control Mechanism

Costing plays an important role in testing not only how management has deployed resources, but in assessing what this deployment has accomplished. Because the effectiveness of academic programs is not always easily quantified, academic performance evaluation may entail complex, sometimes lengthy, and at times controversial cost studies. Whether directed toward academic or nonacademic activities, costing is one of the principal tools for corrective action. Such action, in turn, has its own future cost implications.

The purpose of the Cost Accounting Standard is to ensure that each educational institution's practices used in estimating costs for a proposal are consistent with cost accounting practices used by the institution in accumulating and reporting costs. Only four cost accounting standards may be applied to Higher Education Institutions; namely

1) Consistency in Estimating, Accumulating, and Reporting Costs 2) Consistency in Allocating Costs Incurred for the Same Purpose 3) Accounting for Unallowable Costs 4) Cost Accounting Period

1) An educational institution's practices used in estimating costs in pricing a proposal shall be consistent with the educational

institution's cost accounting practices used in accumulating and reporting costs. The purpose of this standard is to ensure that each educational institution's practices used in estimating costs for a proposal are consistent with cost accounting practices used by the educational institution in accumulating and reporting costs. Consistency in the application of cost accounting practices is necessary to enhance the likelihood that comparable transactions are treated alike. With respect to individual sponsored agreements, the consistent application of cost accounting practices will facilitate the preparation of reliable, cost estimates used in pricing a proposal and their comparison with the costs of performance of the resulting sponsored agreement.

Such comparisons provide one important basis for financial control over costs during sponsored agreement performance and aid in establishing accountability for costs in the manner agreed to by both parties at the time of agreement. The comparisons also provide an improved basis for evaluating estimating capabilities.

However, costs estimated for proposal purposes shall be presented in such a manner and in such detail that any significant cost can be compared with the actual cost accumulated and reported there for. In any event, the cost accounting practices used in estimating costs in pricing a proposal and in accumulating and reporting costs on the resulting sponsored agreement shall be consistent with respect to: a) The classification of elements of cost as direct or indirect; b) The indirect cost pools to which each element of cost is charged or proposed to be charged; and c) The methods of allocating indirect costs to the sponsored agreement.

2) Under this standard each type of cost is allocated only once and on only one basis to any sponsored agreement or other cost objective. The criteria for determining the allocation of costs to a sponsored agreement or other cost objective should be the same for all similar objectives. Adherence to these cost accounting

concepts is necessary to guard against the overcharging of some cost objectives and to prevent double counting. Double counting occurs most commonly when cost items are allocated directly to a cost objective without eliminating like cost items from indirect cost pools which are allocated to that cost objective. The purpose of this standard is to require that each type of cost is allocated only once and on only one basis to any sponsored agreement or other cost objective.

3) The purpose of this standard is to facilitate the negotiation, audit, administration and settlement of sponsored agreements by establishing guidelines covering (1) identification of costs specifically described as unallowable, at the time such costs first become defined or authoritatively designated as unallowable, and (2) the cost accounting treatment to be accorded such identified unallowable costs in order to promote the consistent application of sound cost accounting principles covering all incurred costs.

The standard is predicated on the proposition that costs incurred in carrying on the activities of an educational institution-regardless of the allow ability of such costs under Government sponsored agreements-are allocable to the cost objectives with which they are identified on the basis of their beneficial or causal relationships. This standard does not govern the allow ability of costs. This is a function of the appropriate procurement or reviewing authority.

4) Educational institutions shall use their fiscal year as their cost accounting period. The purpose of this standard is to provide criteria for the selection of the time periods to be used as cost accounting periods for sponsoring agreement cost estimating, accumulating, and reporting.

This standard will reduce the effects of variations in the flow of costs within each cost accounting period. It will also enhance objectivity, consistency, and verifiability, and promotes uniformity and comparability in sponsoring agreement cost measurements (Cost Accounting Standards for Educational Institutions, 2015)[15].

Chapter Summary

Financial accounting enables an organization to have better control and management of finance. It is often argued that since profit is not the objective of educational institutions, the accounting framework, which is relevant for business entities, is not appropriate for educational institutions. The financial statements of educational institution should reflect income, expenses, assets and liabilities in respect of such funds separately so as to enable the users of financial statements such as the contributors, to assess the usage of the funds contributed by them. In this chapter an attempt has been made to examine the accounting system practiced in general degree colleges in Tripura with reference to the period from 2007-08 to 2011-2012.

The Accounting Standards as laid down by the Institute of Chartered Accountants of India(ICAI) are set of neutral principles for drawing up the financial statements so that there is the minimum possible ambiguity and uncertainty about the figures contained in those statements. The main aim of setting the accounting Standard is to bring about uniformity in financial reporting and to ensure consistency and comparability in the data submitted by educational institutions. ICAI, Government of India recommended accrual basis of accounting system, but the study shows that all the degree colleges maintain their books of accounts using the cash basis of accounting which is almost obsolete. It is observed that all the sample colleges maintain books and accounts conventionally which do not follow the statuary provisions and general practices followed by all other educational institutions. Government of India is trying to introduce a uniform accounting system all over the country, but it is found that general degree colleges of Tripura are not at all aware of the uniform accounting system or procedure what is to be followed.

Proper maintenance of this book of account is considered as the barometer for any organization. But no sample college maintains proper books of accounts. There is no uniformity in the proforma of cash book and other books of account maintain by the sample government colleges under the Government of Tripura.

It is found that cash books are not updated regularly and not always properly signed and verified by the competent officials of the college authority. It is observed that many transactions are incurred which is petty in nature, but surprisingly, no colleges maintained any cash book of such kind. Sample colleges do not maintain any ledger for miscellaneous payments like electrical charges, telephone bills, etc. As per provision of the financial rules every government degree colleges are required to prepare annual accounts but no sample colleges prepare income and expenditure statement. Balance sheet is also not prepared by the sample colleges.

In examining the procedure of maintenance of registers and accounts in general degree colleges of Tripura it has been found that there are explicit ways of maintaining the same in each college.

There is some prefix pattern to maintain accounts in an institution. Though the colleges in question do not follow the pattern in an exact way, but a clear idea can be had as cash book, bill register, payroll, fees register etc are maintained regularly. However, strict accounting principle may be absent in the maintenance of such accounts.

Audit of Accounts discloses the weakness and strength of the financial system of the organization. Generally, Directorate of Audit, Government of Tripura is entrusted with the audit of all the government departments while the external audit is done by the Accountant General, Tripura. It is generally accepted rules to perform the audit function at a regular time gap, i.e. after the completion of every financial year, but no such span of time or the periodicity concept is maintained. No advisory activities regarding maintenance of prescribed accounting system or development of accounting procedure on the part of both internal and external auditors are noticed. It is often noticed that two agencies like CAG auditor and internal auditor carry out their responsibility without any preset accounting standards. The entire task of auditing the accounts and financial management of educational institutions is taken very lightly. The control over effective utilization of scarce resources is often diluted.

The opinion of the respondents regarding accounting practices and audit of accounts in general degree colleges of Tripura was also considered to understand the issue in a better way. It is opined by the majority respondents that the maintenance and documentation of records in general degree colleges of Tripura are not proper and adequate. Thus the lack of sound accounting procedure in sample colleges seemed to be a point of concern for the respondents.

Almost all of them think that no verification is done on the accounts on a day to day basis. There is no regular annual internal audit carried out, neither do the institutions have any monitoring mechanism to assure proper functioning of the schemes as stated by most of the respondents. They also opined that both internal and external audit along with academic audit be carried out for smooth running of the colleges.

Thus the accounting standards must be widely accepted in practice in which the statutory obligation should be increased and ensured in consultations with the professional and regulatory bodies, including ICAI, UGC, NAAC etc. The gaps in practices should be seriously detected and checked so as to safeguard the interests of the stakeholders and bodies financing the higher education. The effective information system should be ensured to satisfy the aforesaid users of accounting information.

REFERENCES

1. ICAI. (2012). *Report on Implementation of Accounting Standards in Educational Institutions of Department of Higher Education.* MHRD, Government of India. P-9.
2. ICAI .(2012).*Training Material Implementation of Accounting Standards-With Specific Reference to Educational Institutions.* New Delhi: MHRD, Government of India.Pp-69-70.
3. Op.cit. ICAI. (2012).Pp 11-15.
4. Wagh, A.(2014) . Accounting System in Higher Education: A Study of Colleges in Mumbai City District. *Sai Om Journal of Commerce & Management A Peer Reviewed International Journal.* Volume 1, Issue 12.Pp-18
5. Schaik, F. V. (2004). *Mastering the Transformation: New Public Management, Accrual Accounting and Budgeting.* Retrieved from www. deloitte.com, 13, July, 2010.
6. Nesbakk, L. G. (2010). Accrual accounting representations in the public sector-A case of Autopoiesis. *Critical Perspectives on Accounting,* October, Vol. 12.
7. Thomas, H. B. (2007). Does Full Accrual Accounting Enhance Accountability?. *The Innovation Journal: The Public Sector Innovation Journal,* Vol. 12 (3), pp. 9-14.
8. Mahanta, D.K. (2013). *Financial Management of Higher Education -A Study on Gauhati University* (doctoral thesis), Gauhati University. Retrieved from http://shodhganga.inflibnet.ac.in/, P-166-67.
9. Op.cit. ICAI.. (2012). Pp-9.
10. Op.cit. Mahanta, D. K. (2013). P-167-69.
11. Op.cit. ICAI. (2012).Pp-64-65.
12. Gandhi, M.M. (2015). Financial management of Higher Educational Institutions - with reference to Financing, Pricing, Accounting Standards and Gaps in Practices in Universities and Colleges. *The Business and management Review, Vol-5, No-4,* Pp-299-300.
13. Ibid. P-300.
14. Ibid. Pp-300-301.
15. *Cost Accounting Standard for Educational Institution.* (n.d.). Retrieved December 15.12.2015, 2015, from www.unc.edu/insite /Appendix %20A % 20 Part%2099005.doc
16. Directorate of Audit. (2008). *Internal Audit Report.* Agartala: Government of Tripura.

17. Directorate of Audit. (2009). *Internal Audit Report.* Agartala: Government of Tripura.

18. Directorate of Audit. (2010). *Internal Audit Report.* Agartala: Government of Tripura.

19. Directorate of Audit. (20011). *Internal Audit Report.* Agartala:Government of Tripura.

CHAPTER 6

CONCLUSION

Review of the Chapters

This chapter summarizes the findings; conclusions emerged and recommend some suggestions for improving the prevailing system of management of finance and accounting system of general degree colleges of Tripura. It perhaps requires no mention that the present study deals with the growth and expansion of higher education, source and expenditure pattern, cost structure and accounting procedure of general degree colleges in Tripura.

Chapter 1 of the study deals with the background of the study, statement of the problem, review of existing literature in the field, research gap, significance of the study, objectives, research queries, methodology part, and limitation of the study are discussed.

Major Findings

Objective-I: To analyze the growth and expansion of higher education in Tripura. Against Objective-I, Chapter 2 deals with the growth and expansion of higher education in Tripura:

1. There were no higher educational institutions in Tripura prior to 1947. During the period 1950-51 to 2010-11 the numbers of general degree colleges are increased from 2 in the 1950-51 to 16 colleges in 2010-11 and other higher

education institutions has increased to 21 in the year 2010-11.

2. There were significant growth (350 %) of higher education institutions during the period from 1960-61 to 1970-71 and 60.8 per cent during 2000-01 to 2010-11 in Tripura. The decadal growth rate of higher education institutions in Tripura during the period 1970-71 to 1980-81 was (66.67%) higher than the national growth rate (30.97%). While the decadal growth rate of higher education institutions in Tripura during the period 1990-91 to 2000-01 was quite less (4.5 %) than the national average (23 %).

3. The steady growth of higher education institutes in the West district is also imminent as we find the decadal increase of the number of institutions from 1 in 1950-51 to 7 in 1970-71, 10 in 1980-81, 13 in 1990-91 and 28 in 2010-11 which accounts for 75 per cent of the total higher education institutes of the state.

4. Higher education in Tripura was expanded based on urban area, namely Agartala and adjacent areas under Sadar sub-division. The maximum numbers of higher educational institutions were located in the Sadar sub-division. The data for the period 1950-51 to 2010-11 has revealed that 1 (one) higher educational institutions out of total 2 was established in Sadar sub-division during 1950-51 and increased to 26 (70 %) out of 37 in the year 2010-11.

5. Imbalance growth in terms of location can be assessed in a better way if we compare the number of institutions with the population of the respective areas. Looking into the district wise figure it is found that there is huge discrimination among the districts during the stated period. A similar picture is evident in the case of general degree colleges also.

6. In Tripura decadal growth of number of students in higher education varies from 30.58 per cent to 293.94 per cent. During 1980-81 to 1990-91 the rate of increase was 30.58 per cent, but during the period 1950-51 to 1960-61 this rate was very high as 293.94 per cent. In case of General Degree Colleges decadal growth of number of students in varies from 18.17 per cent to 293.94 per cent. During 1980-81 to 1990-91 the rate of increase was 18.17 per cent, but during the period 1950-51 to 1960-61 this rate was very high as 293.94%. Total numbers of students in the higher education institutes of the state was 495 and of these 350 were in the West district (70.71 %). This trend was maintained all along the decades and even in 2011 we find that out of a total 35,177 students in the entire state, 24,015 were in West district itself (68.27%).

7. Enrolment of girl students is expressed as a percentage of total enrolment varies from 11.91 per cent to 41.88 per cent during 1950-51 to 2010-11. But the trend seems to be a decaling one during the period 1970-71 to 1980-81 in Tripura.

8. The Central Government and the State Governments are making more provision to promote higher education. Such provision is made to increase Gross Enrolment Ratio (GER) related to the higher education. It is the responsibility of the U.G.C. to make more effective regulation over the higher education system in India. GER in Higher Education has improved significantly from 4.05 per cent to 7.82 per cent w.e.f 1970-71 to 2010 -11, but the GER in degree colleges increased marginally from 3.10 per cent to 6.09 per cent. During the period 1990-91 the gross enrolment ratio was significantly less than other period of study both the case of higher education and general degree colleges.

9. According to estimates of the association of Indian Universities, there is a shortage of teachers in higher educational institutions. As a result, today, many colleges seem to be running with a larger number of contractual, part-time and guest teachers, also known as teaching assistants in some states and a small number of regular teacher. If we look into the state of Tripura the decadal growth of teachers in higher education institution varies from 16.33 per cent to 370.53 per cent. There was significant growth during 1960-61 to 1970-71 i.e. 370.53 per cent and lowest growth rate during 1970-71 to 1980-81 which stand for 16.33 per cent where as this rate for India was 50.02 per cent for the same period. Hence, faculty recruitment requires serious attention.
10. Conventional norms such as student-faculty ratios or workload may not be very much relevant in higher education as faculty with various specializations are essential. The financial squeeze has also forced many states to impose an embargo on recruitment of teachers even against existing vacancies. Though the teacher- student ratio in higher education of Tripura is comparatively less than national average yet encouraging but distribution of teachers according to subjects and location is not proper and new teacher positions against increased enrolment are not being created at all.
11. Affiliating colleges are the delivering point of academic programmes prepared by the concerned universities. Thus the sample colleges deliver the academic programme prepared by the Tripura University as affiliating university. But honours as well as pass courses are not equally introduced in every college. Students of Ambedkar College, Govt. Degree College Amarpur, Govt. Degree College Kamalpur, MMD College and Govt. Degree College Kumlung are deprived of availing

different subjects as honours course as well as elective subjects of their own choice. While discussing the matter with the respondents it is pointed out by them that there is a strong disparity in terms of growth, enrollment, teacher-student ratio and course availability existing in the institutions throughout the state.

Objective-II: To examine the sources of finances and expenditure pattern of general degree colleges in Tripura. Against objective-II, Sources of finances, expenditure pattern, and trend in per capita expenditure of government general degree colleges of Tripura are dealt in chapter 3.

1. As per the analysis of financing, the state governments have a major role in funding of higher education and also have the main say in all administrative and operational matters.
2. Higher education budget is fluctuating, as a percentage of the total budget; the figure was 2.89 per cent in the year 2011-12 which has nearly doubled as compared to 1.58 % in the year 2007-08. Apart from the compulsion to allot increased amount of fund in higher education, one can be assured of the fact that there are percentage of increases in budget expenditure of higher education. Thus a shift in the policy towards more inclusive education can be envisaged in the information contained in the study.
3. So far as Tripura is concerned, there has been a substantial rise in higher education budget as per cent of GSDP from 0.57 per cent in 2007-08 to 1.04 per cent in 2011-12 with a high of 1.15 per cent in 2009-10 This rising trend in higher education budget during 2009-10 and 2011-12 may be attributed to the following facts: a)Introduction of revised pay scale for college teachers; b) Fresh appointment of college teachers necessitated by the introduction of new

courses in existing government general degree colleges and fulfilment of posts as vacated due to superannuation of existing college teachers; c)Providing for infrastructure for the introduction of new courses not only in general degree colleges but also in other areas of higher education.

4. Plan and non plan expenditure of higher education in Tripura is decaling from 65.41 per cent to 40.05 per cent during the period 2007-08 to 2011-12. Though annual average growth rate is 34.75 per cent, the annual growth rate of plan and non plan expenditure on higher education is higher during the period 2007-08 to 2008-09 than other periods and negative growth noticed during the period 2010-11 to 2011-12.

5. Expenditure on higher education as percent of GSDP varies from 0.36 per cent to 0.82 percent. During the year 2007-08 this rate was 0.36 percent which is the lowest and highest 0.82 percent in the year 2010-11. If we consider expenditure on higher education in India we observed that during 2007-08 the rate of expenditure on higher education as per cent of GDP was 1.14 per cent and increased to 1.25 percent during 2009-10 and decline to 1.22 per cent during 2010-11.

6. The State Government plays the most important role in providing finance to the general degree colleges of Tripura. During the period of study the contribution of the state government in total amount of funding stays at 86.15 per cent. Other sources of fund, which are prominent are, UGC (3.91%) and different agencies providing stipend and scholarship to the students (8.65%) etc.

7. Annual growth rate educational finance varies from 15.68 per cent to 36.94 per cent during the period 2007-08 to 2011-12. The highest growth rate noticed during 2008-09 to 2009-10. During the period 2009-10 to 2010-11 the

annual growth rate of educational finance is declining and this rate is increased to 18.32 per cent during 2010-11 to 2011-12. It is also observed that compounded annual growth rate of educational finance is 21.98 percent over the period of study.

8. Alternative sources of funds of the GDCs are not found to any noticeable extent. However it is observed that BCA has been introduced in few government general degree colleges under the scheme of self financing courses.
9. Regarding the application of funds in general degree colleges of Tripura shows a prominent aspect that a sizeable amount of fund is disbursed as salary and wages (78.45 %). This is followed by expenditure on stipend and scholarship (7.27 %), equipment (4.63 %) etc.
10. Management of finance becomes necessary when funds allotted are not properly expended or remains unutilized. This calls for serious introspection as un-utilization of fund blocks the objectives of fund allocation itself. In the present case around 3 per-cents of funds remain either unspent or unutilized. This area need to be looked into so that a proper utilization of fund takes place.
11. The respondents were asked about what were the most important factors that need immediate attention for providing higher education in colleges of Tripura in terms of their experiences. The responses of the respondents were obtained in likert five point scale: strongly agreed, agreed, undecided, disagree, strongly disagree. For each factor responses have been arranged and put on the scale. The weighted index of each factor has been arranged and factors according to rank are as follows:
    1. Availability of adequate finance for running and maintenance of colleges.

2. Availability of fund for purchase of necessary capital items.
3. Availability of qualified teachers.

These are the most important factors that are able to provide quality higher education in the college. Again for identifying the factors affecting quality of higher education in college we have also used the factor analysis and the same factors also have been identified. Therefore, it can safely be argued that the crux of all issues is finance.

Objective-III: To analyse the institutional cost, unit cost and expenditure of collegiate education. Against objective-III, Chapter 4 analyses the institutional cost, unit cost and expenditure of collegiate education in Tripura based on relevant information during study period.

1. The analysis based upon the different components of recurring cost. Recurring cost of sample colleges' increase from 15.56 percent during 2007-08 to 2008-09 and 32.33 per cent during 2008-09 to 2009-10 and declined to 24.72 per cent in the year 2010-11 and 15.42 per cent during 2011-12. There is steep rise during the period 2008-09 to 2009-10. Annual average growth rate of recurring cost is 22.01 per cent but the annual average growth rate of general degree college Khumlung is 64.76 per cent where as lowest annual growth rate of Women's College is 10.76 per cent.
2. Per unit recurring cost of general degree colleges of Tripura have been increasing during the period of study except during the period 2007-08 to 2008-09. The annual growth rate from during the period 2008-09 to 2009-10 is 41.73 per cent which is highest while 9.70 per cent during the year 2010-11 to 2011-12 which is the lowest among

the period of study but The annual average growth rate during study period is 14.36 percent.

3. The trend of percentage of salary and wages in total recurring cost shows a constant pattern during the years of study. The notable fact is that the constancy stays at a level of around 87 per cent and all other component stays around 13 per cent.

4. Regarding nonrecurring items equipments constitute the substantial portion of total non recurring cost during the study period followed by cost of furniture, cost of books and journal and cost of computer which are essential items for any educational institution. In the study, it may be mentioned that the information might seem to be incomplete as it does not contain expenditure on land & building.

5. Per unit non-recurring cost of general degree colleges of Tripura have been fluctuating during the period of study. It has increased from Rs 700 in the year 2007-08 to Rs.1200 in the year 2011-12. Non recurring cost during 2007-08 is 3.08 percent of institutional cost, 3.31 percent in 2008-09, 3.14 percent in 2009-10, 2.79 percent in 2010-11 and increased to 2.81 percent in 2011-12.

6. The institutional cost covers both recurring and nonrecurring cost for the maintenance of institutions and imparting education to the students. It is found that the contribution of recurring cost in institutional cost of sample colleges is 96.97 percent. Only around 3 percent is spent for expenditure of capital nature.

7. It reveals that around 84.28 per cent of institutional cost of the sample colleges is spent on only one head, i.e. salary and wages, while a little portion is spent to upkeep the system. However the institutional cost has been showing a rising trend over the years from Rs. 2039.15

to Rs. 4476.36 during the period from 2007-08 to 2011-12 registering 21.91 percent annual average growth. In case of individual colleges, growth of institutional cost of GDC, Khumlung, MMDC, Ambedkar College, DDMC and KNM 62.64, 39.58, 34.28, 30.29 and 29.31 percent, respectively are much higher than the annual average growth rate of Tripura.

8. Regarding recurring cost as percentage of institutional cost, colleges taken individually or taken collectively the percentage hovers around 97 per cent. This percentage has been showing a downward trend 96.92 per cent to 96.69 per cent during 2007-08 to 2008-09. This trend may not be remarkable, but may be considered as an improvement in the management of finance.

9. As unit cost calculation helps in identifying the cost of various activities and courses, the policy makers can decide on suitable ways to check increasing cost or devise methods of getting better returns from these costs. Unit cost per year of education in general degree colleges of Tripura has been showing an upward trend Rs 9600 in 2007-08 to Rs 15600 in 2011-12 which may be taken to be normal and realistic in consideration with the pattern of expenditure evident in the institutions under study.

10. The annual average growth rate of unit cost of the students of general degree colleges in Tripura is 14.26 % whereas lowest annual average growth rate of unit cost is 7.78% of MBB College and highest annual average growth rate of unit cost is 34.53% for GDC, Khumlung. The sudden rise in the unit cost of this college calls for review by the government as the college established during 2007-08.

11. After higher secondary school, a student can become a graduate on completing a course of three years of study. For completion of the study an institution has to incur

expenditure as institutional cost as a whole. Per unit graduating cost of sample colleges is also estimated. It is found that the per unit graduating cost of sample colleges has been increased from Rs. 45590 in 2007-08 to rupees 90320 in the year 2011-12.

12. Correlation between institutional cost / unit cost and components like expenditure on salaries and wages, portion of recurring expenditure out of UGC fund, fuel charges or hiring charges of vehicle, office expenses, expenses out of non government fund, chargeable portion of non-recurring cost (depreciation on furniture, equipment, computer and on books and journal) of all the colleges is positive. But there are negative correlation between institutional cost / unit cost and repair & maintenance, recurring cost on equipments and recurring cost on library/laboratory.

13. Regarding the perception of respondents whether all stakeholders, should be well aware of the expenditure incurred per student/ cost of college education, a majority of the respondents, (96%) gave a positive response. (99 %) respondents were well aware that a salary/wage component is the major share of recurring expenditure of the colleges in Tripura and also (82 %) respondents have realized that the unit cost of collegiate education is rising rapidly.

Objective-IV: To examine the accounting system practiced in general degree colleges in Tripura. Against objective –IV, Accounting process and Audit procedure of general degree colleges in Tripura during the five year period from 2007-08 to 2011-2012 are discussed in chapter 5.

1. ICAI, Government of India recommended accrual basis of accounting system, but the study shows that all the degree colleges maintain their books of accounts using

the cash basis of accounting which is almost obsolete. All the sample colleges maintain books and accounts conventionally which do not follow the statuary provisions and general practices followed by all other educational institutions.

2. Proper maintenance of this book of account is considered as the barometer for any organization. But no sample college maintains proper books of accounts. There is no uniformity in the proforma of cash book and other books of account maintain by the sample government colleges.

3. As per provision of the financial rules every government degree colleges are required to prepare annual accounts, but no sample colleges prepare income and expenditure statement. Balance sheet is also not prepared by the sample colleges. There is some prefix pattern to maintain accounts in an institution. Though the colleges in question do not follow the pattern in an exact way, but a clear idea can be had as cash book, bill register, payroll, fees register etc. are maintained regularly. However, strict accounting principle may be absent in the maintenance of such accounts.

4. Audit of Accounts discloses the strength and weakness of the financial system of the organization. It is generally accepted rules to perform the audit function at a regular time gap, i.e. after the completion of every financial year, but no such span of time or the periodicity concept is maintained. No advisory activities regarding maintenance of prescribed accounting system or development of accounting procedure on the part of both internal and external auditors are noticed.

5. The colleges do not follow a sound accounting procedure seemed to be a point of concern for the respondents (99%). Almost all of them think that no verification

is done on the accounts on a day to day basis. Quite surprisingly, there is no regular annual internal audit carried out. 89% of respondents opined that maintenance and documentation of records in GDCs of Tripura are not proper and adequate. They also opined that both internal and external audits along with academic audits be carried out for smooth running of the colleges.

Suggestions

On the basis of findings of the study and observation arrived the following suggestions are recommended for a betterment of the situations:

1. In order to achieve the preset target of financial planning, efforts should be made to increase Gross Enrolment Ratio among the disadvantaged groups and provide additional facilities to the marginalized sections of the society.
2. Efforts are also needed to bridge the gap between the rural and urban areas in terms of growth in higher education.
3. Financing of higher education needs to be augmented to 1.5 per cent of GDP as recommended by various Commissions & Committees on higher education.
4. It is found that many newly established colleges do not have sufficient finance to run the college nor have any faculty. Therefore, the State Government must arrange adequate finance and manpower before establishing new colleges so that the finance and faculty of the existing colleges need not be shifted.
5. The growth of higher education in Tripura had manifested sizeable regional imbalances within the state. It is, therefore, more essential to have a higher education policy document of the state government to deal with imbalances and other associated matters.

6. The state government has the limited scope and ability to finance the colleges as per requirement of the colleges. Therefore, the alternative source of finances for the government general degree colleges is the need of the hour.

7. All the government general degree colleges in Tripura should take the full advantage of UGC funding and the Department of Higher Education; Government of Tripura should monitor the matter.

8. Government general degree colleges in Tripura should be allowed to prepare annual budget and the funds should also be released as per the approved budget to maintain financial discipline in the colleges.

9. The Department of Higher Education, Government of Tripura should device a formula while releasing grants pertaining to running and maintenance for up keeping the system based on number of students, courses offered number of practical courses, etc. But it should not be based on the mercy of the administrators.

10. In several cases the public funds are not optimally utilized and the mechanism promotes inefficiencies. Therefore, managing the funds of higher education is very much crucial for a fund crunch state like us.

11. The accounting would be based on the principles of accrual system of accounting and the concepts of going concern would have to be maintained.

12. Audit function should be carried out at a regular time gap i.e. after the end of every financial year.

13. The accounting standards must be widely accepted in practice in which the statutory obligation should be increased and ensured in consultations with the professional and regulatory bodies, including ICAI, UGC,

NAAC etc. The gaps in practices should be seriously detected and checked so as to safeguard the interests of the stakeholders and bodies financing the higher education. The effective information system should be ensured to satisfy the aforesaid, users of accounting information.

The above suggestions concerning the various aspects of higher education in Tripura in general education may be undertaken on a priority basis so that the qualitative development of higher education can be achieved at an earlier date.

Conclusion

On the basis of analysis of secondary and primary data, findings of the study, perception of the respondents and the experiences gained during the study, the following observations are put forwarded:

1. The higher education sector in Tripura has rapidly expanded during the era of statehood both in terms of number of general degree colleges, technical and professional colleges as well as universities. The private sector participation in the development of collegiate education in Tripura is not significant. But the expansion of government degree colleges has taken place at the expenses of inadequate finances in the colleges resulting poor performances.
2. There is an imbalance in growth and expansion of higher education in Tripura. In terms of number of institution, enrolment, faculty deployment, academic programmes etc. there is a huge disparity observed among the districts or the subdivisions of the state.
3. All the government general degree colleges in Tripura are recognized by UGC for getting financial aids. But it is observed that most of the colleges are not utilizing

the opportunity fully, it is learnt that many colleges are not even utilizing the fund received from UGC properly within the stipulated time.

4. Apart from UGC, ICSSR, NER and DST are the other sources for funding in colleges, but government general degree colleges in Tripura have not explored these sources to any noticeable extent. Many college authorities are not even aware of these sources of funding.
5. Salary of academic and non academic staff of the colleges constitutes the major part of expenditure in the government general degree colleges in Tripura.
6. Running and maintenance cost for up keeping the system is very less and inadequate. Moreover, there is no formula or parameters for releasing grants pertaining to running and maintenance for up keeping the system.
7. The institutional cost and unit cost of higher education in government general degree colleges are huge and rising.
8. The accounting system in government colleges is founded grossly inadequate. Essential registers and important accounting books are not maintained by the colleges properly.
9. In spite of severe audit observation the college authorities have not changed the defective procedure of keeping accounts and records.

With the improved management of finance by the General Degree Colleges of Tripura, it is hoped that the colleges will be able to contribute significantly towards their goal of dissemination on higher education in the state of Tripura. The findings of present study if followed in its later end spirit it is hoped that the higher education in Tripura will be immensely benefited. The policy makers may formulate appropriate policy for the effective financial management practices in the entire education system of the state. It is very important that financial discipline is urgent for survival and growth of any organisation, governmental or nongovernmental.

BIBLIOGRAPHY

1. Adhav, K & Joshi, D. (2002). Higher Education in the 21th Century. *University News, 40(24),* June17-23.
2. Afzal, S.M. & Ahmed, S. (2008). Student enrolment in Higher education: A Gender Comparison. *University News, 46(30).*
3. Agarwal, P. (2006). *Higher Education in India- the Need for change* (Working Paper No. 180). New Delhi: Indian Council for Research on International Economic Relations (ICRIER).
4. Agarwal, P. (2008). Privatization and Internationalization of Higher Education in the Countries of South Asia: An Empirical Analysis. *Indian Council for Research on International Economic Relations (ICRIER),* New Delhi.
5. Ahmad, S. (2008). Funding to Universities and colleges by the UGC during the 10th plan. *University News, 46(09).*
6. Ahuja, A. K. (2007). *Economics of Education.* New Delhi: Author Press.
7. Anand, S. (2013). Access to Higher Education in India: Cross State Analysis. *University News, Vol-51(31),* Aug-2013
8. Anbalagan, P. (2011). Public Expenditure on Education: A Study of Inter State Variations in India. *IJBEMR. Volume 2, Issue 1.*

9. Andersson,A.E. (2009). *Returns to Higher Education* (Working Paper No-163). CESIS Electronic Working Paper Series.

10. Ansari, M.M. (1988). Financial Health of Universities: A Diagnostic Study. *Journal of Higher Education, Vol- 14,* UGC, New Delhi.

11. Azad, J.L. (2008). *Financing and Management of Higher Education in India: The Role of Private Sector*. New Delhi: Gyan Publishing House.

12. Azad, J.L. (1976). Financing Institutions of Higher Education in India: The Need for a Realistic Fee Policy. *Higher Education, 5 (1976)* 1-7.

13. Banerjee, S. (2011). Quality Higher Education, its Status, Problems & Remedial Policy. *International Referred Reseach Journal*, *VOL-II* Issue 19.

14. Barman, A. (2012). *One Response to Educational institutions to follow ICAI accounting norms. Retrieved Dec. 15.2014,* from www.educat- ioninsight/..../educational-institutions-to-follow-icai-accou.

15. Basant, R. & Sen,G. (2010). *Who Participates in Higher Education in India? Rethinking the Role of Affirmative Action (*ORF Working Paper Series*). Observer Research Foundation.*

16. Bawa, M.S. (2000). Emerging Trend in Financing of Higher Education in India. *University News*, *38(11).*

17. Becker, G.S. (1960) Under Investment in College Education. *American Economic review, Vol-50(2).*

18. Bellew, R. & Destefano, J. (1991). *Costs and Finance of Higher Education in Pakistan (*WPS-704). Policy, Research and External Affairs, Population and Human Resources Department, The World Bank.

19. Bhushan, S. (2008). Financial Requirement in Higher Education during XI Plan Period. In *Higher Education In India Issues Related to Expansion, Inclusiveness, Quality and Finance.* UGC Report.

20. Blaug, M. (1969). *Economics of Education.* England: Penguin Books Ltd, Harmondsworth, Middlesex.

21. Blaug, M. (1982). The Distributional Effect of Higher Education Subsidies. *Economics of Education Review, Vol-2*, Issue-3.

22. Bray, M. (2002). The Costs and Financing of Education: Trends and Policy Implications. *Education in Developing Asia, Volume 3*, ADB Publication.

23. CAG. (2013*). Higher education in Tripura 'ailing'.* Retrieved from http://www.igovernment.in/site/higher-education-tripura-ailing-cag-37300

24. CEDA.(Tribhuvan University) (2007).Financing the Higher Education in Nepal. *Report submitted to South Asia Network of Economic Research Institutes (SANEI),* Islamabad.

25. Central Advisory Board of Education Committee. (2005). *Report on Financing of Higher and Technical Education.* National Institute of Educational Planning and Administration (NIEPA), New Delhi.

26. Chakrabarti, A. (2007). *Higher Education and Research in India: an Overview.* Sitra Reports 74.

27. Chakrabarti, A. & Jogleker, R. (2006). Determinants of Expenditure on Education: An Empirical Analysis Using State Level Data. *Economic and Political Weekly, VolXLI,* April 15.

28. Chakraborty, L.S. (2010). *Determining Gender Equity in Fiscal Federalism: Analytical Issues and Empirical Evidence from India* (Working Paper No.-590). Levy Economics Institute of Bard College.

29. Chaliha, J.P. (2009). Financial Management in Ensuring Quality in Higher Education. In Nath, Hemanta Kumar(ed), *Higher Education in the North East a Perspective.* Guwhati: Purbachal Prakash.

30. Chatterjee,T.K. (1999). Crisis in Higher Education Nature and sources. *University News, 37(4)*, Jan.25.

31. Chattopadhyay, S. (2007). Exploring Alternative Sources of Financing Higher Education. *Economic and Political Weekly,* October 20.

32. Cheung, B. (2003). *Higher Education Financing Policy: Mechanisms and Effects.* Retrieved from www.usca.edu / essays/ vol-5 2003/ cheung.pdf. Dated on 27.09.2014.

33. Committee on Public Finance and Government Accounting (2010). *Changing Times in Government Accounting (A Status Paper).* The Institute of Chartered Accountants of India (ICAI).

34. Das, S.K. (2012). Self-Financing Scheme in Post-Graduate Course of Government-Sponsored College: A case study. *International Journal of Multidisciplinary Management Studies, Vol.2 Issue 1*, January 2012.

35. Das,S.,Chakraborty, K.S. & Dey, N.B.(2015). A Glimpse into Status of Higher Education in India. *Development Dynamics, Vol-2*, January 2015.

36. Das, S., Chakraborty, K.S. & Dey, N.B.(2014). Opportunity of Higher Education in Tripura: A Study With Reference to Disparities among General Degree Colleges. *International Journal of Informative & Fututistic Research, Vol-II,* September-2014.

37. Das, S.,Chakraborty, K.S. & Dey, N.B.(2014). Development of Higher Education in North East India: An Analytical Study. *International Journal of Informative & Fututistic Research,Vol-I,* August -2014.

38. Das,S.,Chakraborty,K.S. & Dey, N.B.(2015). Financing Higher Education: With Special Reference to Government General Degree Colleges of Tripura. *International Journal of Innovative Research & Development, Vol-4,* Sptember-2015.

39. Das,S.,Chakraborty,K.S. & Dey, N.B.(2014). An Analysis of Growth and Development of Higher Education in Tripura: A Review. *Tripura Journal of Social Science, Vol-I,* January-2014.

40. Datt, R. (1969). Unit cost of Education- A case study of Haryana College. In H. N. Pandit (ed), *Measurement of Cost Productivity and Efficiency of Education.* NCERT, Madras.

41. Day, B. (1969). On Costing of Education. In Pandit, H.N. (ed.), *Measurement of Cost, Productivity and Efficiency of Education.* National Council for Educational Research and Training (NCERT), Madras.

42. De, A. & , Endow, T. (2008). *Public Expenditure on Education in India: Recent Trends and Outcomes* (Working Paper No-18). Research Consortium on Educational Outcomes and Poverty. Pp-5-6.

43. Debroy, D.(2011). The Advancement of Higher Education in Tripura. *International Journal of Multidisciplinary Research, Vol. II, No I.* April'11 – June.

44. Department of Higher Education. *Higher Education Perspective Plan 2010-2020.* Retrieved 17.9.2014 from http:// highereducation.tripura. gov.in /pdf/plan-20.pdf

45. Department of Higher Education. *Higher Education profile of Tripura 2012-13.* Retrieved 13.09.2014.from http:// highereducation.tripura. gov.in /pdf/college_prf_15-16.pdf

46. Dhameja, N. (2005). NPOs –Accounting and Financial reporting Framework. *Indian Journal of Public Administration, Vol. L1,* No-4.

47. Directorate of Audit. (2008). *Internal Audit Report.* Agartala: Government of Tripura.

48. Directorate of Audit. (2009). *Internal Audit Report.* Agartala: Government of Tripura.

49. Directorate of Audit. (2010). *Internal Audit Report.* Agartala: Government of Tripura.

50. Directorate of Audit. (2011). *Internal Audit Report.* Agartala: Government of Tripura.

51. Directorate of Economics and Statistics, Government of Tripura. *Economic Review* (Various Issues). Agartala: Planning (Statistics) Department.

52. Directorate of Economics and Statistics, Government of Tripura. *Statistical Abstract* (Various Issues). Agartala: Planning (Statistics) Department.

53. Dutta, P.K. (2007).Quality Maintenance in Higher Education. *University News 45(31).*

54. Finance Department. (2007-08). *Expenditure Budget Detailed Account.* Agartala: Government of Tripura.

55. Finance Department.(2008-09). *Expenditure Budget Detailed Account.* Agartala: Government of Tripura.

56. Finance Department.(2009-10). *Expenditure Budget Detailed Account.* Agartala: Government of Tripura.

57. Finance Department.(2010-11). *Expenditure Budget Detailed Account.* Agartala: Government of Tripura.

58. Finance Department.(2011-12). *Expenditure Budget Detailed Account.* Agartala: Government of Tripura.

59. Ford Foundation.(1971).*The Capital Cost of a University* (Ford Foundation 2288). Fulton Street, Berkely, California.

60. Gaikwad, B.R. and Solunke, R.S. (2013). Growth of Higher Education in India. *International Research Journal of Social Sciences. Vol. 2(8),* 58-60, August.

61. Gandhi, M.M.(2015). Financial management of Higher Educational Institutions - with reference to Financing, Pricing, Accounting Standards and Gaps in Practices in Universities and Colleges. *The Business and management Review, Vol-5, No-4.*

62. Garg, V.P. (1985). *Cost Analysis in Higher Education: A Theoretical Frame and Empirical Results.* New Delhi: Metropolitan Book.

63. Rani, G.P. (2004).Economic Reforms and Financing Higher Education in India. *Indian Journal of Economics and Business, 3(1).*

64. Ghosh, D.K. (1994). Higher Education- Investments, Returns and Mechanism of Maximization of Returns. *University News,* May, 23.

65. Ghosh, D.K. (1999). How Inhabitable is the business concept in the higher education system. *University News, 37(1).*

66. Goel, D.R. & Goel, C.(2008). Higher Education Problems and Prognosis. *University News, 46(37).*

67. Goswami,D. (2011). *Higher Education in India-Growth Expansion and Issue.* Guwahati: DVS Publishers.

68. Government of India. (1985). *Challenge of Education- A Policy Perspective and National Educational Policy -1986.* Ministry of Education, New Delhi.

69. Gupta, K. & Demele, M.(2013). Contemporary challenges in Higher education. *University News, Vol-51, No-32,* Aug.

70. Hallack, J. (1969). *The Analysis of Educational Cost and Expenditure,* IIEP, UNESCO, Paris.

71. Hans-Ulrich, K. (2003). Management Mechanisms and Financing of Higher Education in Germany. In *Higher Education Management and Policy. Journal of the Programme*

on Institutional Management in higher education, Volume 15, No. 1.

72. Hegde, G. (2009). Quest for Quality: Internal Quality System Maters. *University News,* 47(16).

73. Hegde, G. (2008). Towards Ensuring and Enhancing the Internal Quality of Higher Educational Institutions. *University News*, 46(02).

74. Heggade, O.D. (1992). *Economics of Education: A Study of Indian Experience.* Bombay: Himalaya Publishing House.

75. Heggade.O.D. (1998). Finances *and cost of Higher Education in India.* New Delhi: Mohit publication.

76. Hill, S. & Chalaux, T. (2011). Improving Access and Quality in the Indian Education System (Working Papers, No. 885). Retrieved from http://shodhganga. inflibnet.ac.in/bitstream/10603/2094/7/07_absract.pdf

77. Huq, M.S. (1965). *Education and Development Strategy in South East Asia.* Honolulu: East West Center Press.

78. ICAI.(2012).*Training Material Implementation of Accounting Standards- With Specific Reference to Educational Institutions.* New Delhi: MHRD, Government of India.

79. ICAI. (2012). *Report on Implementation of Accounting Standards in Educational Institutions of Department of Higher Education.* MHRD, Government of India.

80. Jenny, H.H. (1996). *Cost Accounting in Higher Education. Simplified Macro- and Micro-Costing Techniques.* National Association of College and University Business Officers. Washington, D.C.

81. Johnson, N.(2009).W*hat does a college degree cost? Comparing approaches to measuring "cost per degree".* Washington, DC: Delta Cost Project.

82. Johnstone, B.(1998).*The Financing and Management of Higher Education: A Status Report on Worldwide Reforms*. The World Bank.

83. Johnstone, B.(2003).The economics and politics of cost sharing in higher education: comparative perspectives. *Economics of Education Review. 23 (2004).*

84. Joshi, A. & Joshi, K. (1997). Quality Improvement in Self Financing Higher Education. *University News, 35(38).*

85. Joshi, K.M. & Kinjal, V.A. (2013). Indian Higher Education: Some Reflections. *Intelektinė Ekonomika, Intellectual Economic. Vol. 7, No. 1(15).*

86. Joshi, S. (2012). *Sustainable Development of the Higher Education Sector in India for Catalyzing Services-Driven Growth* (Working Paper No. 2012/01). Maastricht School of Management.

87. Kalia, S. (2010). *Cost of Higher Education and Financing Practices among Students in Punjab: A Study of Professional Education.* Doctoral Thesis, Punjab Technical University. Retrieved from http://shodhganga.inflibnet.ac. in/ bitstream /10603/2094/ 7/07_ absract. pdf accessed on 5.5.2012.

88. Kamat, A.R. (1969). *Efficiency of Education.* In Pandit, H.N. (ed.), *Measurement of Cost, Productivity and Efficiency of Education.* National Council for Educational Research and Training (NCERT), New Delhi.

89. Kaul, S. (2006). *Higher Education in India: Seizing and opportunity* (Working Paper No-179). New Delhi: Indian Council for Research on International Economic Relations (ICRIER).

90. Kaur, K. (2003). *Higher Education in India (1781-2003).* New Delhi: University Grants Commission.

91. Knight, J.(ed). (2009). *Financing Access and Equity in Higher Education.* Netherlands: Sense Publishers Rotterdam. Retrieved from http://www. sensepublishers.com

92. Komow, B., Khanna, R. & Sharma, R.K. (2012).Journey of Higher Education in India: An Analysis of Post Independence Era. *Asian Journal of Multidimensional Research, Vol-I Issue-I,* June.

93. Rayal, K.S. & Kamble, P.S. (2012). Quality Gaps in Higher Education System in India. *Golden Research thoughts. Vol - I, ISSUE - VIII.*

94. Kulkarni, G.B. (1969). Cost of Education in Commerce College of Bombay 1962-63 to 1966-67. In Pandit, H. N. (ed) *Measurement of Cost Productivity and Efficiency of Education,* NCERT, Madras.

95. Kumar, N.A. & George, K.K. (2009). *Kerala's Education System: From Inclusion to Exclusion (*Working Paper No.-22). Kerala: Centre for Socio-economic & Environmental Studies (CSES).

96. Lbara, E.C. (2011). Funding Higher Education in a Dwindling Fiscal resource allocation: The Nigerian Perspective. *Journal of sustainable development in Africa. Volume 13, No.3.*

97. Mahadevappa, B. (2006). The Meaning of Education Quality. *University News 44(51).*

98. Mahadevappa, M. (2001). Addressing Financial Constraints of State agricultural Universities. *University News. 39(43),* Oct.22-28.

99. Mahanta, D.K. (2013). *Financial Management of Higher Education -A Study on Gauhati University* (doctoral thesis), Gauhati University. Retrieved from http://shodhganga.inflibnet.ac.in/ dated on 15.08.2015.

100. Maheshwari, A.N. (1995). Coping with changes funding for Higher Education. *University News.* May 8.

101. Majumdar Committee Report. (1999), *Report of the Committee on National Common Minimum Programme's Commitment.* Ministry of Human Resource Development, Government of India.

102. Malhotra & Mittal. (2001). *Educational Research in North East India, a Source material.* National Institute of Educational Planning and Administration (NIEPA), New Delhi.

103. Marchang, R. (2012). Higher Education and Inclusive Growth in India. Paper accepted for November 2012, *International Conference*, Taipei.

104. Mehta, B.C. (1993). Financing of Higher Education. *Journal of educational Planning and Administratation. Vol-VII, No.-I.*

105. Mishra, J.K., Abidi, N. & Sharma, R. (2008). *Indian Higher Education: Global Challenges and Local Issues* (JBS Working Paper Series, W.P. No. JIITU/JBS/2008/01).

106. Mohammadi, S.(2012). Implementation of full accrual basis in governmental organizations (Case Study: Shiraz University of Technology, Iran). *Interdisciplinary Journal of Contemporary Research in Busi. VOL 4, NO 2.*

107. Mondal, A. & Mete, J. (2013). Higher Education and Quality Research in India: An Overview. *University News, 51(19).*

108. Mukherjee, R. (2008). Higher Education in India: An Overview and Opportunities for Foreign Participation. *Asia Pacific Foundation of Canada Research Reports.* Centre for Policy Research, Canada-India Policy Dialogue.

109. Mulimani,V.H. (2010). Higher Education in India at Cross Road. *University News 48(09).*

110. Muskin, S. J. Ed. (1962). *Economics of Higher Education.* U.S.: Department of Health, Education and Welfare.

111. Muzammil, Md. (1990). Financing of Higher Education in Uttar Pradesh. *University News,* Dec.24.

112. Nair, P & Kumar, D. (2004).*The Financing of Higher Education –A Broader View.* Hyderabad: The ICFAI University Press.

113. National University of Educational Planning and Administration (NUEPA). (2009). *Facing Global and Local Challenges: The New Dynamics for Higher Education*. New Delhi: MHRD.

114. Newby, H. (2003). The Management of Change in Higher Education. *Higher Education Management and Policy* , *Vol.15, No.1.* P- 17. Paris: OECD.

115. NUEPA. (2009). Facing Global and Local Challenges Country Report: India. In Sub-*regional Conference for South, South West and Central Asia on Higher Education.*Feb.25-26, Vigyan Bhawan, New Delhi.

116. Obester, B. W., Sally, K. & William, M. G. (2011). Cost accounting Standards In Higher Education: Impact of Required Changes. *Journal of Applied Business Research, Vol-17*, No-3.

117. OECD. (2009). *Higher Education to 2030* (Working Paper No-584). Retrieved from http://www.oecd.org/edu/ceri/44101074.pdf accessed on 27.03.2012.

118. OECD. (2003). Higher Education Management and Policy. *Journal of the Programme on Institutional Management in Higher Education, Volume 15,* No. 1.

119. Panchamukhi, P.R. (1965). Financing of Higher Education in India –An Evaluation. In Kaul, J N, (Ed) *Higher Education Social Change and National Development*, Indian Institute of Advanced Study, Simla.

120. Pandit, H.N. (1969). *Measurement of Cost, Productivity and Efficiency of Education.* National Council for Educational Research and Training (NCERT). Madras.

121. Pandit. H.N. (1969). A Study in Unit Cost at the school stage in India: A Design of the Research Project. In *Measurement of Cost Productivity and Efficiency of Education.* NCERT, Madras.

122. Parekh, V. & Manjrekar, P. (2011). Indian Higher Education Sector: Heading towards Transformation. *International Conference on Technology and Business Management,* D Y Patil University (Business Management).

123. Parikh, V. & Saluja, D. (2007). Higher Education, Society and State. *University news, 45(19).*

124. Patari, K. (2009). Financing of Higher Education in Orissa. *University News. 47(13).*

125. Paul B. & Richard A.H. (1986). Concepts of Cost and Cost Analysis for Higher Education. *The Association for Institutional Research,* Number-23.

126. Pradhan, N. (2012. Quality of Indian Higher Education: Policy Perspectives. *University News, 50(31).*

127. Prakash,V. (2007). Trends in Growth and Financing of Higher Education in India. *Economic and Political Weekly. Vol - XLII No. 31*, August 04.

128. Psacharopoulos, G. & others. (1986).*Financing Education in Developing Countries: An exploration of policy option.* The World Bank, Washington, DC 20433.

129. Punnayya Committee. (1993). *UGC Funding of Institutions of Higher Education.* University Grant Commission, New Delhi.

130. *Raghurama. (2013).* Indian Accounting Standards and Educational Institutions. *International Journal of Trade & Global Business Perspectives, Vol -2, No 3.*

131. Rani, P.G. (2002). *Financing Higher education In India in the post reform period: Focus on Access and equity* (Occasional Paper -31).NIEPA, New Delhi.

132. Rao, H. V. (1969). Educational Cost: Concepts and Issues. In H. N. Pandit (ed) *Measurement of Cost Productivity and Efficiency of Education,* NCERT, Madras.

133. Rastogi, S. (2001). Globalization of Higher Education. *University News, 39(35).*

134. Rayal, S. K. & Kamble , P.S. (2012). Quality Gaps in Higher Education System in India. *Golden Research thoughts*, *Vol - I , ISSUE-VIII.*

135. Rena, R. (2007). *Financing education and Development in Eritrea– some Implication. Manpower Journal, Vol. 43, No. 1.* New Delhi.

136. Rizvi, F. &Gorur, R. (2011). Challenges Facing Indian Higher Education. Fearless Nadia, Australia India Institute. Retrieved 2.03.2013 from www.aii.unimelb.edu.au.

137. Salmi, J. (1991). *The Higher Education Crisis in Developing Countries (*Phree Paper Series, Document No. Phree/91/37 (10601). The World Bank.

138. Sambasivam, M. & Raheem, A. A. (2009). Factors Determining Financing of Higher Education in India: An Assessment of Post Reform Period. *Artha Journal of Social Sciences, 8(2).*

139. Sambhu, N.N. (2004). *Cost of Schooling in Kerala: A Study of Private and Institutional Costs under Different Types of Management.* Kerala Research Programme on Local Level Development (KRPLLD) and Centre for Development Studies, Thiruvananthapuram.

140. Sanyal, B.C. & Martin, M. (2006). Financing Higher Education: International Perspectives. *Higher Education in the World.*

141. Saxena,V., Kulsresth, S. & Khan, B. (2010). Higher Education and research in India. *International journal of Educational research and Technology* (IJERT), *Vol-1 (1).*

142. Schaik, F. V. (2004). *Mastering the Transformation: New Public Management, Accrual Accounting and Budgeting.* Retrieved from www.deloitte.com, 13, July, 2010.

143. Schultz, T.W. (1961). Investment in Human Capital. *American Economic Review, Vol. 51, No-1.*

144. Selvam, S.K. (2013). Higher Education and entrepreneurship in India. *University News.50(44).*

145. Sharma, D.L. (1969). Unit cost of educations, our knowledge, gaps and our need. In Pandit, H.N. (ed), *Measurement of Cost Productivity and Efficiency of Education.*NCERT, Madras.

146. Sharma, N. K. (2007). Importance of Higher Education in Trade, Commerce and Industry. *University News, 45(22).*

147. Shollapur, M.R. (2000). Intellectual Resources Sharing between university and industry. *University News. 38(38).*

148. Singh, G. (1969).Concept in and Methodology of measuring Unit Costs in Education. In H.N. Pandit(ed), *Measurement of Cost Productivity and Efficiency of Education.* NCERT, Madras.

149. Singh, J. (2003). Unit Recurring Cost for Regular and Correspondence Course in Punjabi University. *Journal of Distance Education.*

150. Singh, K.P. (2012). Taking Stock of Higher Education in the North-East. *Economic and Political Weekly, Vol-XLVII-No-38.*

151. Singh,Y.V.(2015). Teacher-Student Ratio: Fifty years statistics of Indian Higher Education. *University News*, May 53 (20).

152. Sinha, A. & Chakraborty, K.S. (2010). Management of Higher Education Institutions in Tripura. In *Reflection on Economy & Society.* Akansha Publishing House, New Delhi.

153. Sreeramamurty,K., Sailaja,K. & Appalanaidu, D. (2012). Inclusive Growth and Higher Education In India. *International Journal of Multidisciplinary Educational Research, Volume 1, Issue 2.*

154. Srivastava,R. (2008). Financing Higher education in India –Estimate for 15 % Enrolment under 11th Plan. In *Higher Education in India Issues Related to Expansion, Inclusiveness, Quality and Finance',* UGC Report.

155. Subbiah,A. (1999). Central Governments Expenditure on Education—A Comparative Analysis with its Total Expenditure. *University News 37(47).*

156. Suklabaidya, S. (2009). Quality Assurance in higher Education in Rural Areas in Assam. In NathHemanta Kr. (Ed). *Higher Education in the North East a Perspective*, Guwahati.

157. Sulochana,M. (1991). Financing of Higher Education in Andra Pradesh. *University News,* April.

158. Swaminadhan Committee Report. (1994). *Report of the High Power Committee for Mobilisation of Additional Resources for Technical Education.* AICTE, New Delhi.

159. Thomas, H. B. (2007). Does Full Accrual Accounting Enhance Accountability?. *The Innovation Journal: The Public Sector Innovation Journal*, Vol. 12 (3),

160. Thorat, S. (2008). Emerging Issues in Higher Education – Approach and Strategy in 11th Plan. In *Higher Education in India - Issues Related to Expansion, Inclusiveness, Quality and Finance.*UGC, New Delhi.

161. Thorat, S. (2006). *Higher Education in India Emerging Issues Related to Access, Inclusiveness and Quality*. Nehru Memorial Lecture, University of Mumbai.

162. Tilak,J.B.G. & Varghese. (1991). Financing Higher Education in India. *Higher Education 21. 83-101*, NIEPA, New Delhi.

163. Tilak J.B.G. (2003). Higher Education and Development. Asia',*Journal of Educational Planning and Administration Volume XVII No. 2.*

164. Tilak J.B.G. (2004). Public Subsidies in Education in India. *Economic and Political Weekly*. Jan.24.

165. Tilak, J B. G. (1993). Financing Higher Education in India: Principles, Practice, and Policy Issues. *Higher Education, Vol. 26, No. 1*. In Perspectives on Higher Education in India, Springer.

166. Tilak, J. B. G. (1988). Costs of education in India. *International Journal of Educational Development Volume 8, Issue 1.*

167. Tilak, J.B.G. (1985). *Analysis of Cost of Education in India* (Occasional Paper 10). National Institute of Education, Planning and Administration (NIEPA), New Delhi.

168. Tilak, J.B.G. (2001). *Higher education and development in Kerala* (Working Paper No-5). Centre for Socio-Economic & Environmental Studies, Kochi, Kerala.

169. Tilak,J.B.G. (2015). How Inclusive Is Higher Education in India? *Social Change* .SAGE Publications. 45(2).

170. Tilak.J.B.G (2012). Higher Education Policy in India in Transition. *Economic & Political Weekly, Vol-XlVII No- 13.*

171. Tiwari, R.K. (2009). *Financing Higher Education in India.* New Delhi: Neeraj Publishing House.

172. Tripathi, S.D. (2000). Self-financing courses in Universities and Colleges. *University News, 38(16).*

173. Tulip, P. (2007). *Financing Higher Education in the United States* (Working Paper-44). ECO/WKP (2007)44, OECD.

174. UGC. (2012).*Higher Education in India at a glance.* New Delhi: UGC.

175. UGC. (2013).*Higher Education in India at a glance.* New Delhi: UGC.

176. Vanlalchhawna. (2006). *Higher Education in North-East India -Unit Cost Analysis,* New Delhi: Mittal Publication.

177. Varghese, N.V. & Tilak, J.B.G. (1991).The Financing of Education in India (XIIIP Research Report No -92). *International Institute for Educational Planning* (UNESCO), Paris. Retrieved 15.02.2013 from unesdoc.unesco.org/images/0009/000902/090282eo.pdf

178. Wagh, A.(2014) . Accounting System in Higher Education: A Study of Colleges in Mumbai City District. *Sai Om Journal of Commerce & Management A Peer Reviewed International Journal.* Volume 1, Issue 12.

179. Woodhall, M. (2007). *Funding Higher Education: The Contribution of Economic Thinking to Debate and Policy Development.* World Bank. Retrieved 27.03.2012.from http://www.socscistatistics. com/tests/pearson / Default2.aspx

180. Yash Pal Committee (2008).*Report of The Committee to Advise on Renovation and Rejuvenation of Higher Education.* MHRD, New Delhi.

Websites

http://www.nuepa.org/libdoc/elibrary/articles/2004jbgtilak.pdf

http://education.usibc.com/wp-content/uploads/2010/09/EY-FICCI-report09

http://www.ugc.ac.in/oldpdf/pub/report/12.pdfwww.icra.in

http://shodhganga.inflibnet.ac.in/bitstream/10603/2094/7/07

http://siteresources.worldbank.org/EDUCATION/Resources

http://reimeingam.blogspot.in/2012/09/higher-education-and-inclusive-growth.

http://www.indiaeducationreview.com/news/ugc-consider-new-norms-teacher-student-ratio

INDEX

•••